Reg Twigg was born at Wigston (Leicester) barracks on 16 December 1913. He was called up to the Leicestershire Regiment in 1940 but instead of fighting Hitler he was sent to the Far East, stationed at Singapore. When captured by the Japanese, he decided he would do everything to survive.

After his repatriation from the Far East, Reg returned to Leicester. With his family he returned to Thailand in 2006, and revisited the sites of the POW camps. Reg died in 2013, at the age of ninety-nine, two weeks before the publication of this book.

Survivor on the River Kwai

The Incredible Story of Life on the Burma Railway

REG TWIGG

PENGUIN BOOKS

PENGUIN BOOKS

Published by the Penguin Group

Penguin Books Ltd, 80 Strand, London WC2R ORL, England

Penguin Group (USA) Inc., 375 Hudson Street, New York, New York 10014, USA

Penguin Group (Canada), 90 Eglinton Avenue East, Suite 700, Toronto, Ontario, Canada M4P 2Y3
(a division of Pearson Penguin Canada Inc.)

Penguin Ireland, 25 St Stephen's Green, Dublin 2, Ireland (a division of Penguin Books Ltd)

Penguin Group (Australia), 707 Collins Street, Melbourne, Victoria 3008, Australia
(a division of Pearson Australia Group Pty Ltd)

Penguin Books India Pvt Ltd, 11 Community Centre, Panchsheel Park, New Delhi – 110 017, India

Penguin Group (NZ), 67 Apollo Drive, Rosedale, Auckland 0632, New Zealand
(a division of Pearson New Zealand Ltd)

Penguin Books (South Africa) (Pty) Ltd, Block D, Rosebank Office Park,
181 Jan Smuts Avenue, Parktown North, Gauteng 2193, South Africa

Penguin Books Ltd, Registered Offices: 80 Strand, London WC2R ORL, England

www.penguin.com

First published by Viking 2013
Published in Penguin Books 2014

001

Copyright © Reg Twigg and Clive Medway, 2013
All rights reserved

The moral right of the copyright holders has been asserted

Typeset by Palimpsest Book Production Limited, Falkirk, Stirlingshire
Printed in Great Britain by Clays Ltd, St Ives plc

ISBN: 978-0-241-96511-5

www.greenpenguin.co.uk

This book is dedicated to the lads of the 1st Battalion of the Leicestershire Regiment and the other soldiers of the British Empire who fought bravely in Malaya and Singapore in 1941 only to be brutalized and murdered while held as prisoners of war.

Also to those civilians of Malaya, Singapore and Thailand who showed true kindness to me and others, often putting themselves at real risk of death or beating.

Lastly, to my closest mates during the war, Albert, Jackie and Howard, of which only one came home.

Contents

List of Illustrations ix

Map xii

Author's Note xiii

Prologue: Harry 1

1 A Land Fit for Heroes 7

2 Gone for a Soldier 32

3 Ship of Fools 54

4 Battle Alert 76

5 The Shambles of Singapore 102

6 Hard Labour 119

7 Laws of the Jungle 141

8 Hell Camps 159

9 The Emperor's Murderers 182

10 The Flames at Tonchan 207

11 The First Mosquito 229

12 The River Gypsy 247

13 'You are now free men' 260

14 The Road Home 277

Epilogue: Reunion 295

Acknowledgements 303

Appendix:
   Reg Twigg's Japanese Index Card 305
   Reg Twigg's Air Drop Leaflet 307
   Reg Twigg's Liberation Questionnaire 309

Further Reading 311

Index 313

List of Illustrations

SECTION I

1 Men of the Leicestershire Regiment (6th Division) in a captured trench, Battle of Cambrai, 1917

2 Leicestershire Regiment (The Tigers) helmet plate

3 A card from my father received by us in 1919

4 Ken, me and Cyril, about 1925

5 'Havelock Road Camp, Singapore, February 1942' by Jack Chalker

6 'Slim River, a stop on the railway journey from Singapore to Bam Pong' by Jack Chalker

7 'Appalling conditions on the ammunition trucks carrying POWs' by Leo Rawlings

8 Camp layout at Tha Muang

9 Huts identical to those I lived in

10 Inside a prison-camp hut

11 Life at Kanchanaburi, 1942

12 The kitchen at Konyo 2, 1943

13 Food line at Tha Muang

14 'Building the railway embankment, Konyo' by Jack Chalker

15 'Working on the Thai/Burma Railway at Konyo' by John Mennie

16 Laying the sleepers, 1943

17 Laying the rails

18 'First camp meat, Konyo' by Jack Chalker, October 1942

19 Lieutenant Usuki: the 'Konyo Kid'

20 The 'Silver Bullet'

SECTION 2

21 'Ulcer operation' by Murray Griffin

22 'Hospital ward' by Murray Griffin

23 'Fit parade for work, Konyo 2' by Ronald Searle

24 Unfit for work – inside a typical camp hospital

25 'Dysentery ward, Tarso' by John Mennie

26 Cholera block, Konyo 2, 1943

27 'Cholera camp, Konyo 2' by Ronald Searle

28 'Burning of the cholera dead, 1942' by Charles Thrale

29 'Unloading the sick and dead' by Jack Chalker

30 Pounding peanuts to make butter, Kanchanaburi

31 Men at work on the Railway

32 The three-tier wooden bridge at Hintok

33 A derailed train

34 The Barber of Tarso

35 My home-made blade

36 The cribbage board I made at Tarso

SECTION 3

37 Konkuita, where the railway lines from Burma and Thailand met

38 The bamboo bridge at Konkuita

39 Train on the bridge at Tamarkan, 1945

40 'Bridge over the River Kwai, 1943' by Leo Rawlings

41 'The Blondinis' by Murray Griffin

42 'Journey by train' by Leo Rawlings

43 Bomb damage to the Kwai bridge at Tamarkan, 1945

44 POWs on Liberation Day, 14 August 1945

45 Free men, Rangoon, May 1945; Major McLeod inspects a
    patient

46 Jack Sharpe

47 The Twiggs and the Hilliers camping at Great Glen, 1948

48 Me with Kathleen, Welsh Borders, 1949

49 Annual POW dinner dance, 1957, with Howard and Laura
    Reast

50 Albert Wingell

51 The track along the edge of the Kwai, 1944

52 Return in 2006

53 Konyo cemetery, 1945

54 Walking along the old track, 2006

ACKNOWLEDGEMENTS

Imperial War Museum: 1, 15, 20, 23–5, 27–9, 34, 40, 42, 44, 45

Australian War Memorial: 5–7, 11–12, 14, 16–19, 21–2, 26, 30–31,
    37–9, 41, 53

Thailand–Burma Railway Centre, Kanchanaburi, Thailand:
    8–10, 13, 32–3, 43, 51

Getty Images: 46

Author's collection: 2–4, 35–6, 47–50, 52, 54

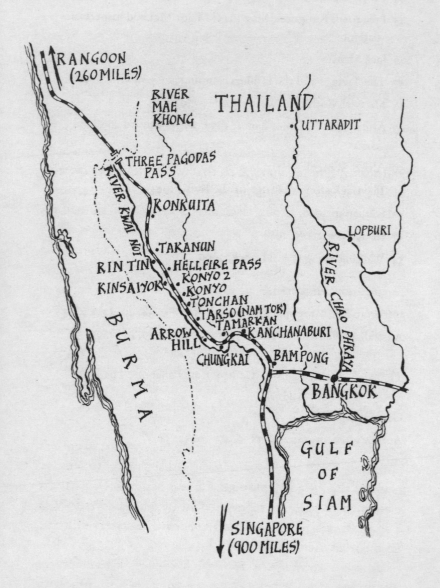

Author's Note

If my father and I walked into a pub together, I'd probably talk to no one and he probably would have talked to everybody. When I remember what he went through at the hands of the guards of the Japanese Imperial Army between 1942 and 1945, I find his survival all the more extraordinary. Not until I was an adult did I appreciate how unusual his attitude was. He was gregarious, a 'cheeky chappie', and he had his close friends with him as he struggled to stay alive while building and maintaining the Thailand–Burma Railway. But he was also a loner, a man driven by a hard childhood to fend for himself. He listened to stories around the fires in those terrible camps and he joined in with the songs of home, but he also trapped lizards and stole food, taking huge chances because he had to in order to survive. He couldn't share his meagre fare with many, so he chose a few – the men he spoke of fondly during my childhood, most of whom did not come back. Men who became crosses in the jungle.

Reg's tough upbringing, the loss of his sister and mother, bred in him a hardness, a resilience which would keep him alive along the River Kwai. It was this that gave him a sense of pride in himself and a purpose. He was happy to be part of a platoon, a battalion, a regiment, but he was essentially Reg Twigg, the tough little soldier's boy from Leicester, a man of his class and a man of his times.

He was a conscripted Tommy, following orders because that was expected of him. So he ran a gauntlet of machine-gun fire at Singapore when it fell to the Japanese. He sat idle in the hospital there when he wanted to fight on. He stayed on duty after the British surrender, charged with not letting British property fall into the hands of the enemy. Perhaps because Reg had a loathing of authority from an early age, he had little time for officers who by and large escaped the worst hells of work on the Railway. The exception – and it was an important one – was the medical officers who helped save his life.

With the hindsight of modern research, we have a more balanced view of this period in history and perhaps a different take on the 'Railway of Death'. Reg had no access along the Kwai to newspapers or radio. Any news he got was second-hand at best and often propagandist rubbish. He had no clock, no calendar, so he is sometimes vague about the exact sequence of events. But he is utterly consistent in his memories and his recall of incidents has never changed. I came to know his mates Howard Reast and Roger Curtis well in the years that followed and their stories always meshed with my father's.

Reg is not bitter about the Japanese people. The culture of bushido, the way of the warrior, which he encountered in the camps, was a way of life for the Japanese. But he was and remains bitter about the cruelty of the individual guards which almost defies belief today and about the fact that the Japanese government has never issued a formal apology for atrocities committed on the Railway.

I am proud to have played my part in putting my father's story together. I am proud of the man, who died two weeks before this book was published and a few months before his hundredth birthday, and proud of the fact that his resilience and his sheer guts got him through. As a child I never understood why he sometimes shouted incomprehensibly in his sleep. It is only now that I fully understand.

And when you have read his story, so will you.

Clive Medway

Prologue: Harry

Harry sits on my bed sometimes, talking. He's skinny. Horribly skinny. Skinny like a man who is going to die. But Harry's dead already. There's a bayonet wound in his side, a dark red hole between his ribs. I can hear his voice. I can see his smile. In the darkness I can even smell him; smell him like he smelt at Tarso, in what they called a hospital. He's telling me he's got dysentery.

Look up the disease today, online or in a medical dictionary. It will stress how mild this is, how easily treated. That's today. In civilized countries. But I am talking about *then* – the time of the Railway. And there was *nothing* civilized about the camp at Tarso. So there was nothing mild about what Harry had got. Amoebic dysentery causes nausea, intense abdominal pain, vomiting and rapid weight loss.

Harry has the lot. He's dying. He's dead. But he's on my bed, chatting away and smiling.

It's a dream, of course. Harry Barnett hasn't sat on anybody's bed for seventy years. But I see Harry regularly and others like him. Jack Clayton. Thompson. Albert and Jackie. All of them. They were my friends, my comrades-in-arms in a badly bungled war. And they come and see me sometimes, in the darkness of my memories, like faded photographs . . .

I didn't go to the hospital at Tarso if I could help it. Only the desperate went there, the walking wounded who could walk no more. But one day I was ordered to take something to the place and I saw Harry, lying on his sack on a bamboo 'bed', a platform inches off the floor. I'd last seen him in the Alexandra Hospital in Singapore, a place with brick walls and a roof, glass windows and metal bed frames. There'd been mattresses and sheets and pillows and everything you'd expect in the medical services belonging to the greatest imperial power in history. *Then* they'd kept us all there pointlessly, because there was nothing wrong with us. We were itching to get at the Japs up-country and they wouldn't let us go because of some ridiculous red tape and the unfathomable decision-making of the high command. *Now* we were all hospital cases and the Japs had come to us.

Harry half lay on his bamboo. His eyes were sunk into his head and his mouth, half hidden under the untrimmed beard, was cracked and bricky-dry. I didn't mean to say it. In fact, it was the last thing I should have said, but it slipped out any-way. 'Oh my God.' Silly little kids of today say this all the time, about the most inconsequential and unimportant things. I said it because I was staring at an old friend, a mate I'd known since our school days, a lad I'd played football with. I said it because I hadn't seen him for over a year and because he was lying there, dying.

'I've got dysentery, Reg,' Harry croaked, forming his dry tongue to get round the words. He didn't need to tell me that. I'd seen it all before.

I knelt next to him, pretending he didn't smell revolting, pretending I wasn't going to be sick. 'How long have you been like this, Harry?' I asked him.

'Just a few days,' he said.

I smiled. I'd seen bigger men than Harry go down with the disease in a day. Thirteen stone six footers reduced to sham-bling, shitting wrecks. I took what little kit he had left – a ripped and ragged shirt and a spare Jap-happy made of rag and some bedding – and told him I'd be back. I held it away from me as far as I could until I reached the bank of that damned awful river and started beating it on rocks, the warm brown water splashing and cascading over the stones, my hands and Harry's kit. Every time I handled the stinking matting I retched, writhing with the pain as I fought to control it.

Then, after I had laid out Harry's kit to dry in the sun, I scooped up river water in empty two-gallon cans and carted them back to the hospital. Nobody stopped me. If the Jap guards noticed, they weren't going to get involved. Just another Englishman wasting his time on a dying friend. I poured the water over Harry and cleaned him up as well as I could. Then I did the same to the bed. I laid him down in his dried clothes and sat with him for a while.

He'd received no treatment. There wasn't any. All the exhausted medical officer could do was to look in on him from time to time. Any food he'd been given by the orderlies went straight through him and we both knew the clean kit and bed and Harry would be covered again by morning.

'I've got to go now, Harry,' I told him when I couldn't stand it any longer. 'I'll come and see you tomorrow.'

I did. And the faces of the men in the beds around him had changed. And they'd changed again when I went back a third time. And a fourth. One by one, the dysentery and malaria cases died. But Harry held on, getting weaker and more pitiful each day. Those nights I sent up a little prayer for Harry. I knew there was no one listening, but maybe I was hedging my bets, for Harry's sake.

One morning on my way to the hospital, I saw Harry up and about. That sounds too breezy. Actually he was with six others, all terminally ill as we'd say today, and they were shuffling along, helping each other, towards the Jap guard-house.

'Where are you off to, Harry?' I asked.

'Don't know, Reg,' he whispered. It was, in some ways, the story of our lives for the past two years. We never had any idea where we were going or why. We just did it. If there was a master plan somewhere, nobody had thought to let us in on it.

You got used to Japanese or Korean swear words in the camps. You didn't really know what they meant but the tone said it all. I heard one hissing in my ear seconds before I felt the rifle butt slam into the side of my head. That was all the provocation they needed; to have the humanity to speak to a dying man. The impact knocked me sideways, my ear was a mass of blood and my head was singing. I was on the ground, checking that I still had all my teeth. Then I felt steel-shod boots crunching into my ribs and I lay still. You're not quite playing dead – even the Japs aren't dim enough to fall for that. You're simply saying, 'I've got nothing left. Just leave me here. I've had it.'

I followed the boots up through half-closed eyes. The put-tees, the breeches, the tunic and the crop-headed face above. It was the Korean guard we all called the 'Silver Bullet'. I could have bet money on it.

Seven walking skeletons were shambling away from the guardhouse as I lay there, feet dragging, shoulders down. If these men had ever been soldiers, they weren't now. The Silver Bullet marched after them, strutting as he always did, shoulders square, back ramrod straight, as other guards led them into a dark trail that disappeared into that impenetrable jungle. I never saw Harry again.

That was the trouble with Harry. He was too weak to work

and too cussed to die. So the Japanese killed him. There was no rifle fire in the trees, no crack of a pistol and no scream. I hope Harry died quickly, a bayonet through the heart, but if I knew the Silver Bullet, he'd have carried out the ritual slowly, making a speech in a staccato, alien language none of us understood before marking out each man for death, making the others watch as their numbers dwindled to that terrified, lonely last one to die. I hope Harry was the first.

And even now, after all these years, Harry sits on my bed sometimes, talking. He can't tell his story now. Neither can Albert, Jackie, Jack Clayton or Thompson. So I'll have to do the talking for them.

I

A Land Fit for Heroes

I still have the postcard. Mum read it to us, me and my brothers, till it became a sort of mantra – 'To my little Reggie. Daddy is coming home soon and Mum and Cyril and you and Kenny and Dad are going to have such a holiday at Christmas, with a Christmas tree and toys for my little boys.'

I was five when my dad came back. And I didn't know what to expect. He had left when I was nine months old and I had no memory of him. If I formed a mental picture, it was of a genie from Arabia, a huge, magical figure looming over us like something out of a lamp. Perhaps this came from some long-forgotten bedtime story about Mesopotamia and Palestine. Much later, I discovered that the 1st Leicesters did fight in the Middle East but most of Dad's stories were about France, where he had fought in what everybody called the Great War.

When I saw him, he wasn't a genie at all, just a man in a rough, khaki greatcoat with a tin hat strapped to his kitbag. We all ran to him, Cyril, Kenny and me, laughing and gabbling as if we'd seen him every day of our lives. We didn't care for toys and trees that Christmas – our dad was the best Christmas present of all.

To the outside world, the one I would come to know all too soon, he was Private Sidney Ernest Twigg of the 1st Battalion, the Leicestershire Regiment. His cap badge was a tiger

with its paws upraised and a banner reading 'Hindoostan' on
its back. The same tiger snarled on the flag over the first home
I knew. It would be years before I knew anything about Dad's
life. Both his parents had died of TB at a time when the disease wiped out whole streets of the poor. So Dad had gone to
live at the Fern Bank Working Boys' Home in Avenue Road,
Leicester. Somebody noticed that the lad had talent – he
could play five instruments – and they sent him to the Gordon Boys' Home in Woking. Lads there generally went into
the army so Sid Twigg became a boy soldier, in the York and
Lancaster Regiment. It was 1902, just after the Boer War –
one of those rare years when the people took soldiers to their
hearts. Sid was sixteen.

Seven years later he married Ethel, my mum. They were at
Wandsworth then and two years after that were living at
Farnborough in Hampshire with their first child, my sister
Constance. The army kept men like my dad on the move and
the 1911 Census lists him as 'Soldier Bandsman in the Yorks
and Lancs Regiment'. His marching instrument was the flute,
although it was usual in those days for all army musicians to
play the bugle, as that was used to relay commands in battle.

It was an altogether older man that we boys climbed all
over that Christmas of 1919. I couldn't estimate people's ages
then, but there was something 'old' about Dad, something
missing, and in those years ahead I'd often see him lost in a
world we couldn't understand, what one of the war poets
called 'the hell where youth and laughter go'. We didn't know
it then, but the Leicesters had had their units increased from
five to nineteen battalions and had fought all over France and
Flanders as well as the Middle East. They had lost 6,000 dead.
That was what my dad had lived through.

The home Dad came back to was a small Victorian terraced

house made of red brick along Healey Street, South Wigston. The home he'd left was the married quarters at Glen Parva barracks in Saffron Lane. I barely remembered it. To me, my world was Healey Street, with its smoke-blackened chimneys and everybody living on top of everybody else. It could have been any street in the world, but it was my street. In our ragged trousers and hand-me-down jumpers we kicked a ball around the lamp posts, shouting excitedly when we'd scored, vanishing like will-o'-the-wisps if a window got smashed. The girls couldn't play football; just didn't have the skill. We'd scuff our ball over their chalk-marked hopscotch and put them off their rhythm in their endless skipping games.

We'd pat the warm sleek hide of the delivery man's horse and get a cuff round the ear from the barrow boy who was trying to sell his wares and didn't have any patience with us kids. From time to time we'd see a motor car, usually passing the end of the street, rattling with its throaty engine or frightening passers-by with its klaxon. We'd stand and we'd wonder. Slowly, the twentieth century came to industrial Leicester.

Death came too. I barely remember them but there were widows in Healey Street, pale, struggling women who would walk around wearing black. The curtains would be drawn for a day or two and neighbours on their front doorsteps would shake their heads and sigh. I knew nothing about the official letters from the government, filled with empty words of regret and the 'Death Pennies': bronze plaques that were sent in little brown envelopes inscribed with the names of the dead. Few of us had dads in those early years. They were away fighting, but none of us understood where or why. It was what dads did.

But in those days, death came to us kids too. You got used to it. Where was Bill? Why wasn't he playing football today?

What about Emily? No one had seen her. And when Constance went, it hit home and hit hard. Because Constance was my sister, the one I went to when I was in trouble. I couldn't tell you why exactly, but Constance was more of a mum to me than Mum was. She was only three years older than me, but she'd listen and nod and put her arm around me, telling me it was all right. Constance had had 'to go away to see Jesus' and wouldn't be coming home. I cried. We all cried. Did I wonder, even then, who this Jesus was who made such demands on little families like ours? Constance was *my* sister, not his, and I missed her.

What actually took Constance away was diphtheria, a contagious disease that killed thousands and came as regularly as the seasons. Anybody could catch it; it was no respecter of persons. It starts with a sore throat and a hoarse voice. Your skin turns blue and your neck swells. It hurts to swallow and your breathing is fast and shallow. The first vaccinations were being developed in the twenties but they weren't ready in time to save Constance. For the rest of us, of course, life went on. As it must. 'Reggie,' I can hear my mum's voice now, 'go down to Dunmore's and buy two penn'orth of broken biscuits, there's a good lad.' I didn't need any more encouragement. The coins were buried deep in the pockets of my short trousers, the ones that reached nearly to my knees, and I was off, running along Healey Street and onto Canal Street, to another world.

After all the adventures I've had I still remember this one. There was a dog that lived in an alleyway between two houses at the end of our street. When you're five a dog seems very, very big and this one would lie in wait for me. It didn't bite, but it barked like hell and ran along with you, snapping and snuffling. Even so, the goal was worth it. I can still smell the

sickly aroma over Dunmore's now. The building was huge
and dwarfed our houses and those tuppenny crumbs were
simply delicious.

I remember it was on one of these trips, running the dog
gauntlet and jingling my change, that I saw two old women
chatting on the pavement. They both looked a hundred but
it was their topic of conversation that stopped me in my
tracks. I could tell they were shocked by what they were
talking about, whispering almost in disbelief. Something
called a Zeppelin had dropped bombs on London. I wasn't
sure what London was but the idea of a flying warship looming out of the clouds terrified me; I watched the skies for
days afterwards.

Most of the men who came home took off their army khaki
and tried to get back to the lives they'd left behind. But Dad
was a regular soldier and khaki was his old life. So, how do
you tell? How do you tell a six-year-old that his father's
going off to war again, somewhere we'd been fighting in for
eight hundred years. And what kind of government sends
soldiers' families to Ireland at the height of the Troubles?
Because we were all going: Dad, Mum, Cyril, Ken and me.
If you read potted histories of the Leicestershire Regiment
today, they'll tell you that the 1st Battalion was sent to Dublin between 1920 and 1922. This sounds very neat and
organized, but my memories aren't like that at all. We sat on
wooden benches on a night ferry. It was raining. I'd never
seen the sea before. Leicester, if you look on a map, is about
as near to the centre of England as you can get. And this
wasn't the seaside I'd heard all about, with golden sands and
rippling surf and buckets and spades. This was the Irish Sea,
wild, dark and deep, lurching under our little boat. Our

world was contained in just two small suitcases, buckled round with a wide strap, just in case. There were no extra coats or blankets. Army families travelled light. We probably drove Mum to breaking point asking when we'd get there, wherever 'there' was. And what it would be like. Remember when you were a kid, how you'd just accept feeling sick from time to time? It went with the territory, didn't it? Like a clip round the ear and impetigo. But seasickness was something else. I thought that night would last for ever.

Dawn was creeping over the docks at Dublin when we berthed. We couldn't actually get off the ship for ages. I suppose there was complicated paperwork and, after all, we were entering a military zone. Men had died only hundreds of yards from where we boarded the train. We kids didn't know this, but it must have made life very difficult for the grown-ups. Was this my first train? I don't know. I'd seen them often enough because the Leicester–Rugby line ran past Canal Street back home. But this may have been my first ride in a carriage. It was third class, of course, with hard, wooden-slatted seats. And it was still raining.

We got to a station. I would find out much later that this was Athlone, a little town in Westmeath, in the heart of Ireland. We were shepherded onto open-topped army trucks; I'd never ridden in one of *those* before. It was cold and uncomfortable and not even the graceful bridge over the Shannon or the greenery of the countryside could compensate for the jolting and shuddering over rutted and pot-holed roads. Then, suddenly, we were there – our new home.

It was a barracks – a home from home. Except it wasn't. A place more unlike Healey Street would be difficult to imagine. The trucks rattled under a wooden barrier that had been raised by soldiers. And the soldiers carried guns; something I'd never seen my dad do. There were heavy iron gates set into a high wall; if I'd been older I'd have realized that this was an outpost, a bastion of civilization at the edge of the world. So we only went outside the barracks to go to school and this was with an armed guard. We were kids. We didn't know about the centuries of hatred, the Irish Republican Army and the Black and Tans. Everything was an adventure and it was made all the more exciting by Dad.

Sometimes he'd hold me up to the window in our little back bedroom as the sun's rays crept over what he called the Blue Mountains. 'There, Reggie,' he'd say, 'that's the magic world. Giants live there. And elves. And little green men. You can see them sometimes, but you'll never catch one 'cos they can't be caught. That's 'cos they're magic.'

We had our own visitor from the world of magic. And she terrified us. Beyond the gates, forever locked, we could see down into the street below. She'd come at different times of the day, look up at us through ancient eyes with a crooked smile on her lips. She led a tattered old donkey, even older than she was, with ragged canvas saddlebags across its back. She'd offer us fruit – an apple or a pear perhaps. We'd never take it. If anyone was tempted, one of us would nudge him in the back and whisper, wide-eyed, 'Don't listen to her. She's a witch. It's poisoned, like in the fairy tales.' I still feel guilty about all this. She was just trying to be friendly and kind. Perhaps she had lost her own grandchildren, who knows? Perhaps she was lonely. In fact, she was just like us, a little lost and very poor.

Army kids. We hung around the cookhouse waiting for the cooks to throw out their hard tack, teeth-breaking biscuits that still formed part of a soldier's rations. The brown paper bags we'd find in the dustbins, British Army, for the use of, we'd tear into strips and roll into 'fags', drawing on the tobaccoless copies as we'd seen the soldiers do with the real things. We also used our hunting skills as dark came down and the lights burned blue in the barracks. We'd creep around the dark corners, scuttling along the alleyways between the high walls. We were looking for cats, but we rarely found them. Actually *hurting* them never occurred to us. But we were amateurs at this. The moggies were the professionals. They hunted – and killed – for a living. They had eyes that could see in the dark better than we could in the daylight. *And they never made a sound.*

I remember standing on the sidelines of the barracks square watching games of shinty played by the men. It is a sort of cross between hockey and hurling, everybody running around after a white cork ball, their curved sticks clacking together in the afternoon. But *nothing* was as exciting as standing in that same barracks square and watching the mail fly in. Looking back, I suppose it was too risky to bring letters by conventional mail van or cart. The Irish Republican Army had neither aircraft nor anti-aircraft guns, so a plane was safe. We'd watch the plane with its double bank of wings like a fly in the distance, getting nearer and nearer and louder and louder until it roared overhead and a canvas mailbag would thump onto the square, sending up a great cloud of dust and gravel.

It was on the barracks square that I saw a pound note one day. There couldn't have been any wind because it would have blown away. It was white and as big as a handkerchief. I'd never seen one before, though I knew what it was. Perhaps an officer had dropped it. Perhaps a squaddie had just collected his pay. I was far too afraid to touch it and ran like a thing possessed for home. The vicious dog, the old crone with the donkey, the giants of the Blue Mountains, they were all chasing me as I crashed into our living quarters. I blurted out what I'd seen to my dad as if I'd stumbled across the Holy Grail or the Ark of the Covenant. My dad told me to go back and get it.

I suppose some people would find this amoral. Stealing by finding, the law calls it, and I should have handed it in to the authorities. What would I have got for that? A 'thank you, lad' and a ruffle of the hair? We lived on that pound for over a week and thought no more about it. I got a large bag of sweets. Perhaps the Jesus who had taken Constance was looking out for the Twiggs after all.

I was eight when the Empire began to fall. Not that I grasped quite what was happening. I remember standing with Dad on the battlements of Dublin Castle as a lone bugler played the 'Last Post', that haunting goodnight I'd heard so often that I took it for granted. The Union Jack, swirling in a stiffening breeze, came down. I wasn't there when another flag, the orange, white and green of Eire, was run up in its place. It was 1922 and, although I didn't know it, the British government had just, in effect, surrendered. And the army had no choice but to go with it.

And then they moved us on again. The army had built Aldershot camp shortly after the Crimean War. It had been a collection of tents and huts to house Queen Victoria's soldiers, but by the time the Leicesters moved in the living accommodation was brick. Married quarters were two bedrooms and a small living room with a fireplace. The kitchen had a cupboard and sink but the tap and lavatory were communal. I slept with Cyril and Ken, three growing boys jostling for space in a two-foot-six bed. The British Army had been in khaki for thirty years officially and longer in practice but this was Aldershot. Headquarters. Us kids watched spellbound as the ceremonial outfits were put through their paces. All the glitter we saw was once combat gear but times had changed and the nodding plumes of the hussars and the glittering helmets of the dragoons only came out on high days and holidays. I remember watching the swords of the cavalry, with their smooth, shell-like handguards and their long, tapering blades. There were no high walls here, no armed guards, just the expanses of meadow beyond the grounds of Laffan's Plain. We ran waist high through the grasses of summer, trying to catch the butterflies on their dazzling flights. We found birds' nests and took the eggs, like all kids did then before the world knew better. But there was more to it than the challenge of climbing a tree, of pitting yourself, in just a little way, against nature.

Somebody once asked me to sum up my childhood in a single word. You don't know how hard that is until you try. Even so, it didn't take me long. The word was hunger. We never, any of us, had enough to eat. Being a regular soldier was a good, steady job and there was always a regular income. It just wasn't enough. Breakfast, at any time of the year, was one round of toast. Dinner was two rounds, bread this time, spread thinly with jam. The only meal you'd recognize was Sunday lunch. We sat quietly at the table – kids were supposed to be seen and not heard in those days – until given permission to eat. There were no snacks, no seconds. The war I would fight as a man exposed the physical deficiencies of my generation. Rickets, flat feet, spinal curvatures – you name it; an awful lot could be put down to the food we didn't get as children.

So our rambles in the meadows weren't just because we were boys out for adventure. We were a foraging army of scouts, calling ourselves 'Commandos' and looking for food. If we found berries, we ate them. If the wild mushrooms were white and fresh-looking, we ate them too. And the pears in a nearby garden became an obsession. September was *the* month, the green fruit ripening to a gorgeous russet. Looking back, I don't know why I took the knife. Perhaps I wanted to share the pears with the others, my brothers and my mates; I don't know. Anyway, I helped myself to Dad's army jackknife with its distinctive black cross-hatched grip which was supposed to prevent your fingers from slipping, except it didn't. I cut my finger to the bone and jumped as I felt the blade bite deep. There was blood everywhere and I had to go home. That was it. I'd been caught bang to rights; you couldn't cover up a wound like that. I was in pain already but I knew it would get worse when Dad belted me for taking the knife in the first place.

In fact, he just took me to the army hospital where an orderly in a white coat cleaned the wound and stitched it. There was no anaesthetic. I just sat on Dad's lap and he held me still while they stitched. I screamed the place down and felt bitterly ashamed of myself. The orderly patted me on the head and said how brave I'd been. I never did feel Dad's belt for this.

I was soon back with the Commandos, hunting acorns. The coal allowance in the winter didn't go far and Dad's pay didn't cover it, so we burned acorns instead. The best ones were to be found beyond the wire, and the sign that read 'Private. Keep Out'. So of course, in we went. The problem with rooting about for acorns is that your head is down and you can't always see clearly through the trees. On one particular occasion, the first I knew of danger was the hissed 'Game-keeper! Gamekeeper!' from a fellow Commando. We knew the man would march us straight to prison. He might even have shot us. So we ran, jumping over the tall grass and the tree roots, making for the fence. I jumped it, but too high and my knee hit my chin so that I bit down on my tongue and lip.

Blood was pouring from my mouth and the lads crowded round me, helping me to stumble along: 'Reggie's wounded.' More army stitches, more pats on the head. I didn't cry this time. I had learned that toughness was its own reward.

I suppose I became a tearaway. I was a scruffy kid, never bathed or cleaned my teeth because I can't remember any-body ever telling me to. I was sharp, skinny and fit. Over time, I realized I could outrun any of my mates and that came in handy, especially when scrumping apples. I was down that tree and out of that orchard long before anybody else and it must have been then I invented a silly rhyme. I said it out loud, then muttered it under my breath as I ran along, the hounds of hell at my heels. 'Kinfi-nob-bleation-mira-moka-kid-comeday-mumday-all-a-mid.' God knows where it came from or what it was supposed to mean, but whenever I said it I got away and that silly eight-year-old's phrase stayed with me.

We fought running battles with gangs of kids from other regiments, throwing stones at each other and ducking behind trees, crawling through the long grass of summer. Our foot-ball matches must have been like the game's early days, before it became a sport. It was just a free-for-all with wild kicking and bruised shins. When we did our 'footballers' falls', it was for real.

And I learned to steal. I'm not proud of it now, looking back. But it was a way of life for kids like me. We were all at it. An old lady kept a sweet shop near the barracks. It was a dark, dismal place with wooden floorboards and planking and it smelt of mothballs. There wasn't ever much for sale but on the counter – about chest height for me in those days – was an open box of Blue Bird toffees. I was never quite sure what the bird logo was supposed to be – was it a swallow or a swift? It didn't really matter; I was just looking at the toffees, wrapped in glittering cellophane. I gave the old girl my wide-eyed look. 'Mother sent me to see if you could let her have a few sheets of brown paper,' I said, a dodger more artful than anything Dickens could have created. Come to think of it, the old lady was like something out of a Dickens novel, with her floor-length skirt and her shawl. I wasn't falling for her kind face; I wanted those toffees.

'I'll have to get them from the back,' she said. I knew that; it was all part of my master plan. 'I won't be long.' I hoped she would be as she rustled off leaving me alone in the shop. I could see the lads outside, peering in through the window. I hadn't drawn a short straw or anything like that; I was just better at this than they were. I waved them in and like a horde of locusts, they descended on the toffee tin. We all took some, but not enough that it showed or I wouldn't be able to pull this dodge again. I waited solemnly once they had gone and thanked the old lady for the brown paper. 'Kinfi-nob-bleation . . .' You know the rest.

I must have been about ten when my world started to fall apart. Mum said to me one day, 'Reggie, take a note for me to the sergeant in the Lincolnshire Regiment barracks will you? He'll give you a bar of chocolate.' I expect my eyes lit up. 'But, Reggie,' Mum held my arm and looked me squarely in the face, 'it's our secret, all right? If you tell anybody, the sergeant won't be able to give you any more.' I didn't question any of this. I didn't understand it. Didn't know that I was helping to betray my dad and break up a marriage. I was never aware of rows between Mum and Dad – although he did throw his Sunday lunch at the living-room wall once. So it came as a huge surprise when Dad was discharged at the end of February 1925. The surprise wasn't that he'd left the army – though he'd given half his life to it – but that Mum didn't come with us. She stayed behind and joined the Lincolns. Ethel Twigg had gone for another soldier.

We all cried, my brothers and I – 'But why can't you come with us, Mum?' Things had happened, she told us through her tears – and we had no idea what – but she loved us and hoped one day we'd understand. And she walked away. I was eleven by now and it seemed like the end of my world. Constance had gone and now Mum – and she wasn't going to Jesus, but to a sergeant in the Lincolnshire Regiment. All the warmth and love in our home left with her that day.

'What is our task?' Lloyd George had asked in November 1918, when I was still playing in the gutters of Healey Street and my dad had yet to come home. 'To make Britain a fit country for heroes to live in . . . Slums are not fit homes for the men who have won this war or for their children.'

Yet here we were, the men of the Twigg family, living in impossibly cramped conditions with friends in Pelham Street, back in Leicester. I shared a bed with Cyril and Ken, the three of us in a freezing room on an iron bedstead with murderous springs. Time had frozen in Pelham Street. Step outside and you'd be stepping back a hundred years. A terraced street in the industrial Midlands as I remember it on Good Friday 1925. It was a raw morning and I could hear the wavering cry from across the road: 'Hot cross buns, hot cross buns, one a penny, two a penny, hot cross buns.' The church bells were ringing all over the city and Dad was already in the back yard, his lean face white with shaving soap and his cut-throat razor wet from the communal standpipe tap there. He was small and wiry like me and he looked even smaller now he was out of his uniform. He never seemed exactly well these days, his chest rattling and wheezing with years of bad food, poor housing and fags, all of it made worse by the filthy wet trenches of the Somme.

The bun seller was wheeling his cart along the street as I rubbed the frost with its crystal beauty from the bedroom window. People came out of their houses to buy his wares but we didn't need them. Mum had sent us boys an Easter egg each so a hot cross bun was nothing by comparison. Then we had to spruce ourselves up because Good Friday was like Sunday and we had to go to a special service at the church hall in Trinity Lane round the corner. We went there for the occasional treat or outing; the vicar hoped we were going there for our salvation.

It must have been soon after this that Dad got married again and we moved to Luther Street, to a home of our own. His new wife was Evelyn Thacker and she came, inevitably, from Leicester. She and my dad had three girls – Peggy, Sheila and Denise, who everybody called Bunty – and I got used to girls in the house once more. Dad's eighteen shillings a week army pension went nowhere and even when he played in a local dance band, we couldn't afford the rent. This was *the* era of the dance band but for a struggling amateur it was no sort of living. So we had to move again. Dad scrounged a handcart from somewhere and we loaded up our few belongings onto it and trundled out to Glenfield, to Kirby Frith Hall. This was a dreadful place, made worse, I now realize, because it had once been a rather grand Georgian country house with a cobbled courtyard and stables. The house was falling apart when a local landlord, Arthur Cart, bought it and converted it into flats. The man was a stranger to scruples and rode around the place in a pony and trap, like a lord of the manor. He whipped the horse for no reason at all as far as we kids could see. Once, it lashed out with its hind hoofs, only to get them tangled in the shafts. Purple with fury, he beat the animal all the harder.

I didn't like him and I didn't like the stables. There was an ancient landau or some sort of coach behind the old, weather-beaten doors, so riddled with woodworm it threatened to fall to bits at any moment. Beneath the outbuildings were more doors that led to the old cellars. These were dungeons, I knew, and untold terrors lurked there.

The Twigg household consisted of a sitting room, two small bedrooms and a tiny kitchen. The floors were flagstone, freezing in winter, and only the sitting room had a fireplace. There was a communal tap in the yard outside and the lavatories were buckets in an outhouse, emptied every day into a huge tub on a cart and spread on the fields nearby. The whole place stank but the mushrooms were legendary!

Coal was unaffordable so the job for us kids was to find wood wherever we could. My mate Bernard and I hit upon a brilliant idea: we chopped down a young oak tree on the estate. Arthur Cart went, as they'd say today, ballistic and threatened to evict everybody if no one owned up. In those days tenants had precious few rights and we went in fear and trembling for days. In the event, Cart didn't evict anybody. It may have just been guilt that I imagined he stared at me more than most at that time.

Dad had got a job working at Snaith's decorators' merchants

in Leicester; this meant a two-mile walk to the centre of Glenfield to catch a bus. I'd go with him sometimes, just for the outing, but of course I had an agenda of my own. There were miles of fields, hedges and woods, a kind of paradise for a twelve-year-old. I'd cut across the fields to school, past a gypsy camp where a fire constantly burned, no matter what the weather. They kept a fox tethered to the wheel of one of their brightly painted caravans and there was always a cheery wave from one or the other of them. I never went too close, of course. It was well known that gypsies stole kids. That wasn't going to happen to me.

As a townie, I loved the countryside, the birds heralding the spring, the fields drowsy with the hum of bees in the summer. We scrumped apples in Smith's orchard next door and played games handed down through the generations, games that have almost disappeared. Tin-a-lerky was a sort of hide-and-seek where the person caught could be released by someone reaching a tin can and kicking it, shouting 'Tin-a-lerky' so we'd all have to start all over again. 'Dicky Dicky Show Your Light' only worked at dusk or after dark and required the ownership of matches! Like half the kids in the world we made trolleys from old pram wheels and raced each other downhill at breakneck speeds. Brakes? Who needed them?

I remember the day I got religion. The way home from school was through the churchyard with its dark yews and grey slabs to mark the dead. It also housed the vicar's shed, which we knew was full of trays of apples in September. We also knew the door was always locked. Then, one day it wasn't. The next day the wrath of God visited us, the vicar in grim conversation with the headmaster. The headmaster's assembly was clearly influenced by this conversation because he told us that stealing of any kind was evil and that God was always watching us. Nobody snitched. There is honour among thieves if you're twelve. But the head's words got to me and when we met up later to eat the apples we'd scrumped, I cracked. 'These are stolen apples,' I said, like Moses coming down from the mountain. 'God will punish us if He's watching.' One by one they all put their apples down, even the half-eaten ones, and we left them to rot under the trees.

It didn't end there. The vicar was clearly an Old Testament man. He and the head identified my best mate, Bob Hillier, as the ringleader of the gang of hellions carrying out a crime wave in rural Leicestershire. So Bob got the cane, six of the best across the polished seat of his trousers from the head. Bob said nothing. Neither did his family. The vicar didn't approach them. He'd have got nothing out of them if he had, just as the Hilliers got nothing from the church. Except, maybe, a few apples!

Compared with Bob's family the Twiggs lived life high off the hog. The Hilliers had moved from White Grit near Bishop's Castle in Shropshire looking for work. All there was in White Grit was an old lead mine. It had been there since Roman times and was all but played out. Bob's dad jumped out of the frying pan into the fire at Kirby Frith Hall because he got a job – I never knew exactly what – from Arthur Cart. The landlord also rented the Hilliers a ramshackle wooden hut in a corner of a field. It had a corrugated tin roof that leaked. There was only one room and two adults and six kids shared it, with no lavatory, water or kitchen. Bob's mum cooked outside on an open fire just like the gypsies. It was more serious for Bob than for me when I saw the light. Not only did he feel the sting of punishment across his arse, he went without food too. Other people's apple cores were an essential part of his diet. What did Lloyd George go on to say in that speech back in 1918? '[The slums] are not fit nurseries for the children who are to make an imperial race.'

Clearly, someone was listening nine years later when the authorities opened the Saffron Lane council estate to families like ours. Mine was the first generation to experience this and even as a thirteen-year-old, I understood what it meant and appreciated it more than I can say. It was nothing short of a miracle. We had three bedrooms, a bathroom, a coal shed and a back garden. All right, so lots of people kept coal in the bath and the dog in the coal shed, but that's what living in a democracy is all about.

From Saffron Lane every Saturday afternoon we all took part in the 'rush', a noisy, happy charge along the streets to watch the children's films at the Grace Road cinema. A man in a posh uniform tried to keep us in line, but our exuberance was usually too much for him. For an hour or two we could forget Bob Hillier's shack, Arthur Cart's viciousness and the vicar's muscular Christianity and thunder across the silent grey plains of the American Midwest in the company of Tom Mix and Hoot Gibson. Or we could cackle helplessly at the po-faced antics of Harry Langdon or Buster Keaton, little men against the world. I once found a bent silver threepenny bit – we called them joeys – and flattened it out with a large stone to look like a tanner. That got me into the pictures for three weeks at tuppence a go.

I became an accidental hero at Lansdowne Road School about this time. I expect my dad gave me advice about 'looking after myself'; most dads did in those days. I don't know how I fell foul of the school bully – perhaps I looked at him funny. Anyway, he promised to get me after school; news got round the grim old Victorian building and a crowd was guaranteed. I was frogmarched by what seemed a cast of thousands to the park and they all formed a hollow ring.

Now there were rules to fighting. You didn't kick your opponent in the balls, you didn't bite him, scratch or pull his hair. After that, it was every man for himself. The bully was bigger than me, which goes without saying, and he came at me fast. I don't know what I was thinking but I actually closed my eyes when I swung my fist and heard it crunch against his nose. It hurts like hell, doesn't it? The shock stops you and your eyes water. For a split second you can't breathe. When the blood began to drip, the bully burst into tears and ran home. I was carried shoulder high.

When the headmaster sent for me it had nothing to do with the fight. Or my indiscipline, come to that. 'Twigg!' one of the teachers had called me over. 'Come to the head's office at lunchtime.' When I got there, I nearly fell over. Waiting outside, in an overcoat and carrying her handbag, was my mother.

'Hello, Reggie,' she smiled. We walked around the block together for perhaps an hour, but it crawled by like years. She asked how we were all getting on, but I knew she didn't include Dad in this. She said she was sorry she hadn't been back to see us, but it hadn't been possible. At no point did she say she was sorry she had left us. There were a thousand questions I wanted to ask her. Why had she gone? What was wrong with us? With Dad? Was life really so much better with the Lincolns? And why wasn't it possible? Why, in two years, had she been unable to catch a train or a bus and come and see us?

When the bell rang she kissed my cheek and was gone, just like she'd gone two years earlier. It had taken me all that time to stop missing her every day. And now she'd brought all that hurt back. I never saw her again.

Christmas 1927. Yes, it was a white Christmas, but there was nothing remotely romantic about this; not in Leicester. The blizzards were bitter and, having just turned fourteen, I was officially a man, making my way, through the slush, in the world. My first job was in a printing firm where the ink got everywhere. It's all electronic today; then it was typesetting with blocks and rollers. We worked a five-and-a-half-day week, finishing at twelve on Saturdays. One particular day, I knocked off early. And as I was washing the ink off my hands in the back yard, I noticed the clock through the open door. Three minutes to twelve.

'What do you think you're doing, Twigg?' The voice behind me made me jump; the boss was suddenly with me in the yard. I could hardly believe my eyes; I'd never seen him on the premises on a Saturday before.

'I finished what I was doing early, sir,' I said, sensing the ground sliding under my feet.

'You're paid till midday,' he snapped at me. 'Not to finish early when you feel like it. Take a week's notice.'

That was it. Sacked. No warning, no second chance, certainly no tribunal against unfair dismissal. And no dole. So I was down the labour exchange as soon as it opened and I also rummaged around in the pages of the *Leicester Mercury*, looking for something else. The something else was a factory in King Street. They made wooden heels for ladies' shoes. My particular job was to 'scour' them, smoothing the leather and wood as the dust filled my mouth, nose, ears and eyes every day. I was green as grass and as the youngest on the payroll fell for every corny old cliché in the book. 'Fetch us a bucket of steam, Twigg.' Off I went. 'A bucket of steam? Only if you've got a left-handed screwdriver.' Where the hell would I find that? It took me a while, but eventually I learned. The shoe-last factory paid piece rate and I was a fast worker so the money was good.

I played football for the Linwood Lane Club in Leicester and proudly put my trophies on display at home. I joined the Saffron Lane Estate Working Men's Club and used to watch the men smoking their pipes. When you're a boyish-looking eighteen and only five foot four you need some gravitas in your life. So I bought some tobacco, borrowed one of Dad's pipes and cycled out to the country, where I lit up. I then threw up. But that didn't last and my pipe and I became almost inseparable.

After that, nothing really changed in my life until 1935. By that time I was twenty-one, a man in the eyes of the law as well as society. I could have stood on my own two feet – lots of men my age had regular girls or even wives by then – but the hardest times had only just arrived. The Wall Street Crash in October 1929 sent its ripples around the world and caused havoc in Britain. Admittedly, the situation was regional and areas like Scotland, the North East and Wales were hit particularly hard. The Midlands, maybe because of the infant motor industry, was better off, but even so money was very tight. In March 1935 Dad got the manager's job at Snaith's Lincoln branch. Did he have a son, they asked him, who needed a job? Dad's move would have left me homeless, so Snaith's in Lincoln it was.

The city still holds a place in my heart. Not because of the great cathedral, magnificent though it was, nor the fact that it rose like a magic citadel out of the flat of the fenlands. I had enrolled in Kirk White's Youth Club and it became my second home. I played left wing for the football team. We didn't train much; just turned up to play on the day and hoped for the best. Our claim to fame nearly arrived, in the spring of 1937 when we were one point clear of Boultham Park Rangers at the top of the table. The deciding game was on our own turf; the tragedy was we'd over-trained the night before at the pub. Just running the next day was a mammoth effort and the League title evaporated before our eyes.

I loved cycling, if I could get hold of a bike. Back in 1930 when I was sixteen, my mate Arthur Barber and I had set off on a marathon trek to Rhyl, over a hundred and fifty miles. We didn't have any money, so had to run like fury when the man came for the penny we should have paid to sit in one of the funny old wicker chairs that they had on the sands there instead of deckchairs. Our tent had already been damaged when we'd camped overnight in a field at Chirk. Curious cattle had ripped it up but a jolly farmer's wife had taken pity on us and resewed it. It was a kind thought, but it was never quite the same again.

At Kirk White I became captain of the club's cycling team. In the thirties a kind of cycling mania gripped the country. The Highway Code was still new and there were relatively few cars about. There were miles and miles of empty roads snaking all over the country, linking little villages where time had stood still. The club had a male and female team and one day the ladies' captain asked me, 'Can we come out with you this Sunday, Reg?' I was still a kid. Football, cycling, the odd bit of camping – these were my passions. I was never a Boy Scout, but Lord Baden-Powell would have been proud of me. I can still remember my hopelessly naive response. 'If you like,' I said. 'Why do you want to come with us?'

The ladies' captain smiled enigmatically. 'We just thought it would be nice,' she said.

The lads clearly thought so too and we set off on a Sunday morning that was summer personified – clear blue skies and the hedgerows dumb in the heat. We got to the east coast, don't ask me where, probably following the Viking Way across to Skegness; 'Skeggie' was *the* seaside resort for land-locked Midlanders. We took off our cycle clips, our shoes and socks, rolled our trousers up and paddled. God knows what the girls did, but as time went on and these summer outings became regular, boy–girl pairs developed, cycling in twos along the empty roads. Sometimes we'd purr past a slower club or meet another on the road. There was always the standard greeting – a wave and a 'Cheerio'. All so innocent. All so long ago.

The factory fortnight had not caught on yet and even week-long holidays were almost unknown. But in 1935, catching a couple of days, we set off from Leicester to Pwll-heli in Tremadoc Bay, north Wales. This wasn't a namby-pamby ride with girls slowing us up, but a serious cross-country trek. I made it with a few mates and my brother Ken, riding an old black butcher's delivery bike, heavy as sin. Two years later, as an incredibly fit twenty-three-year-old, I went back with Arthur Barber. This time we went from Lincoln and this time we rode Dawes racing bikes. We'd have made it in one day but my chain snapped at Harlech so we had to put up there for the night. The land-lady charged us half a crown each for bed and breakfast – and locked our bikes away to make sure we paid! We spent the evening at the Lion Hotel, where beer was served from a half-gallon porcelain jug filled from a barrel in the cellar. We noticed, Arthur and I, that the cellar was reached by a hole behind the bar. There was no trap door, no safety device of any kind, just stone steps disappearing into the darkness. We stayed until closing time and not once did the barman miss his footing and hurtle to his doom. I learned a very useful survival skill that night; if you're faced with an ongoing problem, find a way round it.

I wish now I'd paid a little more attention to the other cycling clubs on the road. This was the late thirties and some of them, I know now, especially ones with maps and earnest expressions on their faces, were probably members of the Nazi Ausland organization, carrying out a recce of Britain against the day.

That day came on 3 September 1939. Nobody was ready for it.

2

Gone for a Soldier

'This morning,' the plummy, tired voice crackled over the wireless, 'the British ambassador in Berlin handed the German government a final note, stating that, unless we heard from them by eleven o'clock that they were prepared at once to withdraw their troops from Poland, a state of war would exist between us. I have to tell you now that no such undertaking has been received and that consequently this country is at war with Germany.'

The prime minister, Neville Chamberlain, was speaking to me and Dad in the front room of 128 Boultham Park Road, Lincoln, as he was speaking to millions across the country. It was a Sunday, 3 September. Bright sunshine bathed the street, which was deserted. There were no dogs barking or kids playing. Not even a bird sang. There was a sense of foreboding I couldn't quite fathom at the time and can't explain now. 'It is the evil things that we shall be fighting against,' Chamberlain explained, 'brute force, bad faith, injustice, oppression and persecution.'

Down at the aptly named Victory pub, I listened to my dad's mates. Chamberlain could put whatever gloss on it he liked – most of the blokes there hadn't voted for him anyway – but in reality, it would be just like the last time. It was less than twenty years since the Armistice and here we were again. The old men remembered; back in 1914 it was all flags and

bands and young lads lying about their age and filling their
boots with crumpled newspaper to make them taller so
they could enlist. It would be all over by Christmas and the
women of England were saying 'Go!' Now it was different. A
dark, collective memory sat in that corner of the pub like a
ghost – the doomed youth of a generation. There'd be no
rush to the colours *this* time, just a nervous, depressed bunch
of eighteen- to forty-year-olds waiting for the buff envelope
to fall onto the front doormat bearing the inescapable letters
OHMS. Above all, in the Victory that Sunday, was the disbelief that the enemy was Germany *again*. Hadn't they got the
message last time? It took a serious follower of the news to
piece it all together, to trace the rise of a Bavarian corporal to
the megalomaniac bent on acquiring living space for a greater
Germany. Most of us hadn't seen it coming.

Thankfully, it didn't come. The thousands of cardboard
coffins mass-produced in London weren't used. There were
no bombs, no hint of what the Germans called *Blitzkrieg*, the
lightning war that would change my generation's outlook for
ever. In France they called it *drôle de guerre*; we called it the
Phoney War. Except at sea, nothing seemed to be happening.
Through the autumn I went to work as usual, played football
and cycled with the lads. The war was happening somewhere
else and might even go away.

But war wasn't going away. The brown envelopes kept
coming and because Snaith's was so short staffed, I found
myself back in the Leicester branch by the January of 1940.
The spring and summer of that year were astonishing and
terrifying. *Blitzkrieg* swept west, swallowing the Low Countries and France and swatting the British Expeditionary Force
aside at Dunkirk. Hitler stood on the coast of France and
trained his telescope on the white cliffs of Dover. In every

pub, every shop, every workplace there were worried, half-whispered conversations. Could we stop them? With what? We'd lost thousands of men and tons of equipment at Dunkirk. On top of that, we had an empire to protect, the pink bits on the school atlas, our troops scattered around the world.

On 18 June Winston Churchill rallied the country with one of his great speeches – 'The whole fury and might of the enemy must very soon be turned on us . . . Let us therefore brace ourselves to our duty and so bear ourselves that, if the British Empire and its Commonwealth last for a thousand years, men will still say "This was their finest hour".' But Hitler had promised his Germans a thousand-year Reich, too. I shudder now to think how naive I was, how politically unaware. For years, some British newspapers had been extolling the virtues of the Nazis and the 'economic miracle' they had carried out in Germany. And now, the prime minister was telling us we had our backs to the wall and Ministry of Information leaflets fluttered through our letterboxes telling us what to do if the invader were to come. We certainly weren't to tell him the way to anywhere and on no account lend him our bikes!

When you're the son of a soldier who fought in the trenches, you have a certain take on life. I didn't learn this Great War song from my dad, but I knew it anyway:

> I don't want a bayonet in my belly,
> I don't want my bollocks shot away,
> I'd rather stay in England,
> In merry, merry England,
> And fornicate my bleeding life away.

The Great War was all about mud, no-man's land, barbed wire, mustard gas, machine guns. No, the infantry had no appeal for me. So I put on my only suit and went down to the recruiting office. It was all formality and forms in triplicate and soldiers too long in the tooth, sitting behind desks. I knew the RAF was up to its neck that summer and any attack from occupied France was likely to hit the airfields of the south first. How about the navy, I asked. This from a local lad living in one of the most landlocked counties in the country. A straight-faced sergeant told me the navy was full. Had I thought about the infantry? I hadn't, not in the way he meant. So I opted for a few more weeks' freedom. The inevitable would come soon enough. On Sundays I cycled along the familiar winding lanes, the cow parsley we called keck high in the hedgerows. I was twenty-six by now and somebody had once told me that Napoleon Bonaparte was this age when he led an entire army into Italy. I had this almost euphoric sense of adventure, a hint of danger, an excitement knowing that I'd soon be doing my bit for my country. Despite the mutterings of my dad's old pals, despite 'the hell where youth and laughter go', I couldn't help myself. I didn't see why I should be called upon to fight for Poland; but I'd fight for England.

Thursday 20 June 1940 was the day I signed my life away. I was standing outside the Tigers barracks at Glen Parva, South Wigston. The Victorian building hadn't changed much since it was built – and not at all since I'd been born there over a quarter of a century ago. I walked through the central gateway, wide enough for a coach and horses, past khaki-uniformed sentries with blancoed belts and .303s at the slope on their shoulders. It didn't cross my mind that these would be the men I might die with. Beyond the outer wall with its small windows and tessellated top the road led to the left past a guardhouse and on to admin offices. To the right were the living quarters and parade ground; a squaddies' nursery.

I looked across to the married quarters which had once been my home. They were deserted now because the army didn't look after its own in quite the same way and army families were elsewhere. I tried to pinpoint the building we'd lived in when Mum still laughed and Constance was with us, but it was all too long ago and I'd been too young. If there were ghosts somewhere in that maze of time-worn red-brick corridors, I didn't see them. Maybe they saw me.

The guardhouse was a hive of activity. A duty sergeant sat at his desk, flicking papers, checking names, stamping pages. We all shuffled forward in the army's time-honoured orderly queue to be issued with our uniforms. We were all excited, grinning and nodding to each other whether we were old mates or total strangers. The government had learned the lesson of the Great War. Back then they had put together lads from the same streets who'd been brought up together, in the belief that it improved morale in the trenches. That's fine, but it wasn't fine when an entire generation from those same streets disappeared in seconds, a single whizz-bang taking out an entire section of the trench. So, in 1940, most of the men in that Leicesters guardhouse were strangers.

At the counter, harassed clerks asked us our chest sizes and our heights and yelled back to orderlies running backwards and forwards in the clothing store. At five foot four, I all but disappeared under a pile of clothing and was whisked away as the clerk bellowed 'Next man!' In my arms I carried denim work clothes (fatigues), an itchy khaki bum-freezer jacket called a 'battledress' and wide-legged khaki trousers. I had a pair of canvas puttees, hobnailed boots, socks, underpants, vest, shirt and – the only fading memory of a once-smart regiment – a Glengarry cap in dark blue with a 'Tigers' badge pinned to it. The shapeless beret would come later and tin hats were only issued in the field. I can say, hand on heart, that nothing in this ensemble fitted me anywhere, but I'd never owned so many clothes in my life. It felt good. Like the three square meals a day felt good. When I was sixteen, I'd asked my dad if I could join the army. He'd said no. Now I know he was probably right, but I couldn't see it that way in June 1940.

On the parade ground, where men of the 17th Foot had once stood, backs ramrod straight in their white-faced scarlet, we met Hell on Earth. He was Sergeant Major 'Porky' Crane, a regular soldier built like a brick shithouse. His bellowing roar ricocheted around the square, bouncing off every stone and rattling your spine. Men like him had been the backbone of the British Army for years. They were legendary for their bark but most of them had little bite, if you kept your nose clean and did as you were told. That said, Porky Crane's job was to bellow us into shape, to turn disorganized, naive, free-thinking idiots into something approximating fighting men.

My first personal brush with Porky came days later when I was trying to look like a soldier on guard duty. He tucked his swagger stick under his arm and looked down at me from his commanding height. 'What's your name, lad?' he growled.

I suppose I said, 'Private Twigg, Sarn't Major,' but I didn't hear any sound come out.

'Speak up, lad!' Porky bawled. 'We don't want Jerry thinking we've gone soft now, do we?' And, mercifully, he moved on.

Sergeant Major Crane took no prisoners. He bawled out privates all day long and then took on officers. If he walked past one and they didn't return his salute with his own vicious precision, he'd quietly rebuke them, stressing the importance of appearance for appearance's sake in front of the men. And of course, he always ended the acerbic dressing down with an immaculately polite 'sir'.

Army living quarters hadn't changed for two hundred years. Our dormitory block was like the old-fashioned Nightingale wards in Victorian hospitals. It was long, whitewashed and had a cold, concrete floor. Iron-framed beds were ranged along both sides of the room with a bed-length space forming a central aisle. There was no heat, not even provision for a fire during winter, and the wash block outside had sinks with mirrors and cold water only. A lot of the recruits found all this difficult, but for me it was heaven, because my army blankets kept me warm in bed and there was plenty of hot food. Perhaps for the first time I realized that my childhood, tough as it was, had prepared me for this; I'd be all right in the army.

Sergeant Moore, of Sixteen Platoon, was our army mother. He must have been in his fifties and was easy-going as far as a regular saddled with a band of no-hopers could be. His gentle morning call still slices like steel through my dreams – 'Wakey, wakey! Rise and shine! Feet on deck! Beds in line! Anyone here going sick?' The question rose to a deafening crescendo and as he'd already marched out again, it was clear that he didn't expect a 'Yes' to that question. It was 6.30 ack emma in the parlance of the army. Bloody early to everybody else.

And three minutes later – you could set your watch by him – Sergeant Moore was back. If we were already up and dressing, he'd move among us, muttering, 'Come on, you useless bunch of mummy's boys, move.' If he found anyone still asleep – and occasionally he did in the early days – he'd approach the bed and in one fluid movement upend frame, mattress, bedding and soldier of the king in one undignified heap on the floor. The spectacle had its own soundtrack too, with Sergeant Moore asking after the sleepyhead's parentage.

'And when I return,' he invariably barked, 'this bed will be made and you will be properly turned out or you will be doubling round the parade ground all day in full kit and after that I'll make you wish you'd never been born.' All this sounds like a cliché today, the stuff of *Carry On* films and 1950s television sitcoms. So try it. Strap twenty-five bags of sugar to your body and run round your local playing fields for a couple of hours. Then see if you still find Sergeant Moore a figure of fun.

That was one reason why I was always up before the man's first visit. The other was that I genuinely liked the army. There is a profound comfort in following orders – I suppose the Nazis found that too. No worries. Shelter, food, sport – all laid on. I just wished I'd been allowed to join before anybody wanted to kill me.

Here I discovered my old boyhood talent – running. In the battalion cross-country race that July I was the smallest runner in the field. There's something indefinable about running cross-country. It's not like an athletics track where it's all adrenalin and hype and then it's all over. It's about staying the course, fighting the pain in your lungs and willing your legs to keep going. I trailed at first as the big runners got into their stride, but one by one they tired and I found myself elbow to elbow with the battalion's best. As I drew level, he put on a spurt. He'd got complacent, I suppose, over the weeks and months and hadn't reckoned on a challenge, especially from a recruit. I stayed with him and with the tape in sight drove myself forward, leaving him floundering somewhere behind me.

Come Sports Day I put myself in for the mile. We were

slogging along on a route march one day when Sergeant Moore breathed in my ear, 'I'm putting my money on you, Twigg, so don't let me down.' I didn't and the delighted old bugger stood me a pint. He never did tell me how much he'd won.

The summer of 1940 was, for me, the summer of Guarding Everything. The perimeter of the camp had to be patrolled, two hours on and four off duty. There were outer and inner guard lines called 'in-line pickets' and you very quickly got used to army speak. I even guarded the Saffron Lane Rec, although quite what the Germans would have wanted the park for if they'd landed was beyond me. Perhaps they intended to indoctrinate the local kids into the Hitler Youth and hitting their playgrounds was as good a start as any. The place was close to my brothers' homes, so I often saw locals I knew and would stand with my .303 at ease, having illicit conversations with them. When I thought the coast was clear, I'd lean the rifle against a tree, stuff my Glengarry cap under my shoulder strap and have a kickaround with the local kids' football.

To the south, we knew, in that long hot memory-gilded summer, the sky was scarred with vapour trails of the daily dogfights they called the Battle of Britain as the Few gave their lives to buy us time. We slogged over open fields and along country lanes, full packs cutting grooves into our shoulders and blisters forming on the blisters in our army boots. Khaki was hot and itchy and the thud and rattle of troops on the road contrasted oddly with the peace of the Leicestershire countryside. Across the fields between Leicester and Market Harborough we played war games, screaming across meadows with fixed bayonets, trampling corn that was golden near harvest time. Sheep would scatter and run every time but the cattle just looked at us or shook their heads as if in disbelief. We crawled on all fours with our .303s cradled in our arms like babies. We snuck up on mates wearing coloured ribbons in lieu of Wehrmacht uniforms and they snuck up on us. It helped that I knew these fields like the back of my hand – they had been my mock battleground for years, when the enemy had been the local farmer or orchard owner. I didn't know then that there had once been real battles on these uplands. To the south lay Naseby, where Rupert of the Rhine's cavalry had ridden too far and too fast to save the king in the Civil War. And to the west was Bosworth, where another king, Richard III, had been hacked to pieces on Ambion Hill. In 1940, hacking away at the unyielding clay to dig slit trenches, we were still playing at war.

But suddenly it wasn't a game any more. We were digging a trench along the edge of the barracks square one day when the air-raid siren wailed. There were NCO shouts everywhere (as if we needed any orders) and we all piled into the new earthworks, spades and kit flying in all directions. I heard the unmistakable snarl of an aircraft overhead and as I looked up, saw the distinctive pale-blue undercart and the black cross of the Luftwaffe. As it vanished into the clouds over Wigston, we heard the roar of explosions and watched the black columns of smoke climbing through the blue. We heard later that the raid had missed the gasworks by 400 yards and several people had been killed in the shops nearby. At the time, I believed the story that the lone raider had been shot down near the coast, heading home. But of course that could just have been propaganda. Whatever the truth, the war had finally come to sleepy Leicestershire.

By winter, with basic training finished, we were old hands; if not exactly battle-hardened, we knew one end of a rifle from

another. Unlike the new lads who moved into Glen Parva as
the conveyor belt of war rattled on. As they moved in, as full
of trepidation as we'd been, we moved out – to the Clarence
Hotel in South Wigston. This was a great barn of a place,
requisitioned by the government because there was, after all,
a war on. The hotel had umpteen public rooms, one of them
named after Gertie Gitana, a music hall artiste my grandad
might have gone to listen to.

We slept on the dance floor on a straw-filled palliasse with
two blankets. It was the warmest, most comfortable bed I'd
slept in but early shaves were still in the yard outside, your
face hit by cold water in the misty light of a winter morning.
When I had a spare minute, I'd take myself back along Healey
Street, the way I'd run to Dunmore's to get some broken biscuits for my mum. And, just occasionally, I'd hear Constance's
long-still voice echoing in my ears; my big sister, looking out
for me as she always did.

Then the war machine moved us on again, this time to the
Co-op in Long Street, Wigston Magna. Down the road was
the cinema, a magnet for girls attracted by the lure of the uniform. It's difficult now to remember how important the
pictures were to my generation. It was here that we caught
snippets of war information in the black-and-white flicks
courtesy of Pathé News. It was propaganda, of course, cleaned
up for our benefit, but in those naive days, which of us ques-
tioned it? We saw the bomb-torn streets of London and the
smoking shells of shops and homes. But we also saw the cheery
faces of civilians and the grim determination of the police,
the fire brigade and the ARP wardens to keep calm and carry
on. But we really went to the pictures for the escapism. Jimmy
Cagney sneered his way through *The Roaring Twenties*; Joel
McCrea built the *Union Pacific* and the girls sobbed quietly

because somebody shot Tyrone Power in *Jesse James*. The back row of the pictures was the place to be in 1940. Everybody seemed to be in uniform and there was a live-for-the-moment attitude that played into the hands of fumbling soldiers who might not be around tomorrow. I suppose the dance halls had the same attraction for some, but there it was usually a case of us blokes leaning on the bar and watching the girls two-step together. It took an awful lot of Ansells Best Bitter for us to summon up the courage to ask a girl to dance.

I was coming out of the pictures in late November and walked into some kind of hell. People were scuttling in all directions as the air-raid siren wailed. The night sky, deep purple and black, was orange in the light of flares and incendiary bombs and we could see the black silhouettes of the bombers high above us until the dense smoke hid them all. This wasn't the first time Leicester had taken a pummelling; the Luftwaffe had hit the city twice before, so you could say we were all hardened to it. I don't remember being scared, not even when the ground shook with the impact of the bomb sticks. We got back to our billet and were told to stay dressed – we might be needed in the town centre. I lay on my bed waiting, listening to the cacophony of war. Explosions shook the night and rattled the Co-op's windows, against the background drone of the bombers. How many planes did the bastards have? There wasn't much ack-ack fire. Those poor buggers, in the sandbagged gun batteries or operating the probing searchlights, must have been exhausted; Leicester wasn't considered that high a risk – not like Coventry down the road – and the place was woefully under-gunned.

In the grey light of the first day of a new month, we marched along our own streets, useless defenders of the people in the People's War. There was debris everywhere – bricks, mortar, window frames, broken glass like crystals on the pavement. The all-clear had sounded about two o'clock and now we had to count the cost of a madman's ambitions. The Grieves factory had made knitting machines yesterday. Now it was a hole in the road. Freeman, Hardy and Willis in Wimbledon Street had made shoes. There was nothing left of it. We helped the fire brigade with their heavy hoses and hauled down the rickety remains of shattered walls. I didn't see any bodies. Perhaps because they were still buried deep in the bowels of their own houses. We didn't talk to each other much. We avoided eye contact. This was going to be a long and nasty business, a war to the death.

And so the targets on the Kibworth rifle range weren't wooden boards any longer. In our minds' eyes, they were the Wehrmacht, all grey uniforms and *Stalhelme* and mindless brutality. We lay on the iron-hard ground of January 1941 with the cold freezing our fingers. We kept our feet flat because the gunnery instructors told us that a sniper could take our heels off at six hundred paces. One platoon acted as lookout while another fired in that huge open field with the ruined windmill, a reminder of more peaceful days. If you've never fired a .303 Lee Enfield, you haven't lived. The thing was a bitch, but it was a bitch that might one day save your life. Its strap wore a groove into your armpit because the rifle weighed 8.8 pounds. And if you weren't careful, you'd trip over it – the barrel length alone was twenty-five inches. It was a bolt action, which meant you had to click the bolt into place for the next shot and it fired ten rounds. There was a rumour that the ordnance department had designed a better version, but it wasn't ready for us. The Mark III's muzzle velocity was 2,441 feet per second and its range was about 550 yards. Anything after that was sheer luck. The official statistics today will tell you they made 17 million of these things, but I only knew one of them. It had a kick like a mule and for weeks I had the bruised shoulder to prove it.

It was one of those freezing January mornings that I resumed my stealing career. On the way up to the range I scrounged four large spuds from the cookhouse and stuffed them into my trouser pockets, well hidden by my greatcoat. We fired our rounds and then took up lookout duty.

The air was crisp and there was a new fall of snow across the range, giving it all a surreal and rather Christmas-card sort of feel. I was with my mate, Private Wigginton, 1st Battalion, the Leicester Regiment, known, inevitably, as Wiggy. 'Come on, Wiggy.' I watched my breath snake out on the air. 'Let's get a fire going. I've got these,' and I flashed the spuds under my coat. Wiggy was up for anything that would improve the daily monotony of life and we soon had a fire crackling just out of sight of the range. Hawthorn hedges make great kindling and I hadn't lost my boyhood touch when it came to lighting fires. We had no saucepan, of course, or water so I went for the direct approach and threw the spuds onto the flames. The outer skins were black and inedible but the insides were great and we chomped away, trying not to burn our mouths.

The firing done, we got into our trucks and rattled back to barracks. Everybody but Wiggy and me was famished and we were late back. Of all the jobs in the army I'm sure that of cook is the worst. You've never got enough rations to satisfy several hundred fit young men. You've got to work in a hurry and on a mass-produced basis. And above all, nobody in the world is grateful for what you do. So God knows how long the cooks had been waiting this particular day by the time we turned up. They filled our mess tins with meat (unidentifiable, army, for the use of), potatoes (minus the four I had liberated earlier, presumably) and cauliflower. I sat at the usual trestle tables, tucking in. Looking up, I noticed the bloke opposite me getting paler by the second. He was staring in horror at his mess plate.

'What's up, mate?' I asked him.

'I'm not eating that lot,' he shouted, pushing his plate away. 'Look at the caterpillars!' I thought he was going to throw up.

I'd already eaten mine. 'It's all right,' I said, trying to be helpful. 'Only their skins are left now. The insides will have been boiled out with the cauliflower.'

'That's disgusting!' he said and left, seemingly disinterested in any pudding that might be going.

'Pass it over here,' I said to his retreating back. 'Thanks,' and I pulled the plate across. His caterpillars tasted just the same as mine; what was all the fuss about?

In the spring of 1941, rumours reached the barracks that we were to be posted abroad. There'd be no more war games, no more playing at soldiers. Now it would be real. That realization brings an intensity of its own. What about my dad? He was still keeping the Snaith's workforce going. My brothers? Cyril had been posted with the RAF by now and God alone knew where he was. Ken had gone, like me, to join the army, but he was a soft, nervous lad and Porky Crane would have had him for breakfast. They'd turned him down. What about my little sisters? Sheila was only six and Bunty barely out of nappies. What about the family of my own I hoped to have one day? Even my childhood friends had scattered. Bob Hillier was with the Eighth Army and everybody knew the Eighth Army was in North Africa. That was the far side of the world. I'd seen the war memorials in the various places I'd lived, the brass plaques at the foot of stone crosses that I'd cycled past on my travels. Would that be it? Would 'Twigg, R., Pte, Leicestershire Regt', carved in cold metal, be all that was left of me?

So I went back to my childhood, to my roots. Some blokes went to the dance hall, to the boozer. I went to the fields of my wild, singing country, to the snowdrops looking for the sun, the crocuses, then the daffodils following close behind. In February the rooks wheeled and flapped in the elms at the Waterhole in Great Glen, building their ugly, awkward nests high and safe above the ground. This was a special, magic place you wouldn't find on any map. Bob Hillier and I used to pick the wild mushrooms there and cook them on a campfire on the banks of the River Sence. Spring came, with that smell of hope which is three parts frost and one part hawthorn. I cycled the lanes and walked the old towpath between Foxton and Kilby Bridge, tripping in the prints of the great horses, gouged deep by their huge iron-shod hoofs pounding the track as they pulled the dragon-fly narrow boats along the canal. Did I really believe I'd never have a chance to see all this again? Perhaps not; but I wasn't taking chances.

Thursday 20 March 1941. Reveille. The bugle notes shattered the morning and we all tumbled out of bed. The sky was a magical blue in the still-crisp morning; it was the sort of day you feel lucky to be alive but, sure enough, some bastard spoilt it. The bastard in question that morning was a company sergeant who called us to silence as we guzzled our way through our porridge. You could have heard a pin drop. Spoons were held in mid-air, mugs of tea sat half-drunk and we all turned to him. This was it. Months of training, tedium, practice and drill. At last it was over.

'Right!' he barked. 'As soon as breakfast is over, I want you lot to get fell in. We're off to Wigston railway station.'

The silence continued. We looked at each other; turned to the sergeant, waiting for more. But he'd already gone; there was no more. Then the noise erupted as spoons hit the porridge bowls again and speculation took over. France. It had to be. We were going back to Dunkirk on unfinished business. No, it would be the Mediterranean. We'd take on the Eyeties, no problem. There again, Egypt made more sense, to reinforce the Eighth Army. I smiled at that one. Yes, Bob Hillier would need all the help he could get. Wait for me, Bob, I'm on my way.

Minutes later, seventy fighting men of the Leicestershire Regiment were lined up on the parade ground, in battledress and Glengarries, confident and ready.

'Parade!' We stiffened at the roar from the company sergeant major. 'Atten-shun!' Our heads came up, our boots clicking in a single leather thud on the tarmac. 'Parade will turn to the right.' A pause. 'Right turn!' And we swung right, seventy men as one, part of something that was bigger than any of us. We'd done this countless times before, but this morning it was different. It was for real. And God help the German who got in our way.

'By the right; quick march!' the order thundered and out we went, four abreast across that parade ground, under the archway, past the sentries standing with bayonets fixed. We'd shouldered our rifles and were striding along Saffron Lane behind the band who were belting out 'Romaika/A Hunting Call', the quick march of the regiment – all the tunes of glory. We marched through South Wigston's main street, past the

hotel which had been our billet. There were people everywhere, cheering, waving flags. We'd never fired a shot in
anger, but here we were, being treated like conquering heroes.
I never wondered how it was that so many civilians knew we
were going. And it was a weekday – why weren't more of
them at work? Was there the odd mum and dad in the crowd,
smiling through the tears at the departure of their little boy?
Was there a girl there who was crying because she'd never see
her lover again? The same questions down the generations,
posed by men going to war.

Most of us knew South Wigston station of old. It had peeling cream-painted woodwork and smoke-blackened red
bricks. Tatty old peacetime posters still told us that 'Skeggie'
was bracing, but we weren't in a holiday mood that day. The
train was a nightmare. With troops already on board there
was nowhere to sit and we all crammed into the narrow
corridors, trying to catch up with old mates and fighting
each other with the continual jostle of kitbags. All the
windows were down and lads were leaning out, chatting to
mums, dads, wives, sweethearts. The guard shattered the
moment with his shrill whistle blast and the carriages
clanked and jolted forward. More tears on the platform, more
fluttering handkerchiefs. But there was no one there to shout
for me.

Word spread as we rattled west. Liverpool. It had to be.
That meant the docks and after that, it could be anywhere in
the world. How many of us, brought up on stories of the
Great War, needed a return ticket? Everybody around me was
drawing frantically on their fags, the conversation dying after
a while, each man alone with his thoughts. I had my pipe –
how quaint that sounds now – and I'd stocked up with all the
St Bruno Flake I could find.

The places we passed through are just signs off the motorway today, names you read without a second thought. We hissed and whistled our way through halts and stations long gone. I knew some of them because of my cycling jaunts to north Wales, but a lot of the lads in my compartment were Leicester through and through. They'd never left the county and the land we rattled through now could have been the dark side of the moon. The youth of 1914 probably felt exactly the same.

We got to Liverpool by the middle of the afternoon, past rows and rows of dismal terraced houses, just like the one I had called home. Liverpool, we knew, had been badly hit by bombing raids, the inevitable fate of a city with docks. Only weeks before, six hundred enemy aircraft had killed over two thousand civilians in the space of days, with as many more injured and homeless. We didn't see any sign of this but nor did we see any cheering crowds. Liverpool was used to men in khaki passing through, on their way to God-knows-where. The Leicesters were just more of the same.

It wasn't until I was off the train that I saw the ship. In the nineteenth century the army called those things 'troopers', ships which carried men to whatever front they were called on to defend. The only ships like this I'd seen before were on the cards in cigarette packets, but now the SS *Duchess of York* reared up before me like a skyscraper, I could barely believe it. Nobody else could either and we all stood like idiots, open-mouthed, until old-fashioned NCO barking brought us back to the reason we were here.

The *Duchess of York* was a two-funnel, 20,000-tonne ocean liner, built by the Clydebank firm of John Brown and used in peacetime to ferry passengers between England and Canada.

She must have been dazzling in her day, but now she was battleship grey in an effort to camouflage her in the Atlantic rollers. The deck was like the Tower of Babel. I'd never heard so many accents in my life and I tried to tie the lilts I heard to the regimental badges. The *Duchess* was a crammed, swaying, floating city, with men jumping to commands, keeping together, moving at the barks of the NCOs. In that madhouse, the NCO regulars who had won their medals already were earning them again, just by maintaining order.

There was a frantic surge at one point as word spread that there were duty-free fags on board and everybody barged their way to the NAAFI counters to take advantage. The men who were serving here resigned themselves to the onslaught. NAAFI, as we all knew, stood for No Ambition And Fuck-all Interest. Within minutes there were hundreds of little flames popping up everywhere and a bluey-grey cloud drifted along the ceilings of each deck. None of us had any notion of the toxic properties of nicotine – that sort of thing was invented long after the war by a generation with not enough to worry about. So a couple of thousand young men inhaled and relaxed and began to believe that, after all, everything was right with the world. Smug, with my St Bruno in my pocket, I looked on as a bemused observer. Like all pipe smokers, I never understood the obsession with cigarettes.

I stood on the aft deck as we steamed out of harbour. Smoke was belching from the *Duchess*'s funnels as we cut through the sluggish brown waters of the Mersey and I drew slowly on my pipe. I was still there as the land disappeared into that hazy line on the horizon where you can't quite see whether it's there or not. There were others there too, having a look at the last of England. I thought again of that one-way ticket, of the handkerchiefs, of the silly, awkward shouts of farewell – 'Keep in touch' . . . 'Look after yourself' . . . 'Don't do anything I wouldn't do'. There was an iron lump in my throat, but my stiff upper lip prevailed. What would Sergeant Moore say? Porky Crane? I took one last look at where the land had been. And I promised myself I'd be back. It might not be tomorrow or the next day. But I would be back.

By mid-evening, as the light was fading, other ships appeared on the horizon, first in ones and twos, then as part of a huge flotilla. I'd never seen so many ships together in one place. We were part of a convoy under the protection of the navy – that branch of the service they'd told me was full. We were all up on deck for this, nudging each other, pointing out the huge black silhouettes matching us knot for knot.

'That's the *Hood*,' somebody said (every battalion has its smartarse) and it was. The Admiral-class battle cruiser, known as the 'Mighty Hood', had been commissioned in 1916 and was renowned throughout the Empire as one of the greatest ships of the line.

'That's *Repulse*.' The same smartarse was pushing his luck now; and we all knew that with ships like these, invincible, unsinkable, the pride of a nation, we'd have no trouble. The only unanswerable question was why, against the biggest and best navy in the world, had the Germans dared to take us on?

The Bay of Biscay has a deadly reputation. Currents, winds, tides? I don't understand a word of it; I'm from Leicester. All I know is that the convoy was suddenly, two days out, ploughing through seas like mountains, the *Duchess* bellying in the hollows, only to roll again and soar to the grey sky, butting sharply downwards in an orgy of spray. The crew were all right but the army were shattered. Decks were awash with vomit and men with white faces staggered around the ship looking for somewhere to lie down and die. I have never felt so ill in my life.

By the third day, this was a memory. The sea itself had washed the decks clean and colour came back to our cheeks. The banter resumed, so did the smoking. There had been no attack and *Hood* and *Repulse* and the rest were still with us, the sun glancing off their gun turrets. One by one our guardian ships veered east with flashing signals, ship to ship, and whooping their sirens. It was the navy's way of wishing us *bon voyage* and good luck.

I remember the next day we were called to parade on the top deck and an officer stood in front of us, at last giving us some concrete information. It had been too dangerous, he said, to go through the Med and Suez, so we were travelling via the Cape. Our destination? Singapore.

I remember our reaction, too. We looked at each other, most of us frowning in confusion. We weren't strategists. Like earlier generations of soldiers, it wasn't ours to reason why. Our leaders, of course, knew best. So we had another pint, another smoke and let nature take its course.

'There aren't any Germans in Singapore, are there?' somebody asked.

'And where the bloody hell is it, anyway?'

The battalion smartarse was just about to tell him when somebody hit him with a knapsack and he decided to keep his information to himself.

Singapore it was.

3

Ship of Fools

As we steered south, the days became gloriously warm and we were grateful for our tropical kit of thin tunics and shorts. Warm quickly became hot and the interior of the *Duchess* became unbearable. We'd got over the hilarity of hundreds of landlubbers trying to cope with swinging hammocks and the ignominy of a quick roll followed by a thud on the floor. No one got off scot free and we all had the bruises to prove it.

I palled up with a Leicester lad called Albert Wingell and we took to sleeping up on deck, if only to avoid the snoring and farting down below. Once we'd reached the South Atlantic, the sunsets were unbelievable kaleidoscopes of colour, the sort that artists can never catch and you see only when you haven't got a camera handy. I'd never seen a night sky so deep black and so studded with stars. It was spectacular but it was alien. You can take the lad out of Leicester, but you can't take Leicester out of the lad and I began to miss the average-looking sunsets of home. Ingrate!

The coast of Africa, which we knew must be lying to our left, came into view one evening as a low black bar above the horizon as the sun set. The pinpricks of light became brighter as we got closer and there were more of them. That evening, I was more aware of the heat than ever. It was sticky and sweaty and my tunic and shirt clung to my body like sticking plaster. As we hung on the deck rails, trying to take it all in, somebody said that this was our first port of call – Freetown in Sierra Leone. There was to be no shore leave so we'd have to watch the dark continent from the ship. And what a sight it was. The night and the town seemed to fizz and jagged lightning flashes struck the mountains of the interior. I knew almost nothing about Africa except trying to draw the bloody map in Geography lessons in school, but it was now a place of awe and beauty such as I'd never imagined.

I had to keep reminding myself that it was actually winter down here, the rainy season; hence the appalling humidity. The day, when it came, was drier, with a warm breeze coming from the west. We were anchored a hundred yards or so offshore in the deep-water harbour that had made Freetown such an important base for the navy. I could see the docks away to our left and the town itself looked about the size of Leicester or Lincoln, but it was so *different*. It was called Freetown because the original inhabitants had been African slaves freed from the cotton plantations of America's Deep South. Apparently, at the time we were there, a tree planted by these men was still going strong in a town square.

I couldn't help thinking that the place looked like a silent film set. Beyond the docks were large warehouses that gave way in turn to small wooden shacks and huts, palm trees and dusty, unmetalled roads. The sound from the odd passing car or truck was muted out to sea and I was back in the Grace Road cinema again, watching an educational newsreel. The vicar would be asking questions later.

Suddenly I saw my first African. A shout came from an upper deck and I followed the pointing fingers. Ebony-skinned

young men, younger than me, I suspect, were swimming out
to the ship, white water marking their wakes. I'd never seen a
black man before – I doubt many of us had – and I was astonished by their ability, not only to swim out to us, but to circle
the *Duchess*, treading water and shouting out in the incomprehensible Krio dialect for money. Whatever distorted view
we had of Africans, it was a two-way street. If the white men
could arrive in a huge ship like this, they must all be million-
aires. Somebody threw a coin – a penny, probably, or a
threepenny bit. Then another and another, with a lot of hilarity. There were a few clean catches and cheers from the rails
but most coins hit the water and the boys bobbed down after
them. I couldn't believe they'd succeed. Neither did I believe
they could hold their breath that long, but they did. An ivory
grin would break the surface and a hand held up the king's
shilling, just like the traditional pay we were taking too. This
went on for an hour or so. We had our entertainment and the
divers had earned, I would imagine, more than most of the
poor little buggers got in a week.

Then the *Duchess* clanked and shuddered back to life with
smoke belching from her funnels as we weighed anchor and
turned south. I suppose many people's idea of luxury is a
pleasure cruise, especially then. The twenties and thirties
were *the* decades of the transatlantic luxury voyage with
images of bands playing, flags flying, cocktails and floating
casinos. Well, the sea quickly palls. We didn't have any of the
golden life; even the hull we travelled on was stripped down
to suit the times and the purpose. We were going to war and
nothing could disguise that. The heat became ever more
stifling and there was no escape from the hypnotic thump
of the engines. The day began with the old ritual rivalry
between the navy and the army. 'Wake up or be washed

away!' a deckhand would shout just before he turned his hose of salt water full throttle along the decks. We moved double-quick, Albert and I, just in time to avoid a soaking. I never did understand the point of this drill. They were washing the salt off the planking with water that contained . . . salt. Maybe it was just as well the navy had been full when I went to enlist an eternity ago. Then we stood on the deck as if it was a parade ground. Our kit was laid out and inspected by the beady, miss-nothing gaze of the company sergeant major. We polished boots and buttons, ironed shirts and darned socks, all those little domestic things that would make us such good wives when we got back! We did PT, stripped to our shorts under a merciless sun, jumping forwards, backwards, side-ways, arms together, knees bend. And we carried out guard duty, rifles at the slope, bayonets fixed. If anybody asked why, miles out to sea in a floating metal cauldron, we were still pretending to be soldiers, you could be sure an understanding NCO would have an answer. 'This is the Leicestershire Regi-ment, lad. Where do you think you are?'

Off duty, I puffed on my St Bruno and leaned over the rail watching the flying fish keep pace with the ship – flashes of rainbow colour skimming the waves with a speed that was astonishing. And I'm afraid the old Reg Twigg was still aboard. All right, there was a war on and I might, indeed, have my bollocks shot away after all, like the Great War song said, but there were still dodges to be carried out. One of the chores we had was to carry out various duties for the ser-geants' mess, and the reward was an ice-cold drink, straight from the fridge, something not otherwise available to the lowest form of animal life like us privates. I'd noticed that this little taste of nectar from the gods was handed over without question.

I was lolling on the rail one night and turned to Albert. 'Fancy a cold drink?' I asked him.

'Not half, Reg,' Albert nodded. 'I keep thinking about those ice-cold ginger ales.' He knew how to push the boat out, did Albert.

'Wait here, then,' I said, beaming and off I went to the sergeants' mess bar. I did my best to look like a man nearing the point of exhaustion, working for the sergeants. 'Sergeants' mess fatigues,' I sighed to the barman. 'Can I have two ginger ales, please?' I wish I'd been able to take a picture of Albert's face when I came back with them. I wasn't in white mess dress and they weren't on a silver salver, but they were ice-cold ginger ales.

'You're a cheeky bugger, Reg,' Albert laughed. 'You'd be on a charge if they caught you.'

'Best not get caught, then,' and I clinked my bottle with his. We stood there, sipping quietly, looking at the stars and thinking of home. For a moment, I was back in that dark little shop in Aldershot, helping myself to the kind old lady's Blue Bird toffees. The trick had been not to take too many. So I would work this ginger ale job once or twice more and then that would be it. But that wasn't the home Albert was thinking of. He was a year younger than me, but he had a wife and kids. He thought about them every day, he once told me, wondering if they were all right and what they were doing.

Cape Town was glorious at night, its welcoming lights trembling against the deep velvet of the sky. Our convoy lights were put out and the sirens whooped our arrival, to be answered by an echoing welcome from all the ships in the harbour. In the Middle Ages, travellers on the sea gave thanks in a church for their safe arrival and wore St Christophers around their necks. This was the wartime equivalent, a hundred whoops all saying, 'Welcome, friend. Glad you could make it.'

I got soaked the next morning by the hose jet on deck. I hadn't overslept or mistimed my move. It was just that I was staring at the sheer, vertical immensity of Table Mountain standing clear against the deep blue of the African sky. It seemed almost surreal, a thing of beauty out of place in a world at war with itself. Here we had shore leave but we had to be back on board by ten at night. And so Private Reginald Twigg of the 1st Battalion, the Leicestershire Regiment, trod on foreign soil for the first time in his life. The sun was warm, the air was sweet and groups of the lads scuttled off in search of beer and women. Call us old fashioned, but Albert and I wanted to reach, if we could, the top of that mountain. 'What did you do in the war, Daddy?' one of Albert's kids might ask him in the years ahead. 'I went mountain climbing, son. With old Reg Twigg.' Everybody we passed was nodding and smiling. There was no resentment, no animosity. We were all in this together and South Africa was, to all intents and purposes, British. Bird Park was dazzling, its trees and lawns bright with a green I'd never seen in the fields of Leicestershire. We sat on the heights with the whole of Cape Town below us and the sea fading to the horizon beyond the great curve of the bay. If they sent us home tomorrow, it would have been worth it for this sight alone.

Then, it got even better. She was wearing a figure-hugging black dress and her shiny black hair hung in ringlets over her shoulders. She was walking towards us as we sat on the lush grass. And, quite suddenly, I was in love. I nudged Albert. 'Look at that,' I whispered. 'Isn't she gorgeous?' She was more than that; she was a goddess. And she was walking right up to us, smiling with a warmth that took my breath away. I nearly panicked, suddenly tongue-tied and useless. I had been one of those layabouts propping up the bar in the dance hall and watching the girls dance back home. I was always more interested in my football or my bike chain than any girl. Now I was paying the price of a wasted youth.

'Hello,' she said, in a clipped accent I'd never heard before. 'Are you new arrivals from England?'

Since I obviously wasn't going to be able to say anything, Albert, the old hand, the married one, came to my rescue. 'Yes,' he said. He was always the master of wit and repartee and I managed to mutter, 'Our troopship got in last night and we've got a few hours' leave.' I said it all in one breath.

She told us her name was Sylvia Cohen and she looked about twenty. I'd never been picked up before so I wasn't quite sure exactly what was happening. 'If you soldiers are free,' she said, 'would you like to come home with me, meet my mother and sister? You could have a meal with us, perhaps, and we could walk to the beach.'

In a blur, Albert and I accepted and caught a bus to West Point, on the coast. The Cohens lived in a nice part of town with bungalows, wide roads and neat lawns. I'd never seen a place like it. Mrs Cohen was a plump, grey-haired lady. Sylvia's sister was older than she was, but with only a shadow of her beauty. If either of them was surprised by the khaki-clad guests, they didn't show it. Sylvia did most of the talking. They wanted to know all about England, to them a fabled land they longed to visit. This made no sense to me or Albert; these ladies already lived in paradise.

In the late afternoon we walked along the white sand below West Point. I put my arm around Sylvia's shoulder and she slipped hers round my waist. I longed to kiss her, but Albert was wandering nearby with the sister and I didn't want to spoil everything by making what was bound to be a clumsy pass. I could see the *Duchess* out in the bay, silent at anchor, but calling me nonetheless. The sergeant major wouldn't understand, I told myself; although, probably, of course, he'd understand very well. The girls saw us to the bus and blew us kisses as we rattled out of sight. I didn't see the sister. I didn't see Albert. I didn't see the bus or the houses and streets we passed. I only saw Sylvia, her hand in front of her, blowing me a kiss so that it bounced off her palm and somehow reached me. A beautiful girl. A girl with a Jewish name. We had no idea in 1941 what was already happening to the Jews all over Europe. Perhaps she did. I never wrote down her address, though I've remembered it all my life – 32 Mount Nelson Place, West Point, Cape Town, South Africa. Did she stand on that beach and wave as the *Duchess* steamed away? I doubt it. That's the stuff of soppy romances written for the girlies. But that face and that blown kiss were always with me in the weeks and months ahead. Thanks for that, Sylvia.

The Indian Ocean was an oven. You had no sense of the sea, of the breeze; and Biscay now felt like a dream. Again, it was already night by the time we saw the black coast of India. Every ship moored in the bay, from ocean liners still plying their luxurious trade in safe waters to dirty old China Sea tramp steamers, hooted out their welcome to us. In the lights from the quay we watched the steel hawsers snake out to the nut-brown men who caught them and lashed them securely. Compared with Cape Town, all bustle and efficiency, Bombay looked tired, old, in need of a lick of paint. Six thousand feet of quay stretched into the darkness and the names of the docks there had a familiar sound to them, Prince's and Victoria.

India was British. In an odd sort of way sailing into Bombay was like coming home. I'd seen the Pathé News pictures of elephants, gilded and howdahed, lines of Lancers, pennons fluttering at durbars and other imperial bashes. We'd been in Bombay for three hundred years and we had no idea all that was about to end.

However, nothing, nothing could have prepared me for the real Bombay. We saw it at dawn the next day. And we smelt it too. We had one day to soak up the subcontinent and we swapped our English money for a handful of rupees. We were barely off the gangplank before we were surrounded by a swarm of beggars who had probably been waiting at the dock gates for hours. They were men, women, children, all of them in rags, all of them with the choking, gag-inducing smell of the starving. They clamoured for an anna, the rough equivalent of a ha'penny, and they clawed, jostled and gouged each other to reach us. Here was a blind man, eyes with no irises staring into the sky. There was a woman with only one arm, struggling against the others. Someone was jabbing me in my army belt buckle. It was a lad; what was he? Twelve? Thirteen? He had no legs and he was scooting along on a little wooden platform on wheels. It was a bit like the home-made trolleys we'd made to race each other at home, but it was nothing like that really. It was half a man's body. First, you can't believe it, the begging. Then you feel sorry. Then you gag from the stench and you know you can't save them all. So you want to get away and you shout and use your elbows. It may be, and I'm ashamed to admit it, some of the lads used their boots. We were squaddies, for God's sake. Did they think we were made of money?

At the dock gates, we all stood stock still. I was looking

into the Abyss, those dark pictures of hell the vicar had described to us in Sunday School. You couldn't see the pavements for people and we stumbled over bodies lying against shopfronts and in doorways. Were they dead, those bundles of rags? Or just asleep? And how could they possibly sleep in that cacophony of noise? Whatever they were, they were lost beyond our comprehension.

People swarmed everywhere. Buses were crammed with them, inside and out, luggage and bodies hanging from the roofs. Klaxons brayed as vehicles tried to navigate the sea of jostling humanity. Shopkeepers, as eager for our annas as the beggars on the quay, called out to us their street cries. Rice. Carpets. Cloth. Tea. I'd never seen so much *stuff*. There was rubbish in every corner; your boots crunched on it constantly. Here and there a scrawny cow with huge horns wandered through a market place. We just stood and stared. No doubt somewhere nearby the battalion smartarse was explaining the importance of sacred cattle to the Hindu and how the British had caused the Indian Mutiny by insisting the sepoys' cartridges be greased with cow fat.

If I close my eyes I can still smell those Bombay streets. The aroma of hot curries from pavement kitchens beckoned, though it was all but eclipsed by the rotting sewage and unwashed bodies. After the grey of Leicester, the colours were unbelievable. Saris of sky blue and carnation pink, turbans of towelling, cotton and silk. Our eyes were drawn, of course, to the beautiful girls, their dark, made-up eyes promising God-knows-what behind their tantalizing veils. Beauty and ugliness hand-in-hand.

A group of us had been wandering for what seemed like hours, keeping our wallets deep in our pockets, politely declining every offer we got, whether in broken English or any one of what seemed a thousand languages. But now we were hungry and whether he had good ears or an exceptionally tuned sense of what the men from Leicester wanted I don't know, but from nowhere, an old man was standing next to us. He was tall, with a hawk-like face and a magnificent grey beard. He wore a white cotton frock coat over loose trousers and his English was amazing.

'Hello, gentlemen,' he said. 'You look as though you are new to the area. May I offer my assistance?'

'We were just looking around, really,' I told him, vaguely aware that my Leicester twang paled alongside his King's English pronunciation. 'You speak very good English.'

'Thank you,' he placed his hands together and bowed slightly. 'We have had a long time to learn it.'

It turned out that he had served in the Great War; I'd seen Indian Lancers thundering in and out of trenches in France in the pictures and since I knew my dad had served in India, felt a kind of affinity with this man. He had a restaurant nearby, he said, and could promise us good food. I expected a flyblown lean-to on the pavement, but it was very modern, the tables covered in crisp, white cloths. I'd never had curry before. Nor rice. Dad had developed a taste for it and sometimes added curry powder to his otherwise English stew. We'd wrinkled up our noses at it. That was foreign, that was. I don't remember who tried it first that day, but it wasn't me. After a few tentative spoonfuls, we all agreed this was pretty good, even if it was probably toned down for English consumption. Meat and two veg? Forget it. We left our tables with much handshaking and bowing as men of the world.

And round the corner, we men of the world were challenged again. It was a warm evening and we felt relaxed and carefree. So relaxed we didn't notice the two girls walking towards us in their light floral dresses. They smiled at us.

'Crikey,' I whispered to Albert, 'is this Cape Town all over again?' It couldn't be, of course. These girls were astonishingly pretty, both perhaps sixteen, but they weren't Sylvia Cohen.

'Hello,' one of them said, her English as good as the restaurateur's. Her heady perfume hit me like a wall. How could anyone smell this good in a city like Bombay? She looked steadily at me, smiling. 'Would you like to have sex with us?' she asked. 'Ten shillings would be enough to have us both.'

I didn't look at Albert. He didn't look at me. For an awkward, agonizing moment, I couldn't find any words at all. Then I heard myself turning them down. There was the ship. There was the war. Sorry. 'All right,' the girl said. 'Goodbye.' And they wandered away in search of real men of the world, or somebody with more time. They were whores, prostitutes, what my grandad's generation called 'unfortunates'. Yet here, in this unbelievable, exotic setting, with their beautiful smiles, their youth, their readiness to oblige, it all seemed so different. Albert could think of his wife when he turned the girl down. What the hell was my excuse?

Albert and I lay on the open deck again that night as the *Duchess* upped anchor and steered away. All around us the talk was of the drinks the lads had had, the girls they'd had. Albert and I couldn't get our heads around that place of contrasts. And already it was the next morning and the deckhand's warning, and India was far behind.

Saturday 17 May 1941: the end of the road, if that's the right phrase to describe a sea voyage. I felt more like a tourist than a soldier as we reached the great fortress of Singapore, the Gibraltar of the East. The British had been here since 1819 when the place with its sixty-three separate islands was taken over by Stamford Raffles and the East India Company. There were a few small warships scattered in the harbour and once again we got a hero's welcome. A band struck up on the quayside and crowds of Malays and Chinese cheered as though they meant it. Perhaps they did.

Army trucks were clattering over the metal chains of the dock and we bundled our kit together for the mass exodus. Top priority for me was my pipe and St Bruno. The rifle came off a poor second best. We rattled through the busy streets of Singapore, through a throng of Chinese, Malays, Tamils – I'd come to recognize them all in the months ahead, but for now they all looked the same to me. Most of them stopped and stared at the lorry loads of their saviours bouncing through their city, but no one cheered. No one waved. It was Liverpool all over again. Did I read too much into it as I looked at their staring faces? Was it a look of hatred? Had the crowd at the quayside just been hired for the occasion? Was this the real face of Singapore, a face that said, 'You British have been here too long. Isn't it time you left?' I shook myself free of that thought. This was Fortress Singapore, as British as Trafalgar Square and impregnable. *And* we'd come, the Leicesters, to defend the place and, along with it, the people.

Bidadari Camp was a sea of white tents in neat rows on ground baked brown and hard by the sun. There was a wooden admin block and a bungalow for the camp sergeant major. Some distance away were the officers' quarters, altogether better built with verandas and flowers.

Soon we were out of the truck, lugging kit and caboodle

and jumping to the snarls of the NCOs. Weeks on-board ship had cramped their style. Here, with the Union Jack flapping overhead in this corner of the Empire, they could give their lungs full throttle. It was three men to a tent; I can smell that hot canvas hole even now. We dumped our gear and formed up on parade on the football pitch to meet the man who would love us as if we were his own.

We all knew that Company Sergeant Major Harry Oates had served with the battalion since Waterloo, though of course he'd only been a squaddie then. He welcomed us with that warmth and understanding that CSMs have been famous for, for generations, the force of his breath parting our hair under our Glengarries. I bet on his wedding day, his 'I do' shattered the church windows and blew off his bride's veil. He reminded us there was a war on. We'd be joining the rest of the battalion at Penang in a few weeks and until then, there were standards. Singapore was, of course, a sink of iniquity and we must not, whatever we did, disgrace the battalion. Perish the thought. Oh, and remember – all prostitutes have VD.

That night we all made straight for the sink of iniquity. We were the king's soldiers and this town was ours, all of it – the bars, the restaurants, the cinemas, the booze and the women. The place was buzzing, warm, cosmopolitan. For the first time in my life, I wasn't at the bottom of the social heap. Wearing the king's uniform in an outpost of empire, you felt, just a little at least, like a king yourself. Today, of course, none of this would find favour, but then it was different. However long ago the British Empire might have left, on 17 May 1941 it was still intact and we arrogant fools were the men who were going to hold it all together. For us enlisted men, the heart of the Singapore world was the

Union Jack Club. Across the road was the famous Raffles
Hotel, its elegant facade disguising the fact that ten years
earlier it had gone into receivership. Officers in immaculate
tropical uniforms and white mess dress sauntered in and
out, continuing their public school and university social
clubs with hardly a glance in our direction. We never crossed
their threshold; nor they ours. We could share a parade
ground. We could share a battlefield. We could even share a
grave. We could never share a club.

The beer was cool and cheap at the Union Jack and the
leather chairs deep and comfortable. Baths were an unbelievable luxury we'd soon come to miss. Even the pipe
tobacco was perfection and I drank for the first time a peculiar American drink called Coca-Cola in its distinctively
shaped bottle. It was refreshing and different, but it wasn't
Ansells.

All night long the rickshaws lined up outside the Union
Jack. They were pulled by hard-sinewed Chinamen in shorts
and bare feet. Their hats were wide and made of muddy
coloured straw and their calf muscles were the size of foot-
balls. I'd never been to London, never ridden in a black cab,
but I naively thought these men were just the Singapore
equivalent, taking taxi fares to wherever they wanted to go.
As I watched them I realized their role was infinitely more
complicated. They were pimps. 'Number One girl very
cheap' was their street cry and they battened particularly on
lads reeling pissed out of the club. 'All prostitutes have VD.'
If Harry Oates had tattooed that on their heads with a ham-
mer and nails, I doubt whether some of them would have
taken the warning to heart.

The club was heaving, the whole place a haze of fag and
pipe smoke and a thousand virgin soldiers jabbering away

excitedly now that we'd finally reached what the BBC continually referred to as our 'objective'.

'Let's have a bash, then,' said a lad from my platoon.

'At what?' I asked him, still vaguely sober at that stage.

'You know,' he nudged me in the ribs. 'The pros – in Lavender Street.'

Lavender Street. Don't be fooled by the name. It stank like a shithouse because that was exactly what was spread on the Chinese vegetable gardens that flanked it. It wasn't a place you'd take your mum or the vicar. But that was just the point. Nobody had a mum out here, the vicar was called the padre and no doubt he'd be sipping sherry at Raffles by now.

I looked across my pint at the lad whose name I've now forgotten. If Albert had been there he'd have talked us out of it, if only because of his wife. But Albert was on duty and maybe my guard was down. I thought of the girls in Bombay, of the Malay women we'd seen sitting, smiling at us, from their tiered doorsteps around the corner from the club. Tomorrow, Reggie, a little voice whispered in my ear, you might be dead. You owe it to yourself to live a little.

'Go on, then,' I said. The three most fateful words in the English language.

The only English the coolie spoke was the price and he was pitch-perfect at that. I saw hardness in his eyes. The girls were a commodity to him; so were we. We tumbled into the rickshaw and he hauled himself into the harness frame and jogged away into the night. The bright lights of the wide streets got dimmer, the streets themselves narrower and dirtier. There was rubbish everywhere and mangy stray cats prowled on their nightly hunt. The coolie never spoke, never glanced back; just ran on like a machine. He'd done this before. Then he stopped and pointed to a small, wooden shanty house, not much more than a hut really.

We walked towards the entrance. 'What a dump!' I said, though secretly I was terrified of it. But what did I expect for what we'd paid? A French bordello with oysters and champagne? Roulette wheels and bobbing flunkeys? A ragged curtain hung across the dark doorway and my mate gingerly lifted it aside. A short grubby passageway ended in a wall and on a low bed against it sat three Chinese girls, all pale, all ill-looking. The air was stale with old sweat and we heard a baby cry from a side room. My mate was unbuckling his belt. I grabbed his arm. 'You're not going with one of those, are you?' I asked in disbelief, CSM Oates's terrible warning pounding in my ears.

'Bloody right I am,' he growled, focusing on the girl to the left. I got religion again that night. Or was it fear? I took another rickshaw back to the Union Jack and waited. My mate was back in half an hour – Casanova, he wasn't – with a half-smile on his face.

'Do you think it was worth it, then?' I asked him, sounding like some sanctimonious mix of the padre and the sergeant major. 'A few minutes' pleasure and days of worrying whether you've caught a dose?'

'It'll be all right, Twiggy,' he said, to reassure himself more than me. 'It's not like love, is it? It's just that you get a bit, you know, in need.' And as he supped his beer, I wondered what his wife would have made of all that.

That night I heard a familiar sound I didn't expect to hear, 'lost' in the East as we were. Right there, in the Pearl of the Orient, was a Sally Army band. They operated out of a non-descript office somewhere in the city and they upheld, with their tambourines and their promise of heaven, the decency the

British had brought to the world, wherever the Union Jack flew. It was all, of course, accompanied by the air of superiority that comes with being conquerors. But it was leavened with humility and with love.

Egg and chips. It's always the things you can't actually get you develop a craving for, isn't it? One night a group of us went out to our first Chinese restaurant. We'd chosen badly; half the battalion had the same idea and the place was packed. It was noisy and smoke-filled. I'd expected what I'd seen at the pictures in the opium dens that Charlie Chan cleared out – all dim lighting and lanterns and dragons. In fact the place was just brick and glass with a wooden floor and neat rows of tables with white cloths, just like the Indian restaurant in Bombay. Looking back, we treated the waiters appallingly, clicking our fingers and shouting 'Boy!' or 'Oi, you!' as they flitted between the tables.

Then came the reckoning. 'I'll deal with the bill,' Ted said. He was loud and brash and jack-the-lad in a way that made me look like a choirboy. When the waiter arrived, he dug first in one pocket, then another. Then he stood up, looking increasingly puzzled and said, 'I'm very sorry, but I've left my wallet back at camp and my mates don't have any cash.'

The waiter's inscrutable face didn't flicker, but he said, in perfect English, 'So what do we do now?'

Ted was momentarily thrown by this. He'd expected hysterical jabbering in an alien tongue and would, no doubt, have dismissed it with all the superiority of a Board School boy from the back streets of Leicester. 'My name's Ted,' he told the waiter, switching to Plan B. 'You come to the main gate of the army camp tomorrow night at six o'clock and I'll be there to pay you. And, just to make sure I bring the right money,' and he took it with a flourish, 'I'll take the bill with me.'

The waiter's face said it all. Without the bill he'd no proof he'd ever served us and I could just imagine the response he'd get from the sentry if he turned up at the gate as Ted had suggested. There were times when I felt bloody ashamed to be British. Bloody ashamed to come from Leicester. This was one of them. Ted never did pay the bill.

It was some weeks later that I nearly succumbed again. I suppose it was the boredom. The Pearl of the Orient had lost its lustre by now and the shops and the stalls and bars had a depressing sameness about them. Bally was a new mate, one of the few in the battalion who was shorter than me. We were out one night, wandering aimlessly near the shore battery where the huge guns of the artillery pointed skywards to defend the Straits. We heard giggling in the half-light and a rickshaw stopped in front of us. Inside were two lovely Chinese girls and they beckoned us over. Was it chance that a second, empty rickshaw arrived just then, or was this the same wily plan the average wide-eyed Tommy could be guaranteed to fall for, time after time?

'You on, Reg?' Bally asked me, his eyes bright.

I must have been having an off night. 'I'm in, Bally,' I said.

'Follow that,' I told the coolie and his immediate grasp of my instructions only dawned on me later. We rattled towards the edge of town, the girls turning back to us and 'cooeeing', as we were urging our rickshaw on. We got to one of those once-grand colonial houses that Stamford Raffles might have visited. Its glory days were long gone and we followed the girls up a rickety fire escape to the side of the building. The fare was extortionate, but the view up the girls' skirts on the metal stairs was some compensation.

At the top, Bally cautiously opened the door. A long corridor lay ahead, lit only by two naked electric bulbs. The walls were flimsy partitions, whitewashed and peeling, but they didn't reach the ceiling. Doors were set into these at intervals and 'our' girls stood waiting for us. One of them sidled over to Bally and took him, almost shyly, by the hand. She led him through one of the doorways and I saw, briefly, a single, narrow bed. This was a brothel and a half, a sort of sex factory operating on what seemed to be a conveyor-belt system. One in, one out. The other girl took my hand. 'Come,' she smiled.

'Er . . . no,' I said. 'I'll just wait for my mate if that's OK?' CSM Oates was standing at my elbow, frowning. The girl walked away without a word and I stood there like a spare part, feeling a complete idiot and suddenly lonely as hell. There was a weird silence. No bed springs. Nothing. From nowhere, a Chinese man was at my side. He must have been some sort of proprietor and he beckoned me into the room next to the one Bally had vanished into. He pointed to a chair against the wall and I climbed on it. Now I knew why those walls didn't reach the ceiling. Either Mr Proprietor could keep an eye on his girls or this was a voyeur's paradise and he saw me as some sort of pervert. Bally hadn't kept the girl waiting. He was already picking up his trousers, his arse pointing in my direction. The girl sat on the bed in just her knickers and was reaching for her dress.

'Hello, Bally,' I grinned.

He nearly fell over in the tangle of his trousers. 'How long have you been there?' he snapped.

I laughed and left the room. The Chinese man had gone and as I waited, Bally's girl, dressed again and cool as a cucumber, walked past me as if I wasn't there, en route to the lavatory. As she closed the door, Bally came hurtling out of his room. 'Come on,' he hissed and the urgency of his tone saw us both running. We were down that fire escape like firemen down a station pole and we hit the ground running, especially when the girl appeared at the top, screaming 'Stop thief! Stop thief!' while the proprietor and another man were charging down another fire escape. Now Bally was a plump little bloke but we did ourselves and the battalion proud in the minutes it took us to reach the shops. Once there, breathless, eyes popping, we did our best to mingle with all the other uniforms. I thought Bally was going to die. His colour was high and he was wheezing like an old steam engine.

'You nicked her money, didn't you?' I rounded on him.

He didn't reply but his face said it all.

'How much did you get?' I asked.

'Fifteen dollars,' he gasped.

'Come on, then,' I said. 'Split it.' After all, I'd just been chased through the night by what I knew must be a machete-wielding maniac and I'd done nothing wrong.

'Like hell!' Bally croaked. 'This is mine!'

I wasn't going to beat the money out of Bally, nor was I going to report him; there's no surer way than that to become a leper in the army. It never occurred to me that Bally's girl might be penniless or that the proprietor might have kicked seven bells out of her for being so careless.

One of my last memories of peacetime Singapore was Happy World. It must have been like one of those eighteenth-century pleasure gardens they used to have in London when anything went in the darkness of the shrubbery, before the prudish Victorians closed them down. There were stalls that sold everything, especially warm Tiger beer. There was a dance hall with wooden floors, not unlike those back home, and, of course, girls. There were also bouncers, Chinese men almost as wide as they were tall. To dance with a girl you bought a ticket from two middle-aged women sitting at a long table near the entrance. The girls wore Western clothes, smelt of cheap perfume and never refused a soldier. After the dance you could take your girl to a table, preferably in the hall's darkest corners. But you had to buy drinks and the cost was extortionate. Many was the Leicester squaddie who left Happy World decidedly unhappy.

And then we all left Singapore. For a while at least.

4

Battle Alert

Thinking about it, Singapore's railway station wasn't all that different from South Wigston's. Except that it was swarming with Malays and Chinese, of course, still going about the daily business of trying to run an empire.

The country we rattled through, going north, was fascinating. It was lush and green and there was water everywhere. Women and oxen stood knee-deep in the paddy fields and little Malay children stopped and waved to us, the soldiers from so far away. The roads were littered with bicycles and slow, lumbering bullock carts and here and there were little villages with mud roads and bamboo huts, their roofs heavy with the grass-like palm fronds called attap. It was the jungle that drew me, dark and impenetrable until the drooping branches nearly reached our carriages and a troop of chattering monkeys ran at us, leaping over each other and darting back. I'd never seen so many in one place before and they seemed to be daring each other to take chances, to get as close to the snorting, wheezing engine as they could and to stare at the strange, khaki-clad men beyond the grimy glass.

Butterworth sounds as if it might be in the heart of Lancashire or along the leafy lanes of Surrey. Actually, it's a ferry port to the island of Penang, our new destination. We'd got there in six hours with a couple of stops to have a pee and stretch our legs and we stood looking at the newly built airfield. However, there was something odd about RAF Butterworth. The personnel were there in their powder blue but there were no planes. Don't worry, came the cheery answer to a casual question from one of us. New Spitfires and Hurricanes were on their way. We'd stopped at a tiny station near some crossroads and our short march to the jetty was instantly interrupted by Malay street vendors carrying a world of merchandise on their backs; I didn't even recognize some of it.

Penang was an island paradise. The jungle-clad hills gave way to palm trees that hung heavy in the heat and the beaches were as white as the snows of Leicestershire, except they petered out into a sea of unimaginable blue.

The ferry was an old drive-on, reverse-off type, black and chugging. You could dip your hands into the warm sea and watch the shoals of fish, rainbow flashes under the water, enjoying the sun just like we were. Lorries took us to a camp on the edge of Georgetown, named in honour of the mad, bad old king the Americans hated. There were pineapple plantations and coconut groves stretching as far as the eye could see. After PT and rifle drill, I got used to lolling in the sun drinking cool coconut milk. What a war.

Welcome to the army, boys! Until now the only career soldiers we'd met were the NCOs with lungs of bronze back home and in Singapore. Now *everybody* had more experience than we did. The inmates of the camp at Penang had been there and done that; this was the battalion's base. We were the new boys and we were expected to keep our mouths shut and show the necessary degree of respect.

I didn't. At least I didn't the day I ran into Private Daniels. Maybe it was because I was a bit older than the other recruits;

maybe it was because the sun and the sand and the coconuts had made me too relaxed. Daniels was an Irish giant, a sort of Finn McCool who probably lived in those Blue Mountains beyond Dublin my dad had told me all about. He was usually perfectly pleasant, but on this particular day he looked a bit down in the dumps.

'What's up, then, Paddy? Just found out the missus ran off with the milkman?'

I must have hit a nerve because you could almost feel the silence. Everybody was looking at Paddy, wondering what he'd do. They didn't have long to wait. He lifted me off the ground by the throat and that was only his left hand. His right, about the size of a sledgehammer, was curled into a fist in front of my face. 'You think that's funny, do you, you little runt? Well, maybe you'll laugh even more when you see the shape of your new face.'

I could hear rising voices around me, though whether they were people urging Daniels to put me down or whether they were urging him on in his plans for plastic surgery, I have no idea. It was all I could do to breathe. Suddenly I was on the mess floor, gasping for air. I saw Daniels's boots move away and an air of normality descended.

'Learned something, have we?' a battered old soldier asked. Actually, he was more old lag than old soldier.

'He almost strangled me,' I croaked, my larynx throbbing.

'Just be thankful he wasn't in a bad mood,' the old soldier chuckled. Then, he got serious. 'And in future,' he said, looking me straight in the eye, 'don't get cocky unless you've had permission.' I didn't.

Penang was indeed a paradise. Twice a week 'Jigger' Johnson and I walked along the white sand until we were away from

the others. Then we'd strip off and rush into the gentle break-
ers, splashing around like kids. He was a dollop of lard was
Jigger, despite all the PT and the fitness. I was the scarecrow
I'd always been and it must have looked like a B-feature film I
knew they'd never make – *Laurel and Hardy Bare All*. It was
that day or the next that we found a turtle. We'd never seen
one before and it was lying in the surf, quite beautiful and
quite dead. The flies hadn't got to it yet and its shell was an
exquisite brown-green. I remember looking out to sea, the
creature's home, and wondering how it came to die.

Friday nights were the social high spots in Georgetown.
There were a few bars and a fleapit but when you're as bored
as we were, you could always spend your pay on liquor and
watching an old film whirring away on a clapped-out pro-
jector. We went through the motions, of course, because it
was unthinkable not to. Smartness inspection was a formality unless the duty officer was Sergeant Holmes. He failed
me every time, so it was out with the blanco, the button
stick and the gun oil. I hope Holmes enjoyed the torture he
inflicted, but he never seemed to. In all my time at Penang I
never saw him smile.

He still wasn't smiling when he came to see me one day.
'Twigg!' he called. 'South East Asia Command Games.'

Running, of course, was in my blood. Whether it was away
from dangerous dogs, orchard keepers and farmers, old witches,
the giants of the Blue Mountains or Chinese pimps, I was
bloody good at it. I'd beaten the best runners in the battalion,
both at home and out here. The Command Games were a sort
of Army Olympics and I trained every evening for them, bringing ridicule on myself with my breathing exercises.

'Yes, Sergeant!' I all but leapt into the miserable bugger's
arms.

'I've put you down for the boxing,' he said, straight-faced as ever. I was dumbstruck. I wasn't even bantamweight – and what if they put me in the ring with Private Daniels?

I never found out what I'd done to upset Sergeant Holmes or why he'd so misread my athletics skills. I may even have asked Albert Lockton about it. He was a sort of battalion fortune teller, sitting on the edge of his camp bed, staring dismally into a crystal ball. You didn't cross his palm with silver, which was just as well really because his news was never good. 'There'll be a war,' he would say with his flat Leicester delivery and deadpan expression. 'Some of us will die.' Thanks, Albert. And as blinding glimpses of the obvious went, that had to be the top of the tree.

I remember walking along the beach one glorious sunset evening. The darkness came down with such suddenness that the fireball of the setting sun didn't last for long. I heard a dog barking somewhere in the distance and, looking up, began to pick out the stars – the Southern Cross, Orion's Belt, the Plough. It's then that you think of home. Dad and my brothers and sisters. The mates I'd known. Were they all safe? Would I see them again? September brought no answers, but it brought an end to the idyll of Penang. There would be no Games after all. They'd been cancelled. We were going up-country. At last, we weren't playing games any more.

Sungai Petani means, roughly, farmer's river. I didn't realize when I first saw it just how much a river would come to fill my life. This was another tented camp but it stood in the middle of a rubber plantation and on the first morning, as I stuck my head out of the tent, I saw a Malay woman among the trees. She moved silently, like a ghost, collecting fluid from the rubber trees. She'd sliced V shapes on the trunks and the sap dripped into cups fastened below each cut. The only sound was a distant whooping of monkeys on their jungle trails. Never once did the woman look across at us. It was as though we didn't exist.

Training continued as always, but there was a greater urgency about it. We moved forward line abreast, our rifles at the ready across our chests, and every now and then picked out a target. This was the enemy. We charged, screaming, with arms extended and bayonets fixed. Many a sapling went down before the charge of the 1st Leicesters, but somehow I didn't feel ready. Doubts start to creep in, especially with the jungle all around you. Had that Malay woman not seen us because, in her eyes at least, we no longer existed? I'm not the superstitious type, not prone to jump at shadows. Even so, I couldn't get Albert Lockton and his mournful prediction out of my mind. 'Some of us will die.'

We hadn't been up-country long before the unbelievable humidity got to me. There's no wind. No breeze. Whether you're marching or charging or just standing still, it's like you're in a shower. You're running with sweat and any exertion is exhausting. I'm no military historian, but somewhere I'd heard that on campaign, disease has always killed more men than die on the battlefield. Not that my first problem felt at all fatal; it was just bloody annoying. Thousands of itchy red dots appeared all over my skin. 'Prickly heat,' said the medical officer and gave me some cream. To be honest, it didn't do much good and for the first time I got a sense, maybe foreboding is the word, that nobody seemed to have a clue what to do in this climate and this terrain. We were all working along British lines, as if we'd been operating somewhere in Europe. They had different rules out here; even the jungle had its own.

I was still scratching and wincing with the pain of my red, lacerated skin when an old Malay came over to me. He did odd jobs around the camp and his grasp of English wasn't bad. 'Prickly heat,' he said. I just looked at him. Was he going to offer me some useless cream or tell me to see the MO? 'Best way,' he nodded enthusiastically, 'stand in rain no clothes. Make you feel better. It good.'

It was the rainy season of course and the downpours came most afternoons with a monotonous regularity. I stripped naked and stood at the edge of the jungle, feeling the raindrops beating down on my agonized body. It was heaven; it cooled down my hot itching. I felt my sanity coming back. It was so good that long after the condition had gone I took to standing naked in the rain. It wouldn't do in Leicester High Street but out here nobody seemed to notice. I passed the word to anyone who would listen. And I never thanked the old Malay. His was one of those little kindnesses you meet along the road sometimes. I should have thanked him.

Another kindness, although we paid for it, came from Nappi. We'd been in the camp for a day or two when this short, crisply dressed Indian came to our tent and made us an offer none of us believed. 'Excuse me, sirs,' he said. 'You want me shave you before you wake in the morning? Very cheap.'

'You what?' somebody laughed. 'Shave us while we sleep? Pull the other one.'

'No, sir,' the Indian wasn't smiling. 'No joke. You wake up already shaved. Very good for sergeant major.' Now he smiled. We did too. Nothing ventured, nothing gained, so I took him on. Anyway, it was impossible. A dry shave would hurt like hell and a wet shave, with lather and a cut-throat, would be bound to wake me up. Next morning I jumped at the sound of Reveille shattering the jungle morning and

1. Men of the Leicestershire Regiment (6th Division) in a captured second line trench at Ribecourt during the battle of Cambrai, 1917. 'Dad was in the trenches to the end of the war. He was gassed and saw mates killed around him but he was lucky. Maybe it runs in the family. I think all the Twiggs came through both wars.'

2. Leicestershire Regiment ('The Tigers') helmet plate. Helmets were not worn in the field after 1900, but as Sidney Twigg was a bandsman he wore it ceremonially. By the time of the First World War, helmets, which gave little protection, had been replaced by tin hats.

3. '"To my little Reggie, Daddy is coming home soon", received by us in 1919. I can't remember the card arriving but we were so excited when it did. This was the first time I remember seeing him.'

4. 'The three of us: Ken, me and Cyril. I know Dad was still in the army so it was about 1925 and I was about eleven. That year our mother left us.'

5. 'Havelock Road Camp, Singapore, February 1942' by Jack Chalker. 'That's just the sort of place I found Harry Foley. I went up the ladder and then shouted, "Anybody here from the Leicesters?"'

6. 'Slim River, a stop on the railway journey from Singapore to Bam Pong' by Jack Chalker. 'I was put on that sort of carriage. We were so cramped you could hardly move.'

7. 'Appalling conditions on the ammunition trucks carrying POWs' by Leo Rawlings. 'Mainly it was mixed trucks, some open, some like this one, but that is how it was inside.'

(IWM ART LD 6032)

8. Camp layout at Tha Muang. 'I wasn't at Muang but this is how the camps looked. They were made from bamboo and attap. They weren't all exactly the same, but our huts were generally in rows of some kind.'

9. 'The huts are identical to those I lived in. I just had a loincloth but some blokes managed to hang on to shorts for a while, but they wore out in the heat. We often called the loincloths "bollock bags".'

10. 'The inside of my hut was like this. We slept on the platforms side by side and head to toe. We sat around and talked after work or on a Sunday.'

11. Life at Kanchanaburi, 1942: (*above*) queuing at the canteen;
(*below*) chopping wood outside the cookhouse.

12. The kitchen at Konyo 2, 1943. 'That looks right. I slid down the bank at the back so I could be first in the queue. You had to get food and there was no point in hanging back.'

13. Food line at Tha Muang. 'One day my mess tin went missing. I left it hanging around and somebody nicked it. So you'd use anything you could. I used an old tin and we had a mug for tea.'

14. 'Building the railway embankment, Konyo' by Jack Chalker. 'I did that. You'd search around for rocks to carry up to the embankment. Somebody else then bashed them down to make the foundations of the railway track.'

15. 'Working on the Thai/Burma Railway at Konyo' by John Mennie. 'I used a pick a lot. You broke up the ground and widened the clearing. It was hard. Others cleared rocks by hand as the picture shows. Even though you got beaten if you slowed down, it was better than working inside with men with disease.' *(IWM ART 16712 (1))*

16. Laying the sleepers, 1943. 'Two men to a sleeper, then the tracks went on top. The Japs used to get us to push in bricks and earth underneath to make it solid. The Japs then brought the rails up by train and we laid them on top.'

17. Laying the rails. 'It must have been early on or these men came late to the railway because they've still got shorts and hats. I was in a loincloth in no time because clothes and boots just rotted.'

18. 'First Camp Meat, Konyo' by Jack Chalker, October 1942. This was the first meat in the camp that the prisoners had seen. 'The caption says the Commandant tortured the buffalo – that would be the Konyo Kid. At another camp I got the bladder of a steer and tried to eat it – it was like rubber.'

19. Lieutenant Usuki. 'Everyone knew him as the Konyo Kid. He was very violent indeed. He'd parade around criticizing and usually instructed his men to do the beating, then carry on overseeing things. Even if you moved on parade, you would get a beating. He raved and shouted.' He was executed after the war.

20. 'The Silver Bullet (in the middle). He took pleasure in violence and killing. He loved the power and was one of the guards that killed Harry.' *(IWM HU 29175)*

absent-mindedly rubbed my chin. It was smooth as a baby's bum. So was everybody else's. No nicks. No blood. No lather. Nappi was simply a genius. To this day I have no idea how he did it.

The deeper you go into the jungle, the more of the world you leave behind. Georgetown had been much, much smaller than Singapore and Sungai Petani was much, much smaller than Georgetown. The whole place was a shanty town, built entirely of wood, and the population was mostly Malay. The handful of Chinese here were sullen and very traditional. The women wore tight dresses down to their ankles and hobbled on deformed feet, bound to stumps, as their mothers and their mothers' mothers had for generations. The local brothel was run by a fat Malay woman, probably in her thirties, whom we called Mexicali Rose. Any evening you could find her sitting outside her bordello, calling out to anything in khaki. There were two restaurants that served egg and chips (isn't it amazing how the British can always manage to take their gourmet delights with them wherever they go?) and a rickety old cinema that was actually a hut with a corrugated tin roof on which the rain drummed incessantly. So bored were we one night that we got into the place via the balcony and, after a few beers, pelted the cinema-goers of the Leicestershire Regiment with sticky, over-ripe bananas we'd bought from the market. Then we ran, laughing like pissed hyenas, looking for more beer.

To walk to our training ground, we had to cross the jungle first. It was a hostile world, dark and forbidding. Ants the size of cockroaches marched across our path, in columns four abreast. They *really* knew how to march, never deviating, never hesitating, swarming over any obstacle, including our army-issue boots as if we weren't there. The Malay woman collecting her sap had ignored us; so did the ants. Huge spiders' webs stretched from branch to branch, superfine and invisible in the sunlight until it was too late. They wrapped around you, clinging to your face, your nose, your ears. The huge black and yellow spiders whose trap you'd just sprung would come at you, undaunted by your size. And why not? They had more eyes and legs than we did and could wrap up a helpless enemy in seconds. Many was the six-foot Leicester lad who would end up squealing like a girl knocking one of these things away. We all did it and in the end no one noticed.

There was no swigging from our canteens until the order came. We were allowed to sing as we marched and, perhaps because of my dad, I was usually the lead in a Great War song:

> If you want the old battalion,
> We know where they are, we know where they are,
> We know where they are . . .

The originals of Ypres and the Somme were hanging on the old barbed wire, but we'd seen precious little of that on this jolly so far and we hadn't even seen an enemy. In fact, apart from the jungle, it wasn't quite clear who our enemy was. By the end of the march, the song intended to maintain the pace had dried up and we all collapsed on the ground, filthy, sweat-stained, exhausted. I wasn't thinking of the Command Games any more.

I was Number One on the platoon mortar and my mate Albert was Number Two. It was actually an Ordnance SBML two-inch mortar and, to be honest, I wasn't very impressed with the thing. It weighed 10½lb, which made it heavier than the .303, and of course you had to carry your ammo as well – bombs with fins that held either high explosive or smoke or even flares for night work. We were shown the traditional way of operating the mortar. One man aimed the thing while another loaded it. The first man operated a trigger mechanism at the breech and in theory the bombs would hurtle to the ground 500 yards away, creating murder and mayhem in the enemy lines.

'Now, Twigg,' Platoon Sergeant Benny Watkins said. 'See that tree stump?'

I did.

'That's your target. Off you go.'

I crouched in the time-honoured position, lining the thing up through the collimating sights which reminded me of a spirit level with its bubbles for elevation. 'Bomb in,' I shouted to Albert and he duly did the honours, fins first. I pulled the trigger. Nothing happened. I steadied the tube, took aim again and fired. Again, nothing. Smoke was snaking out of the muzzle and the officers who had been watching looked as if they were recreating the retreat from Mons. Sergeant Watkins hadn't moved.

'Well,' he said quietly. 'You know what to do, lads. Get on with it.' We knew what to do. Run like mad. But an innate discipline kicked in and I carefully unscrewed the barrel, now very hot, from the base. The smoking fin had broken away from the bomb casing so Albert and I lifted the thing out and looked at Watkins. He nodded silently, pleased that men under his command either had nerves of steel or were the luckiest pair of herberts west of the China Sea. We reloaded the mortar, fired it and shattered the tree stump with a frightening speed and precision just as the officers returned from their reconnoitring position. As they moved away, satisfied, Benny Watkins looked down at us. 'Almost made soldiers of you then, lads,' he said. 'But next time, I might not be there.

Them little yellow bastards might have got me, especially if I have to keep telling you lot what to do!' Benny Watkins *was* the British Army. He was shorter than me, but like a lot of little men – Nelson, Napoleon, Attila the Hun – he more than made up for it with sheer, in-your-face guts. He'd been a regular for years and at bayonet practice he always encouraged us to see the sapling, the tree, the swinging sandbag as a 'little yellow bastard'; it made the lunge all the more deadly.

Then we moved on to Jitra. This was another tented camp way up on the border of Siam (which they'd now decided to call Thailand) and the 1st Leicesters dug in as though for the duration. The jungle was thicker here than anything we'd met before and the work was hot and heavy. We washed in the daily downpour with the drops bouncing off us like pebbles and we fought a war of attrition against the teeming insects that swarmed around us.

Late in October the whole battalion moved up and D Company manned the road to Kampong Manggis. We *knew* nothing. Everything was rumour and counter-rumour based largely on the speculation of the Singapore-printed English-language newspaper. Benny Watkins had been right; the enemy was likely to be those 'little yellow bastards', the Japanese. What did we know about them? Again, nothing. I don't remember the battalion smartarse adding to the conversation but the older hands told us they were all tiny – about Reg Twigg's height, they said – and were very short sighted. They couldn't hit a Lavender Street brothel with their clapped-out rifles. None of them could see at all in the dark, so at least there'd be no night attack. Hadn't they been flexing their muscles for years here in the East, though, somebody asked. Weren't they actually battle-hardened veterans whereas the Leicesters hadn't fired a shot in anger since 1918? Well, yes, perhaps; but just look who they've been fighting against – the bloody Chinese, for God's sake. It'd all be very different up against the British Army.

It was now that the monsoon proper hit and I realized that the daily downpour was just a light drizzle by comparison. The trenches we made filled with water as soon as we'd dug them and we found ourselves up to our knees in mud, our boots all but sucked off by the bloody stuff. Keeping dry in our tents was impossible and we slept on wet beds with the water rushing under us and the rain like machine-gun fire on the canvas overhead. And the rain brought out the wildlife like never before. Huge croaking frogs sulked silently during the day, only to open their throats as darkness fell and the chorus was deafening. Snakes swam silently in the trench water and there were shrieks and much jumping up the slippery banks until we realized they were harmless. Leeches weren't harmless. They were big; they were black and they clung to your body. They had a knack of slipping inside your uniform and sucking the blood out of you before you even noticed.

'Bugger off!' 'Shit!' 'What the fucking hell . . . ?' The intellectual conversation of the slit trenches was almost all caused by the discovery of leeches. Knocking them off did no good so whoever had a fag on would pass it round so we could burn the buggers into oblivion. Just one touch on the back end would make them let go; we liked to imagine with a silent scream. But even so, in the end you could say it was Leeches 1, 1st Leicesters 0. We stayed out of the trenches except for essential maintenance.

This misery dragged on into December. Rain. And more rain. No news. No attack. It was an odd sense of isolation deep in the jungle of the Malay peninsula, knowing that a world war was being fought somewhere else and that we weren't part of it.

In the Hawaiian islands across the Pacific, in a different time zone from us, it was Sunday 7 December. President Roosevelt called it a date that would live in infamy. The Japanese launched their attack on the American Pacific Fleet at Pearl Harbor. The 'little yellow bastards' hadn't even declared war first. The rather more clued-up among us realized, if we hadn't already, that these people played by different rules. In fact, it looked as though there were no rules at all.

The other news was worse. The Japanese had hit Hong Kong too. And Hong Kong was ours. The battalion moved to Battle Alert. Our officers told us now that the Japs had invaded Thailand and that we'd already abandoned our forward positions. Today, you can read all about it because it's in the history books. Then, we had no detailed information at all. On the 8th, four divisions of the Japanese Imperial Army under General Yamashita landed at Singora, Pattani and Kota Bharu. They had tanks and air cover. We had neither.

We simply weren't ready. We'd put up barbed wire and the Engineers had laid some anti-tank mines, but the incessant rain had held us up badly. We all knew now that it was just a matter of time until the soldiers of the 1st Leicesters would be called upon to fight. The history books will tell you we were poorly trained, what some of our officers would have called the Second Eleven in keeping with their largely public-school traditions. I don't know about that; I've got nothing to compare us with. I only know that, in the end, there's nothing that can prepare you for a battle. The only way you learn is by fighting one.

The mortar practice went on. We had a different platoon

sergeant now – Watkins had been moved to another company – and he told me, on the 9th, to set the thing up on the slimy edge of a rain-filled trench and set the sights on a crossroads in a ramshackle village about 200 yards away. Rain and trenches. Talk about history repeating itself. I could just see my dad sitting in the City Arms at home, nodding over his pint. 'See. I told you so.' And so I became what may have been the first casualty of the war in Malaya.

Albert dropped in the bomb fins; I squeezed the trigger and the blast of the ignition rammed the mortar tube down into the soft mud until it flopped over. It was now horizontal rather than at the usual 60° angle and the bomb hurtled into the nearest tree, sending a shower of branches and leaves down on our heads. When we'd recovered from the noise and shock, I pictured the headlines in an imaginary battalion newspaper. 'Twigg hit by twigs!' If we'd done that in the face of a Japanese onslaught, God knows what the result would have been.

The bad news just kept coming. We heard the next day that both our capital ships, the *Repulse* and the *Prince of Wales*, had been sunk in a battle with Japanese planes from Indochina. We just looked at each other. We all remembered *Repulse* as part of our convoy on the way out, her awesome power, her sleek lines, her big guns. What we hadn't known was that her nickname was *Repair* because she was so often in various ports for refits. The *Prince of Wales* was a far greater loss. She was new and, as they'd say today, state-of-the-art in terms of naval warfare. The loss of life was appalling. Rumours ran that the ships went down because they had no air support and we remembered the naked runways at Butterworth. Where the hell was the RAF?

The tension in the camp was cranked up more notches than

we realized. The rain still hammered down, the frogs still croaked and we guarded the trenches with our capes soaked through and the drops running in rivulets off our helmet rims. We had orders to challenge anyone approaching from the jungle or the road to the north and the password was changed daily in case the jungle itself had ears. On the night of 10 December someone emerged from the blackness and the sentry challenged him. There was no reply. The sentry swung his .303 in front of him, calling the challenge again. Still nothing. No password. No response. So the sentry fired and Private Ron Maine of the 1st Leicesters fell like a stone. Ron was our first death and it stunned us. Where had he been? Why didn't he give the password? We didn't even have time to bury him. And the sentry? I don't know who it was or whether he ever spent a peaceful night again.

Dawn on 11 December 1941. That day, I understood the strange withdrawals of my dad for the first time. The poetic phrase for it is 'baptism of fire' but you don't feel very poetic when somebody's doing his level best to kill you. And that's how you see it. The 1st Leicesters were part of a bigger unit of the 11th Indian Division; other units had been mauled by withering Japanese fire in outposts to the north over the last two days. You take comfort from the scale of things – the thousands of men you know are deployed in Malaya. But when it comes right down to it, every single gun in the Japanese Imperial Army is pointing just at you.

Ours not to reason why, of course, so we stayed where we were. There was a lack of communications. Right hand. Left hand. There was nothing new in this; my dad told similar stories when he was in a certain mood, of the Ypres salient. All day we waited, talking quietly, speculating, trying to control our nerves. I've never seen so many fags smoked and

I thanked God and the NAAFI for my St Bruno. That night I swear the frogs were croaking in fluent Japanese.

Dawn on 12 December. The gunfire we'd listened to the previous day seemed further away. Surely, the Japs weren't retreating? And if they were, who the hell was driving them back? We got news that a dispatch rider sent the previous day with orders for us to move had been killed, so effectively we were cut off. By late morning the officers had come to a decision. The company would be split into four, each section comprising about twenty-five men led by an officer. We'd fight our way through to the coast and march south. Captain Ley led us west by whatever jungle track we could find. Using the road would be suicidal. We hadn't seen any aircraft but we knew the Japs had the skies to themselves and we'd be sitting ducks. We found shelter that night in a brick shed in the middle of nowhere. God knows what it had been used for but it stank to high heaven. It had no windows and an uneven brick floor below ground level. Lying in fetid water and rubble, I'd never slept so deeply in my life.

In the morning we were moving again, Ley navigating west with his compass. The mud got worse, heavy and dragging us down as we tried to keep up some sort of acceptable pace. If it was torture to our legs, it was worse on the nerves. We still had no idea where the Japs were, but common sense told us they should be to the north, to our right as we slogged on. By now, of course, they could have surrounded us so an attack might suddenly come from anywhere; or everywhere. Then we hit the river. As if we hadn't seen enough bloody water coming out of the sky, there was more of it here; a twenty-yard-wide torrent of brown foam, surging downstream to the sea and carrying jungle debris with it. Maybe a strong swimmer could have crossed it, but we were exhausted and carrying kit and I knew of at least three lads who couldn't swim at all. But, miracle of miracles, there was a bridge. If you've ever seen a jungle bridge, you'll know you can't understand how the things stay up. They all look like they've been built by a madman whose grasp of physics is fleeting. Either that, or they're the most complicated aids to suicide ever invented.

Captain Ley decided that two men should try the bridge out. It looked lethal enough even if the Japs hadn't booby trapped it. The first man was Albert Lockton, the gloomy fortune teller. I often wondered afterwards if he'd had time to gaze the night before. He and his oppo edged out onto the rickety contraption and the handrail moved. They were nearly halfway out when the rail bulged outwards and Albert lost his balance. For a second, he seemed to hang in mid-air like a freeze-frame. Then Albert, rifle, pack and, no doubt, his crystal ball plummeted into the foaming water. He made no sound and the weight of his kit dragged him down. For a second, perhaps two, no one moved. Albert's oppo was scrabbling back along the bridge and Captain Ley and I dropped our kit and jumped into the water. It took all my strength to withstand the current; all I could see was swirling mud. We both dived, the foul-smelling water filling our noses and ears. Each time I came up for air, I had to look round for the captain and for the watchers on the bank. The water disoriented me and I had no idea where I was. Ley called, 'Nothing, Twigg?'

'Nothing, sir.' I was fighting for breath. 'Can't see a thing.'

'There's nothing more we can do. Come on.' And we helped each other ashore. Ley didn't want another man's death on his conscience. Then we tried the bridge again, careful, on that swaying death trap, to stay wide of the point where Albert had gone. I was saturated, my sodden uniform clinging to me everywhere and my boots full of water. Below us the torrent roared and foamed, its victim claimed. What was it Albert had predicted? 'Some of us will die.' He got that right.

The next river had no bridge and would have been a shallow stream in the dry season. Now, if anything, it was more deadly than the last one. This one we'd have to wade through. Ley told us to clip our rifle slings together to make a long belt but this still had to be lashed to the far bank. 'Who's the strongest swimmer?' Ley asked. I can't remember whether Private Webster actually volunteered but his name seemed to be top of the list. 'Think you can make that?' the captain asked him.

'Soon find out, sir,' Webster told him. He stripped to his shorts and lashed the rifle slings around his waist. Then he was in the water, up to his knees first, then his waist. We played out the belt ready to haul him back in if the current won. But Webster was good and despite buffetings from floating flora that must have hit like sledgehammers, he dragged himself up onto the far bank. Then, of course, the Johnny Weissmuller of the 1st Leicesters had to do it all over again to release the belt tie from the far side, or we'd have had no slings for our rifles. We'd already left God knows how much kit behind in Jitra.

The heat gets to you. It saps your strength, fills your lungs and slows your reactions. The sweat dripping from your eyebrows stings and burns and your nose drips in sympathy. So you breathe through your mouth and your tongue gets thick and parched. Men start to look into the distance, wondering just how big this jungle is, how far the track winds. My mate Albert Wingell looked like that soon after the second river crossing.

'I'm not going to make it, Reg,' he muttered when I asked him how he was. I'd never heard that sort of talk from Albert before. Ron Maine, even Albert Lockton had gone. Anyway, they were comrades, but they weren't mates. Albert was a mate.

'Don't talk like that,' I scolded him gently. 'We'll be all right. Just got to stick to it and keep watching out.'

He didn't react.

'Here, Albert, give me your kit.' I was already hauling it off him. 'Have a break for a while.'

He half-smiled. 'Thanks, Reg,' he said.

Don't ask me how I coped with two rifles, my own kitbag and Albert's but cope I did. Don't give me a bloody medal. Don't give one to Private Webster. Just get us out of this. Another night. Another abandoned jungle hut. Another sleep like the dead.

Captain Ley reckoned the next day that we must be close to the coast. The jungle would thin soon, he estimated, and we'd be seen from the air. Twenty-five men moving together attracts attention. We didn't know the Japanese Imperial Army had 1,500 planes but we knew it would only take one of them to cut us to pieces. Ley divided us into groups of six and our objective was the coast. Then we were to head south and find the rest of the battalion.

'See you later, Reg,' Albert said that morning. The kit rest had done him good and he was back, more or less, to his old self. I shook his hand. 'You keep your head down and your chin up,' I said and laughed. Then he hauled the rifle over his shoulder and vanished along his jungle trail. I never saw him again. Another dad had gone for a soldier.

*

The rain stopped as if somebody had turned off a tap and, slogging along behind Lance Corporal Starkey, we found the coast in a few hours. I've never been so grateful to see anything as that sea and we marched south towards Penang. We were moving in single file now, six tired, jumpy lads from Leicestershire with the hostile jungle to our left and the white beach to our right and the wild surf beyond. Expecting a Jap attack any second, we came to a fishing village. The coast was littered with them, attap-roofed huts, slung nets and little, bobbing boats. A large mob of Malay men were coming towards us, faces grim, eyes fierce. And they carried sticks and knives. We weren't sure what they knew. Had the Japs been through here already? Or had the villagers just heard news from the north and realized that the British, for all we were walking, were in full retreat?

Starkey wasn't taking any chances. He only had one stripe on his sleeve, but he had to make a split-second decision just like a general. He ordered us to level our rifles. He then told the natives – in English, of course – to keep back or we would fire. They may not have spoken fluent Leicestershire, but they understood the universal language of six .303 muzzles. However we couldn't hold this position for long. Then somebody remembered a rowing boat a few yards back. Sailors we weren't but we were between the devil and the deep and while two of the lads kept their rifles on the crowd, steadily creeping forward, we dragged the boat into the surf and everybody piled in.

We only had two oars and no sail so we kept close to the shore and breathed a collective sigh of relief as the Malay mob faded to specks against the dark backdrop of the jungle. Up to this point I'd never been shot at in my life. It's so ordinary and matter-of-fact you don't know what it is at first. There was a 'zip' as a bullet hit the water to our stern. Then a second near the bow. We crouched as low as we could but whoever was firing from that damned jungle was no sniper and nobody was hit.

You lose track of time on the water, but we must have been heading south for a couple of hours, each of us taking turns to row. 'Shit!' one of the lads suddenly shouted. 'I've lost my oar.' The sheer force of the current had ripped it out of his grip and now we were helpless. Ever tried rowing a boat with one oar? You tend to see the same bit of water rather often. So the wind and the tide guided us after that.

Then the keel ground into soft mud about fifty yards out and the beach seemed a very long way away. We weren't consciously thinking about quicksand but a man had drowned already and nobody wanted to see that again.

'We've got to get to that beach,' Starkey said.

'We're knackered,' somebody else said. 'We'll never make it.'

Silence.

'So what are we going to do?' I thought somebody had to say it. It might as well be me.

Silence.

Had they all gone deaf? 'Corp,' I nudged Starkey. 'What are we going to do?'

Starkey was crying quietly to himself. He was tired. He had no answers. There were generals like this in Malaya in 1941. I don't know how long we sat there, the merciless sun beating down on us. Then it dawned; the others were all looking at me. I was a day away from my twenty-eighth birthday, the grandad of the unit in their eyes. Surely *I* had an answer.

'Right,' I said, a man with a mission. 'I'll try and make it to shore. If I do, you blokes follow me.'

'You'll never make it, Twiggy,' one of them said, concern on his face.

'Somebody's got to do something,' I said. I wasn't needling Starkey but to him it probably felt like it. I was stripping to my underpants. 'I'll leave my kit here. It'll only pull me down. But if I make it,' I let my eyes burn into each of them, 'bring it over. Especially my pipe and tobacco.'

So I was over the side, feeling a bit of an idiot when I sank up to my ankles. I waded beachwards and found myself being dragged down. I was up to my thighs in clawing, sticky mud. I didn't know whether this was quicksand or not – you don't get much of it in Leicestershire – but I pushed on, kicking my legs forward against an ever-growing mass of glue. Then, I felt firmness under my left foot, then my right. I staggered out onto the sand, covered in mud up to my crotch. 'Kinfi-nobbleation-mira-moka-kid-comeday-mumday-all-a-mid.'

'All right, lads,' I called. 'You'll be OK. Don't forget my pipe!'

I saw them shoving their uniforms and boots into their kit-bags and it wasn't until they were all ashore that I realized nobody had brought my gear over and the boat was drifting away. 'Weren't you bringing it, Jack?' somebody asked. 'No, Tom. I thought you were.' Those blokes could pass the buck for England. So off we marched, five British soldiers in tropical battledress and an odd-looking idiot in baggy underpants, bare feet and no rifle.

After our reception at the last village, we were ready for the next one. But the locals were friendly. They smiled and invited us, in broken English, to stop and have a drink. We were taking chances here because this could have been a delay-ing tactic linked with the Japanese. In the event it wasn't and they plied us with black, sweet coffee, the first we'd had since leaving Jitra. They hadn't seen anybody; not Japs nor the British. But then, this place was so remote they might well not have realized they'd been part of our empire for the last century. They gave me a red sarong before I left which was touching if a little conspicuous and off we marched again as if I was some sort of regimental mascot!

Starkey had got himself together by the time we reached the next village. This lot were hostile. A mob gathered on the outskirts, pointing, unsmiling, jabbering loudly.

'Let them see the rifles,' Starkey ordered. We were, of course, one down now – mine. How threatening I could have looked in the sarong, I don't know, but the .303s did the trick, probably because we were desperate enough to use them, and the mob stayed back until they became a blur against the jungle.

That night, sleep was a luxury. No longer trudging through the jungle, we weren't as physically exhausted as we had been, but now we knew we had to watch for Malays as well as Japs. We lay down with trees to our backs and were grateful for the soft, soothing breeze from the sea.

By mid-afternoon of the next day, we were close to Butterworth. Although my swollen feet hurt like hell, our spirits were lifted. We'd soon be back with the battalion, fed, watered, reclothed (in my case) and ready for whatever the 'little yellow bastards' were going to throw at us. But there was no one there. Actually, that's not quite true. We caught sight of other bedraggled men, handfuls like us, all looking for some semblance of a camp or defensive lines. I even saw a knot of them in a rowing boat heading for Penang, waving to us as they went. It was late by the time we found the cream-painted school. Thirty men lounged outside with three officers. At last, something approximating a platoon. There were certainly odd glances, but no wisecracks at my appearance. We didn't know then that men could go mad in this jungle. Perhaps they all assumed I was the first example. The local Malays were friendly and gave us gorgeous, thirst-quenching hot coconut juice to drink. There was no food. And actually, precious little safety, for all our sudden increase in numbers. We slept like the dead.

The Malays had gone the next morning, which was an ominous sign. These people had known the jungle all their lives. Perhaps they smelt death. Fags were passed round as the officers talked among themselves. Their decision was to follow the main road south to Singapore, but again we had to move, for safety, in small groups. And again we had to negotiate the sea. The road could only be reached by a little ferry boat and the ferryman was demanding payment. Who paid him? The officers, digging deep in their pockets. I couldn't help smiling at this. Here we were, a retreating shambles of a unit, with everyone (except me) armed to the teeth and we were haggling over the price of a ferry. The Japs would have shot him.

So we marched south again, in pairs on both sides of the road, with the jungle for cover. Every time we heard an engine we dashed into the undergrowth. My oppo now was Wigginton who'd shared those over-baked spuds with me on the frozen ridges of the Kibworth range back home.

'Look what I've got,' he grinned, ferreting in his kitbag. It was a small tin of condensed milk.

'Well done, Wiggy. That could be useful.'

Another hostile village. More snarling and spitting. More raised rifles. Word must have reached here by now. The British had once been masters of the East and now the British were in full retreat, running from an enemy we still hadn't seen. Half an hour later we saw the other face of Malaya, that mixed-up outpost of empire we were supposed to be defending. A middle-aged Chinese man came out of his bungalow and called us over. 'Hungry?' he asked us and when nobody answered, he asked again. 'Hungry? Come, I have rice. Please. Eat.' We couldn't believe this. Through a garden gate a whole team of Chinamen were bringing out vats of boiled rice. Starving as we were, we were soldiers first and we queued up in an orderly fashion as if Porky Crane had been with us.

It was Wiggy's finest hour. 'Here you are,' he said, triumphantly producing the condensed milk. Rice pudding! Absolutely fantastic. Maybe he was paying me back for the spuds.

We thanked the Chinaman profusely. He and his family had put food in our stomachs and restored a little of the pride we'd once had. We certainly had a spring in our step as we took to the road again. I often think about that man and wonder what happened to him. He had nowhere to go and would probably have stayed there until the Japanese arrived. They had been fighting the Chinese for years. I dreaded to think how they might show their gratitude. Anyway, he probably thought the British would be back soon. A flag that had fluttered over this country for so long couldn't possibly be hauled down in just a few days.

We were hot. We were thirsty. We were tired. And it was hours before we reached a river, which might have been the Krian. What was left of the road bridge was a twisted heap of buckled iron and concrete. We all stood there in silence. This was what a bombing raid could do; I'd seen it in Leicester. Now the Japs had done it here, trying to cut off our retreat. Then, on the opposite bank I saw somebody in uniform. Thank God it was a British one.

'Who are you?' a plummy voice called.

'The Leicesters,' our sergeant shouted back. 'We were cut off at Jitra.'

'Right. We'll get you.' Rowing boats appeared from nowhere. It quickly became obvious that we'd blown this bridge ourselves, the Engineers planting explosives to delay the invasion. At the field kitchen we had corned beef and biscuits. I'd never tasted anything so marvellous. I was quite sorry to say goodbye to the sarong, but people would have talked so into the bin it went. I scrounged odds and sods of uniform and tried to look like a soldier again. We were debriefed by the unit commander. He announced we'd be on a train south to Singapore for a health check and then we'd be deployed elsewhere.

As it turned out, there was no elsewhere.

5

The Shambles of Singapore

The Alexandra British Military Hospital in Singapore was brand new, set in grounds of mown lawns and surrounded by low white buildings of the colonial style. The views were marvellous and I remember sitting on my bed wondering why nobody else seemed to be aware there was a war on. The Mitsubishis snarled overhead like hornets and when they weren't machine-gunning anything on the ground, they made two or three passes and banked north to the mainland. I now know that they were taking photographs of every building, every road, every army installation on the island, and that with each click of the camera, the impregnable fortress got a little bit less impregnable.

The usual targets were the docks, the airfield and naval base at Sembawang. We'd hear the ack-ack batteries open up and we all knew the island had no air-raid shelters. The odds were beginning to stack up and it didn't look good. I told anybody who would listen – doctors, nurses, the hospital cat – that I was fine and could get back to the battalion. Stay put, they said; wait until you're passed fit. The irony was that I *was* fit. Most of us were. We'd spent days in the jungle but none of us was actually hurt.

'Reg Twigg!' a familiar voice called out to me as I wandered back to the ward one day. 'Bloody hell; all this way to meet you here!' I couldn't believe it. Sitting there, smiling at me, was Harry Barnett and I hadn't seen him for five years. We'd been to school together in Leicester and scorched the grass in many a football match. After my move to Lincoln we'd lost touch, like you do, but we were soon nattering away about happier days before the Japanese Imperial Air Force was trying to kill us. He'd had it rougher than me; he'd been with the 5th Infantry Division at Jitra, taking the full force of the Japanese attack. Like me, he felt fine, and like me, the only thing keeping him out of the front line was army red tape. He was itching to get back to it all. I have to tell you we weren't heroes. Sitting idly under fire with no means of fighting back gets to you. I may as well still have been wearing my sarong!

Soon enough we were both discharged and Harry's company was dispatched to join another unit. It was the last I'd see of him until that dreadful reunion in the hospital at Tarso.

Even once we were out of the Alexandra we were still kicking our heels in inactivity. They housed us in a smart bungalow on the edge of Singapore town and we had Christmas with most of the trimmings. I bought myself a new pipe to compensate for the one quite possibly still bobbing about in an abandoned fishing boat somewhere in the Andaman Sea.

Two days later, action at last, that is if you call a move to the Reinforcement Camp action. From here men were sent to front-line units and we all knew, because we heard the distant gunfire, that serious fighting was going on in the jungles of the mainland. There were hundreds of us here, keyed up and ready. On the first evening I joined in a mass singsong. There was as much beer as you could drink – about five pints in my case; after that I was on the floor! – and there were hearty choruses of 'When They Sound the Last "All-Clear"'. I have to admit it sounded better when Vera Lynn and the Mantovani Orchestra performed it, because we weren't exactly a regimental Glee Club. Over our pints, puffing away at fags and pipes, we'd ponder over and over again – what the hell were the generals doing? There were thousands of us in Malaya, the cream of Britain's fighting elite. If the Japanese could advance through that bloody jungle, so could we.

Then came the word. We were going. Your stomach falls through your arse at the same time that your heart fills your mouth. As a kid, I remember facing some scary ride at the annual fair: you wanted to go on it, but you were terrified at the same time. We collected our kit and marched to the station, rolling out of Singapore across the Causeway to the mainland. That night we slept in the open on the hard ground away from the train in case of air raids. Who was the stupid bastard who said the Japs couldn't see in the dark? It was odd – I'd almost missed the frog chorus and here it was again, all around us. It was like coming home.

We climbed on board again in the morning and the engine hissed and snorted into life. Looking out of the grimy window I thought I was seeing things. I'd passed that hut yesterday. And that pile of logs. We were going back down country, all the way back to Singapore. Know that nursery rhyme about the grand old Duke of York? Well, I was one of those 10,000 men, marching up and down in some sort of collective idiocy. So we drank and smoked and fretted and pretended to be Vera Lynn all over again at the Reinforcement Camp. We'd reinforced nobody and we hadn't been told a damned thing.

Sunday 8 February 1942. Thirteen thousand battle-hardened troops of the Japanese Imperial Army, none of whom could hit a barn at a thousand paces or see in the dark, came ashore on the north-west of the island at night under cover of a massive artillery barrage. At dawn on the 9th, another 10,000 arrived. We didn't know the numbers then, of course, or who they were. For the record they were the 5th, 18th and Imperial Guard Divisions and we outnumbered them nearly three to one. The Engineers had blown up the Causeway to delay the invasion but that hadn't stopped the attack and the Australians in the north couldn't hold them. I was no longer with my platoon. We'd become scattered since Jitra; the others were God knows where all over the Malay peninsula and I was with a bunch of men I scarcely knew at all. All day on the 9th we took up positions, moved, fell back, regrouped. Around us Singapore burned. You've probably only seen a battle in the pictures or on television. It's neat and ordered and makes perfect sense to everybody and there's usually a hero, from Errol Flynn to John Wayne, you can identify with. That's rubbish. A battle is a mess. There's no direction, no overall plan. Our officers were as lost and useless as we were, dodging shells and scanning the skies for raiders. In the end you just hope for a miracle; that you might see, in the clouds of war, the Angel of Mons.

Singapore Golf Club had been opened in 1924 and became Royal when the king visited shortly before the war. I'd never aspired to that kind of life. It was an expensive business, what with club fees, pink gins and quails' eggs. The place had a legendary wine cellar, deep, opulent leather chairs where the umpteenth generation of colonial planters looked down their noses at the squaddies of the king. This was to be the Hougoumont of the 1st Leicesters, that farmhouse on the Waterloo battlefield that bore the brunt of the fighting that day. It was a golf club, for Christ's sake – long, low bungalows, undulating greens and bunkers, flags fluttering at its eighteen holes. How the hell are you supposed to defend a place like this?

To the north were dark woods where the Japs had taken up position. And this seemed to sum up everything about Singapore in those insane February days. They always got there first, to the best positions, to the high ground. Every move we made was in the murderous open, under a fierce sun as if we were on a spotlit stage. Even their mortars seemed a heavier calibre than ours and the beautifully manicured lawns became pockmarked with bomb craters. Cedar branches crashed in all directions and a constant withering fire came at us out of the dense cover of the woods. It could only have been minutes before we were hopelessly separated, cowering in our slit trenches and popping up every now and then to fire back. I couldn't see an enemy and just banged away uselessly into the trees.

In situations like this you fall back on the old ways, the surest remedies. They'd done the same thing in the Great War. Nobody had a radio and a heliograph was out of the question, so what could you do? You send a runner. And who would that be? The best runner in the unit, of course.

'Twigg!' I recognized the roar of my CO, Major Bowley. We were in the Reserve position at the clubhouse by now; this was both good and bad. Good because we weren't lying in a bunker with sand blasting into our eyes. Bad because if a single high-explosive shell landed on the building we'd all kiss our arses goodbye. I scuttled over to him. 'Sir!' I slapped my helmet in what passed for a salute in the heat of battle.

'You'll be my runner, Twigg.'

In fact there wasn't a chance to run anywhere that day before darkness fell and the rate of fire with it. There were no high explosives, so the Japs couldn't have brought up their artillery yet. Grateful for small mercies, we collapsed on whatever bit of ground was nearest. There was no food and

no chance of sleep. From my trench in front of the clubhouse
I realized that, come dawn, I'd be the first into action. I went
over my bayonet drill in my mind. All that charging over the
fields of Leicestershire with Porky Crane, slicing our steel
through saplings and sandbags, that was make-believe. Would
it be the same, I wondered, when a thousand of Benny Watkins's 'little yellow bastards' were running towards me,
screaming '*Banzai!*'

That watchful, wakeful night was unreal. Singapore blazed,
with huge columns of black smoke vanishing into the darkness and the sky over the docks a bright vermilion. At least
one thing was certain. There'd be no more pointless shunting
backwards and forwards of trains. We were totally cut off
now. The Angel of Mons wasn't going to rescue us and anyway, that was just a myth.

Shortly before dawn all hell broke loose. The rattle of rifle
fire, machine guns with their staccato rhythm, the thump of
mortars. Bullets sang as they danced past my head and the
machine guns ripped up the grass in neat, deadly rows. At my
back, most of the windows of the clubhouse had gone, crystal
fragments like hailstones on the concrete. It was odd, but in
the thick of the fighting I didn't actually feel scared. It was a
day's work, like moving rolls of wallpaper at Snaith's. You
don't think about a bullet's impact, how it will puncture your
tin hat at 500 paces, how your skull will disintegrate like egg-
shell. You just keep working, jerking the bolt of your .303
when the mortar shells run out, reloading the clip, firing
again. As long as you heard the 'zing' of a bullet, you were
alive. That had to be enough.

Then a colonel – I never found out which one – ordered a
counter-attack. You've seen it in football a thousand times. It
goes against the run of play, it's designed to wrong-foot your

opponents, throw them off balance. That's fine on a football pitch, but in a slit trench in front of a bungalow being shot to pieces, it's rather different. He ordered one of the lieutenants to silence the fire from the woods.

Now I've never had much time for officers. Maybe it was ingrained in me by my dad; maybe I just saw them as authority figures when I was a kid, like the headmaster and the vicar. But I had to feel sorry for this one and I respected him for his answer. There was an appalled look on his face and he said flatly, 'No, that's just suicide.'

'Do as you're told!' the colonel snapped back. I don't understand the weight of command. I've never had a battalion looking to me to make split-second life and death decisions, so I don't know; but it seemed to me the British Army collapsed at this moment. If the colonel's only answer was 'because I tell you', we were all going to hell in a handcart.

The lieutenant wasn't going quietly. 'It's madness,' he said. 'We'll be shot down before we get a hundred yards.' I hadn't heard the magic word 'sir' in this entire conversation. And I couldn't believe it as the colonel unbuckled his holster strap and rested his hand on his Webley butt. 'Do as you're told,' he said quietly, 'or I'll have you shot.' In this insane moment, we all knew he meant it.

The lieutenant drew his men together, signalling them into line along the trench. 'Fix bayonets!' A platoon sentenced to death. I saw their faces. Grim. Silent. The lieutenant had his Webley in his hand as he jumped out and hurtled forward. His men were with him, weaving and dodging as if they could see the bullets coming through the air towards them. They didn't scream or shout as they had been trained back at Glen Parva. Their bayonets were fixed but none of them got remotely within lunging range of the Japs. They died against a wall of grey smoke, their bodies twisting and jerking as the bullets ripped into them. Some came back, bleeding, pale, wild-eyed with terror. This was what my dad had faced in the corner of some forgotten field. I couldn't count the dead, but there must have been twenty or thirty corpses lying out there on that bloody green and one or two of the still living whimpering, calling out for help. We couldn't help. *I* couldn't help. I couldn't move. Nobody moved. And I felt sick. Sick with the slaughter, yes, but sick too at the stupid, pointless waste. Who sends boys with rifles out into the open against machine-gun nests? Well, the donkeys who led the lions on the Western Front had done it. Had we learned nothing from our one million dead?

But the colonel was still brimming with ideas. He wanted to reach an artillery unit nearby and I expected, as runner, to be given a dispatch. Instead, the colonel took Major Bowley, his own runner and me with them. The rifle fire became murderous a few yards out and I hit the ground, the other runner dropping next to me. As I lifted my helmet rim I couldn't believe the sight. Bowley and the colonel were not only still on their feet, they were actually *walking* forward, discussing the situation as if they'd been sipping brandy and sodas at Raffles. There were bullets zipping everywhere but the officers were still going, so, a bit embarrassed, the other runner and I scrambled up and ran after them. We never did find the artillery unit; we just ran back the way we'd come.

But the day hadn't really begun. Before lunchtime (not that we had any!) Mitsubishi Zeros came screaming out of the distance, their bombs ploughing up the ground and their machine-gun bullets tearing into the already shattered earth of our trenches. We knew that on the clubhouse roof was a machine gun that fired tracer bullets. What we thought we could achieve I don't know, but we'd been pinned down for over twenty-four hours and I, for one, wanted to return the compliment. A mate and I ducked into the clubhouse. The floor was awash with smashed bottles and the bar was riddled with bullet holes. We went up the stairs during a lull in firing and out onto that roof. Maybe the ground troops were resting and letting the planes do the work, because the rifle fire had almost stopped. I'd worked a machine gun before so I knew what to do. My mate aimed the thing and I fed in the ammunition belt. We kept our heads down but were relatively safe from ground fire at this height and just hoped their mortar fire was a bit off!

A fighter-bomber came low and level from the west and we opened up. The gun kicked like something demented and the shell-casings flew everywhere as we blazed away. The line of tracers arced into the sky but we were always playing catch-up, the bullets sliding past his tail fins. Then he saw us and the plane banked steeply with a roar of its engine. It wheeled against the treetops and came for us, like a demon wasp. A plane coming *at* you, as opposed to flying past, is even harder to hit. Years later, I saw Burt Lancaster machine-gunning a Jap plane out of the sky in *From Here to Eternity*. It just doesn't happen. We realized he would drop his bomb on the clubhouse before we could get to those stairs. So we ran for it, clattering on our hobnails down the stairs as the machine-gun bullets from the Kawasaki ripped up the roof's asphalt in neat rows of white-hot metal. His bomb missed the clubhouse but hit the ground, too near to us for comfort. We were both knocked off our feet by the impact, showered in mud and debris. Enough heroics for one day.

We pulled back that night, abandoning the clubhouse entirely and digging in, deep in our own woods across the green from the Japs. The course lay like no-man's land between us. Only the barbed wire and the tin cans of Ypres were missing. How did that old song go? 'If you want the old battalion, we know where they are; they're hanging on the old barbed wire.' Well, this battalion's casualties still lay out on no-man's land, the flies droning around the corpses. No winding sheets. No service for the dead.

'Twigg!' I jerked myself free of the sight as dawn crept over the golf course. It was Major Bowley. 'I've left my tommy gun in the clubhouse. Go and get it.'

There was no 'please'. No 'there's a good fellow', no apology for the fact that the man was a bloody idiot to leave his weapon behind in the first place and was now sending me out against half the Japanese Imperial Army to get it. What was I supposed to do? Refuse? Tell him to go to hell? Face a court martial? I nodded, taking a deep breath. I was the battalion runner, for God's sake. I could do this. True, short distances weren't my forte, but nothing's perfect when you've taken the king's shilling. I crawled to the edge of the trench, wondering whether their snipers were awake yet, then stood up and ran like mad, weaving, dodging, keeping my head down and my body low. I wasn't going to win any Battalion Games this way, but I might just stay alive.

I suppose it was about 200 yards to the clubhouse and nobody fired anything on the way there. I grabbed Bowley's gun and started back. The line of trees still looked silent and safe and for a ludicrous moment I imagined the Japs had pulled out and gone elsewhere to cause mischief. I'd just reached open ground when I heard a sound I knew rather well. It was the loud, shrill whistle of a falling mortar bomb.

I threw myself forward as the ground jumped under me and I was pelted with pebbles and mud. It sounds ridiculous, but you really do look down, just to check that all your bits are still there. They were, so I was up again, running like stink until I reached our trenches. The major was pleased to get his gun back and he didn't comment about me getting a VC or anything so I got back to my unit.

'You were lucky there, Twigg.' Somebody clapped me on the back. I was. Like I'd been lucky on the clubhouse roof and all the previous day. You can use any analogy you like – it's a lottery, it's the turn of a card or the throw of a dice. The kid in me saw it as a deadly game of tig. Move fast, you stay alive. Slow down, play it wrong, second guess the bullet you can't see, the one with your name on it, and you'd be out there, in pieces on no-man's land, crying for your mother.

The potted histories of the Second World War, the ones written for armchair generals and war-gamers, will tell you nothing much happened in Singapore on 12 February 1942. In fact this was the day the Japs brought up their heavy artillery. I thought the machine guns and mortars were rough; this was unbelievable. My dad's generation on the Western Front had dug deep shelters against artillery, the huge shells that gouged great craters in the ground. We only had slit trenches; you might just as well try to hide in a golf bunker. Screams punctuated the explosions that filled your brain and hurt your ears. Men were thrown around like broken dolls, blood and limbs everywhere. After only minutes of this you were disoriented. Everywhere was a wall of noise and the raw, alien smell of hot metal. Mud and earth and clods of grass thudded onto your helmet and shoulders, stones hissed through the air like shrapnel. I don't know what actually hit me but as I reached the trench at the opening barrage I felt a searing pain in my right leg. I just had time to see my thigh oozing blood when an Indian soldier who'd been alongside me, landed on top of me, pinning me to the floor of the trench. Half his back had been blown away in a tangle of shredded tunic and flesh. I could see his backbone and ribs gleaming white and crimson and I could see he was dead. The shell must have hit him direct and snapped his spinal cord. I eased myself into a sitting position, sliding what was left of his body off me. His lips were drawn back, his teeth bared, and he was staring sightlessly at the trees that arched like a canopy over us. By comparison with him, my leg was nothing. The heat of the shrapnel had probably cauterized the gash and it was hardly bleeding at all.

Finally, it stopped. Or I think it did. Had the shooting ended? Or was I too deaf by now to tell? My heart was thumping like a drum trying to break out from my ribcage, but other than this, silence. Then the cries began and reality returned. I read later that the Duke of Wellington once said, 'Next to a battle lost, the saddest thing is a battle won.' I wouldn't know about that because we had lost this one. And 'saddest' doesn't come close. But the silence of those seconds was the worst of all and in a weird sort of way I was glad when I heard the inevitable whimpers and sobs. It meant I was still alive.

Still the Japs did not come. I dragged myself out of my trench, straightening my tunic and trying to wipe the sticky blood off it. I couldn't. There were shell holes all over the ground, dotted with the dead. Medical orderlies with redcross armbands were scurrying out to them, risking God-knows-what else the Japs might throw at us. Their job was impossible, but with unbelievable calm, they gave the dying water and cradled their heads, talking quietly to them because they couldn't handle the silence either.

'I need a volunteer,' I heard a voice near me say, 'to check the forward trench.' I'll never know why but I was the one with my hand in the air.

'Well done,' the sergeant said grimly. 'Come with me.'

The forward trench was on a slight rise in the ground, maybe a hundred yards away. We ran forward, crouching and weaving, expecting machine-gun fire to cut us down. There was nothing. We reached the trench together and jumped into it, both of us with our rifles and bayonets at the ready. Nothing. The place was shot to buggery but it was deserted. So we ran back again.

I don't know how long we waited. The medics were lifting men where they could onto makeshift stretchers and an officer appeared, checking the lines. He looked at the dark blood sticking my shorts to my leg.

'You'd better get down to the Victoria,' he said. 'Get that seen to.'

I just stood there, numb with delayed shock, I suppose.

'Now!' he barked. 'Go on!'

And so I limped away from the only actual battlefield I've ever stood on. I hadn't seen the enemy at all, although you could say I'd felt his firepower. At the Victoria Hospital, they cleaned and dressed my wound and I waited to be sent back to the golf course. 'You needn't go back, Twigg,' an officer told me. 'The casualties are coming in thick and fast now. The Japs might cut off the water supply and I need a guard on the hospital gates.'

Ours not to reason why. The battalion was still bleeding, if not on the golf course then in the streets of the Gibraltar of the East. And I was guarding a hospital gate. In fact for the next twenty-four hours all I did was stand at ease, to attention and at ease again, saluting officers. What a way to run a war.

Had wars always been like this? Bombing raids were sporadic but devastatingly effective. The ground shook as if to emphasize the terror everyone was feeling. Panic-stricken civilians tried to keep it all together. A bit like me on the golf course, they probably thought the best thing to do was to keep working as though hell wasn't breaking out all around. But we'd all heard stories of Jap atrocities against the Chinese and most of the population were Chinese. You could almost smell the despair. Was I supposed to save them, with my gammy leg and my 500-yard-range .303? Standing by that hospital gate all day gave me too much time to think. There were rumours of a running fight to get off Singapore Island, do a Dunkirk out here in the East, save what we could of the fighting men and the equipment. It didn't happen. With the golf club went the fresh water reservoir next door. The Japs now had both.

The morning of 15 February 1942. I saluted the grim-faced officer who came to find me. 'It's all over, Twigg,' he said. 'We're surrendering. You remain at your post and don't let anybody take or destroy any military property.'

If that doesn't sum up the double-think of the British Army I don't know what does. We'd given up, except Private Twigg of the 1st Leicesters. He was supposed to carry on fighting, because who else was going to take or destroy military property except the Japanese Imperial Army? But the man had gone, the sun glancing off the pips on his fallen shoulders; he was just as beaten as the rest of us.

I felt . . . I can't describe how I felt. It was a physical pain in the pit of my stomach and I've never felt anything remotely like it since. I pulled myself together and ignored the last order I'd just received. What if *I* took military equipment? What if *I* destroyed it? I walked to the temporary stores nearby and helped myself to all the rifles I could carry, a handful out of the 17 million made. I walked down to the docks, blackened with fire and still smouldering after three days. There were half-sunken wrecks in the water and knots of men standing around, looking lost in the fog of war. I threw a bundle into the sea and went back for more. I did this four times. It wasn't much of a gesture as gestures go, but I felt a little better for it. At least the Japs would never get thirty of our guns. I never went back to the Victoria Hospital.

It was later that day I had my first glimpse of the Japanese Imperial Army. Klaxons roared to clear the streets and a convoy of dust-painted open-top cars swept in a cavalcade of triumph towards Raffles Hotel. The Rising Sun fluttered on their pennons. These were the men who had cut us to ribbons on the golf course, the men whose speed and guts had driven us out of Malaya and now, no doubt, out of Singapore. That afternoon I saw a tall, grey-haired man in ludicrously long shorts. He was wearing a solar topee and was walking with Japanese officers. An ADC stood with him, a Union Jack in his hand as he disappeared into a building. The man was General Arthur Percival and he signed the official surrender documents at half past eight that same night.

There were men milling around everywhere. As Winston Churchill wrote years later, 'There may have been 100,000 of them, but they were an army no more.' I didn't join them. There were no faces I recognized immediately – the 1st Leicesters were scattered – so I looked around for somewhere to sleep. For all that Singapore must have been under Japanese martial law by now, I didn't see a single soldier as I climbed into an old abandoned bus parked down by the docks.

It wasn't the most comfortable night I've ever spent. A bus seat is hard and unyielding and I was completely unarmed for the first time in months (if you exclude the sarong incident). If it hadn't dawned before, it did now and the thought hit me like a wall. This wasn't the 11th Indian Brigade, the Leicestershire Regiment, the 1st Battalion or Sixteen Platoon. This was Reg Twigg, the soldier's lad from Saffron Lane. And Reg Twigg was going to survive; if needs be, on his own. Bizarre as it sounds, I found a shaving kit in the bus as well as blades and a towel. I was determined to take some minor comforts with me, whatever the 'monsters of Nippon' decided was going to happen next.

I walked to the town centre. Order had been established here, every building was in Japanese hands. Their soldiers stood around with watchful eyes and bayonets fixed. We were herded into a central square and a Jap officer climbed onto some sort of podium and looked down at us all. I didn't like the smirk on his face. His English wasn't bad.

'You are now prisoners of the Japanese Imperial Army. You be good and we will be good to you.'

They marched us to the sea, to the prison called Changi which the British had built for civilian criminals and which would now become our home. There were thousands of us and the route was lined by civilians. Some laughed and joked and pointed, enjoying our humiliation in defeat. Most, though, were silent and looked at us in a mixture of sympathy and disbelief. The mightiest empire in the history of the world had gone, not with a bang, but a whimper.

Years later I read Churchill's memo to General Wavell, in overall command in the East in 1942. It told him that Singapore must not be allowed to fall, that men must die in the streets and their senior officers with them. Yet Percival had surrendered. You can read the figures for yourself today. The Japanese losses for the whole Malayan campaign were less than 10,000 men. We lost 138,000, killed or captured. They expected their campaign to last one hundred days; it took them seventy. And General Yamashita, their commanding officer, admitted that he never expected to be able to take Singapore. Today, although there are those who try to find excuses, the fall of the Gibraltar of the East is regarded as the worst military defeat in modern times.

If you know your ancient history, you'll know that Spartan mothers were prouder if their sons were brought back lying dead on their shields than carrying them, because it was a sure sign of courage. The Spartans didn't understand surrender.

And neither, it turned out, did the Japanese.

6

Hard Labour

The Changi peninsula housed the gaol itself, the army barracks at Selarang and, as events turned out, a large area
which became a prisoner-of-war camp. The civilian population went into the gaol itself, which immediately became
overcrowded. We were formed into rough lines, but there
was no real structure. There were Australians there, with
their slouch hats and a bolshie attitude to authority that
made us look like choirboys. There were Indians, less
pleased than their dads had been to fight for the British
Empire. We didn't know it at the time but the Quit India
campaign really got underway only weeks after we'd left
Bombay. And there were Malays; God alone knows what
they felt about all this. The Aussies, the Indians, the British, we were all far from home, fighting for England
'following a falling star'. But this was the Malays' own
country and it was occupied by the most brutal regime in
the Far East.

One of our own officers ordered us off in threes and we
were put into a tiny, one-roomed adobe hut which could just
about house our sleeping bags. Apparently it had been used
by Indian labourers; what had happened to them I have no
idea. We hadn't had a square meal in days and we lined up for
our food ration. Our own cooks, the men we grumbled about
and who grumbled about us, stood on the other side of the

trestle tables doling out the grub onto our mess plates. I just stood there, looking in disbelief. The meat and veg of last week had been replaced by a lump of white, boiled rice. It wasn't even salted.

'That's it, mate,' a cook said in response to my dropped jaw. 'Move along there.'

I found a seat somewhere and took stock. We were thousands. Our officers were as impotent as we were. Having pips on your shoulder was a guarantee of nothing in this hellhole. So the old Reg kicked in, the scrawny kid who scrumped apples because he never had enough to eat; who pinched sweets from the old girl in the Aldershot shop; the cocky squaddie who roasted stolen spuds near a snowbound rifle range. Here, Private Twigg was one of thousands served up on a plate to a barbarous conqueror. But as Reggie, he might just make it.

The Jap guards left us pretty much alone. They knew we had nowhere to go. Swim out from Singapore in any direction and the sharks will get you, if exhaustion doesn't do the job first. Try and pinch a boat of any kind and they'll shoot you. So we had relative freedom to wander about. The first place I wandered to was the water's edge, filling an old two-gallon drum with seawater. I boiled it dry and used the salt to flavour my rice, or even licked the damn drum itself to replace the salt I was losing in the fierce heat of the day.

Did I say our officers were powerless? They were, but *form* was everything. Yes, there was a war on. Yes, we'd surrendered. But there were standards. And there was a system. So I was made batman to Lieutenant Savage of the Leicesters. Quite a bit of the man's kit had gone but I spat and polished what I could and tried to play the game. In fact, the game worked quite well. The officers at Changi still, astonishingly, had a mess and one day I told the lieutenant how I'd kill for a smoke. The next day he came back with a tin of Sir Walter Raleigh. All right, it was American tobacco, but a smoke is a smoke and I spent that night with my pipe looking out over the harbour where the Japanese warships now crowded and those great British guns, which should have been our salvation, stood black and silent against the darkness.

There was too much time to think that night at Changi but as we sat cross-legged by the fire beyond the huts I heard an extraordinary story about a Leicester soldier who'd been at the Alexandra Hospital when we surrendered. He'd been shot in the head at Jitra and was lucky to be alive. He was lying on a stretcher on the floor of the hospital when the Japs arrived and was expecting, like everybody else, a civilized, respectful and orderly capitulation. Unarmed, with his head heavily bandaged, the most he thought he'd have to do was to raise his hands, the symbol of giving up the world over.

Instead, he heard screams from the room next door. Terrified, he rolled off the stretcher and with his back against the wall, hoped to escape notice as the Japs arrived screaming and bayoneting doctors, nurses and patients. Through the open door he could see bodies lying, too many to count. The screaming and clamour seemed to subside and he looked again only to see green canvas boots coming towards him. Suddenly, a Jap sergeant knelt beside him, looking into his face and speaking perfect English. 'What regiment?' he asked.

'Leicesters,' the soldier mumbled through his wired jaw.

'Jitra?' the sergeant asked.

The soldier replied, 'Jitra.'

'It is an honour to know you,' the sergeant said extending his hand while he snapped something incomprehensible to the men at his heels. Then he turned back to the astonished bloke. 'I have left orders not to touch you. I am going to take over the big guns now.' And, as he walked away, the killing continued.

The soldier just lay, frozen in terror, until some other survivors found him. He'd no idea why he'd been spared. He wasn't the only soldier in the hospital; it was yet another example of the incomprehensible mindset of the Japanese. What kind of people were they? The soldier's name was Fred Shenstone and in old age he recorded his amazing experience for future generations.

Years later I would read that one of the first Europeans to work with the Japanese was a Jesuit missionary called Francis Xavier. He wrote, '[The Japanese] are a people of good manners, good in general and not malicious; they are men of honour . . . and prize honour above all else in the world.' The only problem was that Father Xavier couldn't speak Japanese, so perhaps his summary was a little optimistic.

Hunger. It was the one word I've used to sum up my childhood. Now I felt it again at Changi where tasteless rice was the only order of the day. I was sitting on the grass outside my hut one evening when I smelt cooking. It was rabbit, I felt sure. Drooling, I followed my nose to a hut nearby where a bunch of men crowded around an open fire, which crackled and spat into the night.

'Where'd you find the rabbit, lads?' I asked, hoping there might be enough to go round us all.

'Rabbit?' one of them asked. Another pointed to the tabby fur hanging like an empty glove nearby. I walked away, telling myself the animal wasn't big enough for all of us. And I hadn't – yet – got to the camp cat stage of hunger.

In April they moved us from one hut to another. Our new

homes were along Havelock Road, named after a hero of British India and they seemed to be purpose-built. The huts were long and narrow with a central aisle and men sleeping in pairs on raised wooden platforms. There was even an upstairs, reached by a rickety old ladder. Space was at a premium but we hadn't much kit anyway, so we coped. I didn't know anybody here so I popped my head up into the 'bedroom' and called, 'Anyone here from Leicester?'

There was. His name was Harry Foley and he'd originally come from Nottingham, but found himself out of work and had met up with a baker's delivery man who worked for Frears and Blacks. Harry had used this link to get a job with Frears and had ended up marrying the friend's sister.

'What's his name, Harry?' I asked. 'I've got a mate who works for Frears.'

'Bob Hillier,' he said.

I never calculated the odds. Two strangers, bound by khaki and defeat, thousands of miles from home. And we both knew Bob Hillier. When that sort of thing happens, you have to believe there's some kind of plan, don't you? Some point to it all.

In those weeks, the Japs kept us busy. We were marched along dusty roads to the docks, to clear debris and remove bomb damage. We whistled 'Colonel Bogey' as we marched. Don't ask me why this particular tune should be so associated with the Burma campaign. It had no particular significance for us and the number of testicles the Führer had seemed totally irrelevant at Changi.

On no account, we were told, were we to have any dealings with the locals. But one day that changed. It was a small token of kindness, but it's amazing how such little things keep your spirits up, especially when the rest of the world is going to hell in all directions. A middle-aged woman came furtively out of her little wooden house as we waited to be marched back to Havelock Road. She checked to see that the Jap guards weren't close then came towards me and quickly slipped three hen's eggs into my hand. I was thunderstruck and was still trying to gabble out my thanks when she nodded, smiled and scuttled away. It would be some days before I realized the risk she took. Had I known, those eggs would have tasted even better than they did.

To the south of the island was Keppel Harbour. It was a shambles because of the bombing and we had to put it right. With every swing of my sledgehammer under that blazing sun I reminded myself that this mess had been created by the Japanese themselves and we were the slave labour restoring it to some sort of original condition. They let us cool off after a few hours by dipping into the sea but the sun was so hot that the salt dried almost at once on our skin and that took its toll. My lips erupted into sores, ugly, painful and leaking pus. Even getting the slimy rice down was purgatory. I went to the MO and saw a look on his face I would see a thousand times in the months ahead. He had nothing that could help.

But a local Chinaman could. We were working near a brick kiln that was operated by Chinese labour and one day, when the guards were far enough away, he beckoned me over. Weeks earlier, I'd have ignored him. I knew men who would have cuffed him around the ear for his insolence. He disappeared into a hut and came back with a little bottle of what looked like milk. With a mixture of broken English and handsigns, I let him smear this stuff on my lips. I went back the next day for a repeat prescription and again and again. Before a week was up, the sores had gone and never came back. God knows what was in the bottle or why the Chinaman had risked his life to help me, but it worked and he did. Little acts of kindness. Little glimpses of love. And there was nothing I could do for him in return.

Our conquerors were enjoying their moment in the sun. The guards would strip off in turns and run naked into the sea, splashing and laughing like kids at Skeggie. Then they picked on a young German woman who acted as our interpreter. She was crimson with embarrassment but the Japs ran round her, bollock naked, squealing with delight at her blushes. One of their sergeants, the rank they called *gunso*, was an arrogant bastard and set the tone for what was to come. If they spoke any English, they chose not to and our Japanese was non-existent, so if the German lady wasn't around, communication was all a bit of a lottery. His name sounded like Harc and he was just over five feet tall. He strutted around as though he owned the world – which, in terms of Singapore, he did – and shouted at us for no reason. The Japanese language is harsh and staccato. Even a friendly greeting sounds like something between a curse and a snarl. But Harc's rantings were followed up with pushes and slaps, so we got the general gist. Somebody looked at Harc funny one day and the *gunso* beat him to the ground and kicked him with his Japanese Imperial Army boots. We just stood there and watched.

You're probably thinking – what spineless bastards! Why didn't they *do* something? The bloke was a midget and we outnumbered the guards something like ten to one. Let me answer that one with six little words – 'This Is What Happens To Looters'. It was a sign – in neat, carefully crafted English letters, pinned to a platform on our way to and from the harbour. On the ground below it was a raised podium with ten wooden poles jutting upwards. I know there were ten because I counted them every day – twice. On the top of each pole was a human head, stuck there by the nation that had promised to be good to us. They may have been looters. They were probably Chinese or Malay. At the very least they were human beings. And if the Japs did that to looters, they could do it to anybody. Anybody who answered back, didn't move when told, looked at them funny. *That's* why we stood there and watched the *gunso's* beating. The flies droned around the bloated heads whose tongues protruded from blackened lips. The eyes were rolled upwards, a deathly white in the rotting faces.

And one morning, I nearly saw what led to that ghastly spectacle. We were marching past the scaffold holding our breath against that unmistakable stench of rotting flesh, past a knot of Jap soldiers who were standing alongside the road. Kneeling in front of them was a Tamil – there were many in Singapore – and his hands were tied behind his back. He was crying, tears trickling into his mouth, his nose running. Then his head was rammed forward and one of the Japs swept a sword upwards. I'd seen officers carrying these things over the past weeks but I didn't know how deadly they were. I didn't want to know. I marched blind for the next few seconds because I closed my eyes. All I heard was the downward slice of the blade and a thud as the Tamil's head hit the ground. That night there were eleven poles on the scaffold.

It was a couple of days later that something akin to panic set in. We were working as usual, our backs and arms in agony as we hauled and lifted rocks and concrete slabs, our nails chipped and our fingers raw. Suddenly, there were guards everywhere, armed to the teeth and screaming at us. We didn't understand the commands or the significance of the truck which rattled and barked to my right. There were maybe thirty people in the open back, Chinese civilians of both sexes. Four guards stood with them and an open car with more guards followed. The truck coughed and growled past us, making for the beach. I was struck by the faces of the Chinese. They were pale and solemn, as if they were going to a funeral.

They were. While our guards yelled at us, 'OK. Work. Work,' we heard the familiar staccato of machine-gun fire coming from the beach. We looked at each other. We were listening to an execution squad in action. 'Work. Work.' Our heads went down. We didn't want to go to that beach party. Soon after that the truck rattled back empty.

Amazingly, we had Sundays off. It meant nothing to the Japs of course and, looking back, it was all part of the weird cat-and-mouse game they played with us. The other six days were hell – I lost weight along with everybody else, with the hard labour and lack of food, but it looked worse on the big men. You could see bones sticking through shirts plastered to bodies with sweat. The padres still held church services for those that cared to attend but for most of us Sundays meant rat hunting. If you look up the fauna of Malaysia today you'll find there are three types of rat native to the Far East; brown, black and Muller's. They were all the same to me, horrible crawling things with wet, spiky fur made so by the sewage they lived in. They'd sit up, sniffing the wind and play leap-frog over us as we slept. A fellow prisoner, a frustrated poet who'd missed his way in life, called them 'lords of the night'. I wasn't so impressed and I kept a sort of running total as I splatted them with a shovel. One Sunday a professional joined us. He was a mastiff, with a few other varieties thrown in, and he was brindled and battle-scarred. He could smell our prey and leapt around, barking and snapping, his tail wagging sixteen to the dozen. We knew that rats liked rotten wood and we found an old fallen tree trunk which looked perfect. We hauled it over; it fell to pieces in our hands with that unmistakable smell of fungus and decay. Then the biggest rat I've ever seen leapt out, coming straight for us. The mastiff caught the thing in mid-air as it bounded along the trunk. The rat squealed and twisted, trying to bite its attacker, but the fight was hopeless. The dog's jaws closed and blood spurted everywhere. He flipped the twitching animal and swallowed it whole.

Is this a metaphor for us against the Japanese? No, it's just a story about a dog, a battle-scarred survivor I came to admire enormously.

August 1942. Dates had become almost meaningless for us. We'd been imprisoned in hopelessly overcrowded barracks for nearly seven months and one day was much like another. News had been replaced by rumour. Information was propaganda. But, like a breath of fresh air in the sweltering heat of Keppel Harbour, we did get something from outside. It was tangible and it was ours. And we had one each. It was a parcel from the Australian Red Cross, the first decent food we'd had since February. August was the month when the Japanese government stopped any Red Cross ships coming into the Pacific so this would be the last outside help that any of us would get. I kept it close and added it to my little store of treasures, my towel, my shaving kit, my pipe and the little Walter Raleigh tobacco I had left. When you're a prisoner, when hope has gone, and you're having a low day, such silly, petty things become hugely important. It was that month too that a particularly persistent rumour began to circulate. We were going up-country, leaving Singapore island. You take comfort in routine: the food, however little and monotonous

and bad; the work, however hard and back-breaking; the
screams and slaps of the guards. It is your life and you get
horribly used to it. We were institutionalized, part of a system which, however grim, was *our* system. How would we
– how would *I* – cope with a new one?

That said, I wouldn't be sorry to leave. Singapore nights
were a curse and a blessing. The air was cool and the stars
bright, a dazzling glory high overhead. I had watched them,
only the other way up, from the decks of the *Duchess of York*
and the rambling leafy lanes of Leicester. In my mind I could
see and hear the rooks building their nests at Great Glen and
I could see myself wandering that towpath by the old canal. It
was a curse because I knew all that was long ago and most of
it far away. There was a kind of infinity in those stars. They
shone night after night no matter what us silly bastards here
on earth were doing to each other.

Was there some sort of purpose to all this, I wondered,
probably along with 99 per cent of my fellow prisoners.
Smoking my pipe in those Singapore nights, I came as close as
I was ever going to, to finding God. But He was always hid-
ing somewhere.

The rumour came true some time in October. We were told
to pack up because we were moving out. I stashed everything
I had into my kitbag, especially the Red Cross parcel with its
chocolate, packed tight at the bottom. The bags were loaded
onto trucks and we were told we'd get them back later. All we
carried was a small canvas bag slung over our shoulders for
personal kit like tobacco and shaving gear.

We marched to Singapore station, as straight-backed as we
could after nine months of rice and hard labour. We whistled
'Colonel Bogey' with a spring in our steps. We expected

trains. That was how modern armies had moved their troops behind front lines for seventy years. We had no idea where we were going or why.

We were prodded with bayonets and herded like cattle along the platform. That was because we were being loaded into cattle trucks. They had steel roofs and wooden sides of horizontal slats with six-inch ventilation gaps between them. Thirty-five of us were crammed into each coffin-like box on wheels. The men against the sides had the best of it because they could breathe properly and feel the wind in their faces. For me in the centre, the heat was intolerable and I heard someone screaming from another truck. I didn't know what claustrophobia was in those days but I heard that day what it could do as a man went mad. The doors crashed closed, locking into place. Silence. Men looked at each other, noses pressed together, buttocks against hips and shoulders jammed. Lying down was impossible. You could just about sit if you could fight your way down. Fighting your way back up again was something else.

Then we moved. The carriages jolted and banged, rattling with an unearthly noise as the train gathered speed. Just when you thought you'd got your balance right, the carriage swerved and swayed, throwing you sideways to ram some poor bugger up against the wall. I heard some new army expletives on that journey.

There was no toilet. We'd had no food or water since Changi but now it was a blood-red sunset. At first we peed through the slats, everybody negotiating with everybody else to change places for the purpose. Shitting was out of the question and I held on. Some of them couldn't, however. Dysentery rode that train with us and there were groans as men fought their way to a corner to shit where they could.

21. 'Ulcer Operation' by Murray Griffin. Japanese soldiers stand guard over an operation performed by prisoners on a tropical ulcer, probably without the use of anaesthetic.

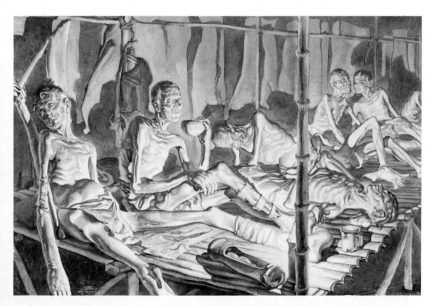

22. 'Hospital Ward' by Murray Griffin. Gaunt figures lying on beds in a hospital on the Burma/Thailand railway.

23. 'Fit parade for work. Men with malaria, ulcers, beriberi and dysentery, Konyo 2' by Ronald Searle. 'In the morning the sergeant shouted, "Anybody reporting sick?" He'd then get one of our officers to look at us along with the Jap doctor.' *(IWM ART 15747 79)*

24. Unfit for work – inside a camp hospital. 'It was like that. You had to take one day at a time. You didn't know if that day was your last … he looks really bad.' *(IWM HU 4569)*

25. 'Dysentery Ward, Tarso' by John Mennie. 'The smell was horrible but it was open so the air helped. It was the sort of place I found Harry Barnett, but he was away from the others on his own. I'd been looking around to see if there was anyone I knew to help them. You could hear the groans at night. It made me a hundred times more determined it wouldn't be me but I still needed luck – I was very lucky.' *(IWM ART LD 7292)*

26. Cholera block, Konyo 2, 1943. The white article on the left is a cholera victim awaiting burial. In the foreground are blankets returned for reuse after burial. 'That's Konyo 2 – I've walked down there. The cholera was after I left but I got involved with cholera at another camp.'

27. 'Cholera Camp, Konyo 2' by Ronald Searle. 'We tied the bodies down flat and carted them off to be burned. I had to do that. At the start I felt bad about it but you got used to doing it and it just became another job to do.' *(IWM ART 15747 103)*

28. 'Burning of the cholera dead, 1942' by Charles Thrale. In a clearing in the jungle prisoners lift corpses towards the fire; the dead lie in the foreground. 'The fire would be in a pit and we'd stack wood around the bodies to keep the fire going.' *(IWM ART 15417 60)*

29. 'Unloading the sick and dead' by Jack Chalker. POWs supervised by Japanese unload stretchers at Chungkai hospital camp. 'I went from Konyo to Tarso on a boat like that when I had beriberi. The dysentery cases were all but dead. Getting away from Konyo probably saved my life.' *(IWM ART 15417 60)*

30. Pounding peanuts to make butter, Kanchanaburi. 'I didn't do that. These men were officers who never worked on the track. I wouldn't have minded a bit of that.'

31. 'This is what we did. British officers sometimes came to the line at the big camps and "oversaw" us working but did not work themselves.'

32. The three-tier wooden bridge at Hintok. 'This was a typical construction, all propped up with virgin wood out of the jungle. The whole thing built by hand. It was one mile south of Hintok and was one of six trestle bridges north of Konyo. The viaduct I worked on at Rin Tin was made the same way.'

33. A derailed train in the background. 'We had to lift and move the rail with crowbars and a British officer would check it was level and then talk to the Japs. When they were satisfied our officer said, "All right, solidify." This meant we had to thump earth and stones in and around it.'

34. 'I was nicknamed the "Barber of Tarso". I offered to shave people as I wanted to keep busy. I sat my "clients" on a tin and I had a fire going with water always on the boil.'

35. 'This blade served a number of purposes – gutting fish, slicing off bits of pumpkin and even skinning lizards.'

36. 'I made this cribbage board in the Tool Shed at Tarso after I'd found a piece of old wood in the jungle.'

Dropping shorts and pants was difficult and some didn't have time. The smell became indescribable, the overcrowding even worse as we tried not to stand in it.

Night was appalling. The train rattled on, heading north relentlessly through endless black jungle. Nobody spoke. Whatever conversation there had been had long ago dried up and the only sound was the occasional snore of men sleeping standing up like cattle. That and the retching as some poor bugger threw up over the man he was standing next to. My mouth felt like a badger's arse, my lips and tongue so swollen I couldn't even wet my lips with saliva. All night long I remembered the words of the Jap officer when we'd surrendered. 'We will be good to you.' When was that going to start? Could this possibly be as good as it was going to get?

It wasn't until morning that we had a 'comfort break'. I couldn't believe the silence at first. Nor the fact that the endless swaying and buffeting had stopped. In fact the nerves in my legs felt for hours as if we were still moving. Having a shit in a field, albeit with no paper, was luxury itself. Men staggered out of the trucks like wrecks, their shirts stiff with vomit, their boots and shorts black-brown with shit. We tried to behave like soldiers and queued in an orderly fashion for a cup of brackish warm water and a handful of rice. How they spoilt us.

Then we were off again in our jolting, clanging hellholes. Men who had been against the slats were now on the inside and everybody tried to avoid 'shit corner' as far as that was possible. What snatches of conversation there were, were depressing. 'We've been here before,' the men muttered, peering through the slats. You might think one bit of jungle looks very much like another, but that's not quite true. They were taking us, our conquerors, up to the Thai border, the way we'd come south from Jitra. What for? Was this some sort of new humiliation? To visit the sites of our recent defeats?

For three days and three nights we clanked and swayed north, getting weaker and more hopeless with every jolting hour. More and more men fell ill and 'shit corner' became impossible to avoid, so we took turns to stand in it, putting our arms with difficulty across our noses to staunch some of the smell. Late on the fourth morning we ground to a snorting halt alongside a painted sign that said Bam Pong. I don't know if the battalion smartarse was still alive or whether he was with us in that bloody charnel house of a carriage. But somebody told us this was Thailand. We'd come all the way up the Malay peninsula, all nine hundred miles of it.

I couldn't see a station, just a stretch of scrubland beyond the tracks and paddy fields as far as the eye could see. Not many of us could get out of the trucks unaided now and we were all pretty much impervious to the shouts and bayonet prods of the guards. Something like three hundred of us formed an orderly queue to take advantage of a water pump standing alone on a concrete base nearby. The chance to drink and wash off the stink of three days was like heaven beckoning. 'Come on, Jackie,' I said to a lad whose chest I had been jammed up against for the past twenty-four hours. 'Let's wash it off in those fields.' We couldn't drink the filthy water, of course. One of the first things they taught us out East was that Nasty Things lived in water courses out here. But as hundreds and thousands of Malays and Thais lived up to their waists in water every day we assumed it wouldn't hurt our skin. Soaking there in that cool, shallow water after the journey we'd had was indescribable.

Over our evening delicacy of a cupful of boiled rice with

no trimmings, an officer trailing his sword behind him told us in broken English that our train journey was over. There were a few cynical cheers from men too tired and too depressed to care about the consequences. We were here overnight.

The dinner had been exquisite. The hotel was even better. Two stinking attap huts alongside the track were our sleeping quarters and we shared it with half the insect population of Thailand. The stench was appalling because the huts were built on jetties out over the paddy fields and everywhere reeked of rotting vegetation and wet. The mosquitoes, those tiny little bastards that my old teacher told us had brought down the Roman Empire, buzzed like a cloud at sunset over the water. They were waiting, like the Mitsubishi Zeros had waited north of Singapore, to regroup and attack us en masse, dive bombing and biting in their zeal to bring down yet another empire. Jackie and I read each other's minds and without a word slipped outside. That night we slept in the open, so shattered we didn't need a blanket; so shattered we didn't, for a while, feel hungry.

It wasn't Sergeant Moore screaming us awake the next morning, tipping our beds over and calling us his 'orrible little men. It was Benny Watkins's little yellow bastards, shrieking and kicking us upright. There weren't many words we could make out in their rat-a-tat delivery, but 'Speedo! Speedo!' topped the list and we instinctively skipped to it when we heard that. Because we were British and because we were soldiers, we joined a breakfast queue for our morning rice. It was gone in minutes, a slushy pap you didn't need teeth for. Even as we gulped it down, the guards circled us. 'Speedo! Speedo!' There seemed more urgency than usual this morning.

'Fall in!' a stentorian voice rang out. I didn't see who it was and probably wouldn't have known him if I had, but I knew the sound. He was an NCO, the backbone of the British Army, and he expected us to respond. And respond we did. We stood to attention, even men who could barely stand, and we marked off and divided into two columns.

'Parade will turn to the right.' That was an officer; public school. He probably wasn't still wearing his rank badges, any more than the NCO was, but he was still in command. This could be Glen Parva, Knightsbridge, Aldershot – it didn't matter where. We were the soldiers of the king. And we'd taught half the world how to march.

'Forward march!'

And we did, our boots crunching on the sun-baked mud of a road that led to nowhere.

Midday, with the sun right overhead; the sky too bright to look at, the heat too fierce to ignore. Nobody was singing, nobody whistling. 'Colonel Bogey' and the tunes of glory had quietened, first to a croaked whisper, now to nothing. We didn't look at each other, just kept our heads down and concentrated on the rutted road and the black sweat stains of the shirt of the bloke in front. The pace had slowed to a crawl as the stronger ones became the shoulders and legs of the weakest. Every few yards the Japs marched with us, bayonets glinting as a reminder of who called the shots in Burma now.

As we slogged through the little villages they called *kampongs* the locals watched us. They'd never seen Englishmen like this before and they also knew there was nothing they could do for us, even if they wanted to. But there were exceptions. Like the woman who had given me eggs as we trudged back from Keppel Harbour, so now another one gave me a bunch of bananas. They were small and green, but they were food – manna from whatever the Thais called heaven. I took them without slowing and thanked her through thick and blistered lips. She was lucky. The guards could have caught her, slapped her around, raped her or just skewered her with their bayonets. Perhaps she had a son about my age or a kid brother. Whatever her reasons, I thank her again today. It was an act of unprompted humanity from someone I would never see again.

If a man went down, he was kicked upright again by the steel-shod boots of the guards. Those who couldn't walk any further, who had just given up the ghost and lay there mumbling, those who had no mates capable of lifting them, were dragged off, the last we saw of them. The guards had stopped yelling '*Mai e susumé*' at us now. I assume it meant 'move out' or 'quick march', and we were long past doing that. But there was no '*yasumé*', no 'rest' or 'stand at ease' for the rest of the day.

It was late afternoon by the time our destination came into view; scattered low buildings that became houses as we neared them, with scruffy, open-fronted shops and a town sign that read Kanchanaburi. In some ways this place was the start of the rest of my life. We learned to call it Kanburi and if I was climbing Everest, this would be my base camp. It was a one-street hellhole, dusty and with mangy, wandering dogs everywhere, sauntering along that one road with their tails between their legs. It was as if they were mimicking our appearance after hours on the trek. We limped into what seemed to be an improvised camp, a square with attap huts on three sides and a guardhouse, rather more substantial, facing them. The Jap accommodation was some yards away.

Jackie and I sat a little apart from the others once we'd got our pap ration and I slipped the bananas from my haversack. I couldn't believe it. The green fruit had turned brown in the space of a few hours and the flesh was stinking and inedible, even for men as hungry as we were. The huts were full of suffering soldiers, lying cheek by jowl on the raised bamboo platforms that would be our beds for the next three years. Jackie and I slept in the open again, our feet in agony and every muscle stretched and strained.

It was the next morning I saw it clearly for the first time. It was a wide river, brown and sluggish, the largest I'd seen in the Far East. The swollen streams we'd negotiated in the retreat from Jitra looked like trickles in comparison. For the record, this was the Kwai Noi at the point where it met the Kwai Yai and flowed together into the Mae Khong. These were names we heard later. They would have been meaningless at the time; those dark waters that still swirl and eddy in my dreams.

After morning pap I lined up to be inspected by the MO. 'Anything untoward, Twigg?' he asked.

What was I supposed to say? Well, I've lost two stone, sir, and I feel as if I've been run over by a steamroller, but apart from that, tickety boo, thanks. I didn't think he'd appreciate the levity so I pointed out a red patch on my right calf. It had been bothering me throughout the previous day but I put it down to a mosquito bite rubbed by my sock after the long march. It wasn't that simple.

'That's a tropical ulcer,' he said grimly. 'You'd better stay here. We don't have anything to treat it but we'll do what we can.'

'I want to go with my mate, sir,' I told him.

The bliss of ignorance. I didn't have the first clue what he was talking about. But *he* knew. He knew that these ulcers develop and take most of your leg with them. The skin blisters and blackens. The tendons shred and contract so you can't walk. The flesh darkens and falls away so that your bones show. The pain is appalling and you'll never get a night's sleep again. To me, it was a red patch on my skin. Nothing, really. No need to make a fuss.

The MO had probably seen it all. He was a busy man with no equipment and no outside help and he had a thousand cases to cope with. If he'd ever had a bedside manner he'd quickly lost it along the Kwai and barrack-room lawyers like me who knew better than he did, he had no time for at all.

'All right,' he sighed, 'but it's at your own risk. Next.'

The march that day was different. We weren't on the road any more; we'd been split into groups, following narrow trails twisting into the jungle. We seemed to be some sort of advance guard, what centuries ago they'd called the Forlorn Hope, the poor buggers out in front of the enemy to draw their fire. Except the enemy were marching with us, one at the front and one at the rear of our little column of twenty. Slowly it dawned on me that we had another enemy now; the jungle itself.

Don't read this book in the cool comfort of your armchair. Read it in the hottest greenhouse at Kew or the Eden Project. Feel your clothes cling to your body, see the print on the page blur and smudge with the sweat droplets from your chin and eyebrow ridges. Don't spend minutes there, spend all day. Spend every day. And don't eat anything except pap rice. If you have the strength left, try to imagine the branches above you draped with deadly snakes, the undergrowth full of spiders no less deadly. Then you'll have *some* idea of what the jungle is all about.

I could literally feel the energy draining away from me.

The humidity was unbelievable yet there was no water. The tiny streams we saw were slow moving and stank to high heaven, almost solid with the putrefying debris of the jungle. It wasn't as dense as Jitra, but it was thicker and darker than any wood I'd known back home. The hamlets we came upon seemed deserted; we saw no one. But the dogs were there; and where there are dogs, there are people. The dogs barked at us and ran away. By midday my tongue was swollen to the roof of my mouth as I watched the guards swigging from their water canteens.

We took a break on the banks of the river – *yasumé* at last. That damned, awful river. There was no food and no water. So I just got to my feet and walked into the Kwai. A few others followed. There were no shots, no screams from the guards. They just lay beside their rifles, barely noticing what we were doing. We sank into the brown, flotsam-filled water up to our shoulders and drank. We drank deeply like you do when you've had no water for six hours and the temperatures are in the eighties. It probably tasted revolting and God alone knew what it contained, but it was a life-saver that day and Ansells Best Bitter didn't come close to it. We didn't splash around and behave like idiots because we were too exhausted. Then it was harsh grunts from the guards – '*Mushi, mushi* [quickly, quickly] *speedo*.' And we were on the trail again. My clothes never dried for the whole of that day because of the humidity and sweat.

The coolness of night was a blessing and we lay on the jungle floor, too tired to worry about what was scuttling around and over us. One sight did bother me, though. On the branches of a dead tree, strikingly white in the dark green of the jungle, sat two vultures. You've seen them in zoos and aviaries, safe behind mesh and glass. There was nothing between me and these birds. And you've no idea how big they are until you've seen them in this setting. Or how beady their eyes are. Or how murderous their beaks. I took comfort in my belief that these were the cowards of the bird world. They only attacked carrion. In other words, you had to be dead already to interest them. And I had no plans for being that just yet.

The vultures were gone by morning and we were on the track again. There was no pap this morning; no food at all. And even the guards' rations seemed to have run out. So it may have been a sort of collective delirium when we all saw a little old woman coming along the track towards us. Thai women age quickly so it was impossible to guess her age, but I'd say she was in her sixties. She wore a cheap blue suit that reminded me of pyjamas and she had the usual straw coolie hat on her head. Across her narrow shoulders she carried a wooden yoke, like the old prints of milkmaids you see in junk shops back home. She was gabbling away and we understood none of it, but the meaning was clear enough. She poured some of the contents of her bucket into a tin cup and held it towards me and then to the next man. I sniffed it. Chicken? It was warm. It was food. So I tasted some. All this was done while still trying to march and she was no doubt giving me her best sales pitch. It was soup. And here, in the middle of nowhere, was a Thai woman selling it. We still had money in our pockets so we all bought some, nobody daring to stop or break ranks. With a series of hand signals she told us to leave the cups along the track and no doubt she picked them up later. Did I say 'chicken'? It would be some weeks later that I realized, but I should have said 'snake'.

The jungle by moonlight is, no doubt, magic. If you've got a full belly, a pipe of St Bruno, a few cold beers – oh, and Miss

Sylvia Cohen for company. Without all that it was just dangerous. Tired and weak we tramped on, stumbling over roots now invisible in the half-light. But the fact that we were still marching after dark meant we must be nearing our next destination. The track opened into a clearing, pale under the moon, and we could make out the now usual pattern of attap huts on three sides and a guardhouse. We stood there while the guards disappeared inside. Later a British officer came out from under the attap. My experience of officers up to this point was not good. This one was as clued-up and sympathetic as he could be, given the limitations under which he was forced to operate. This was Tarso, he said. We'd be moving in the morning, but for now, we were to fall in for rice. The huts were full, but he gave us half a blanket each to sleep on the ground.

Where were we going tomorrow?

'A place called Konyo.'

7

Laws of the Jungle

Tarso was a sort of base camp, more so I suppose than Kanchanaburi. It was difficult to keep track of time and to remember exactly where we were. The occasional officer might still have a watch but we fell back on the ancient way of time-telling – watching the unforgiving sun and its approximate position in the sky. The only point of reference we had was the river, a constant whose stink and gurgling I could well have done without.

The prisoners of Tarso were a mixed bunch of British and Aussies. We looked like some sort of Neanderthal tribe, with long hair and beards. We were men from a clean-shaven army in a clean-shaven decade and we hated being hairy. The odd officer might sport a 'tache, but the rest of us were used to a good shave every morning. I still had my safety razor and one blade and I used it when I could, but the guards went through periods of intense nosiness and it wasn't wise to let them know we had any luxuries. Rank badges, even uniforms were becoming a thing of the past, so you didn't always know who to salute (before we stopped bothering altogether) or who to be nice to. You often had to wait for a bloke to talk to you before you knew which side of the world he came from.

We wandered around aimlessly, stomachs grumbling from lack of food. Speculation was rife. There was talk of a railway, to be built out here in the middle of nowhere. We were going to build it. I'd never heard such bollocks in my life. Nobody could build a railway through country like this, rock and bamboo as far as the eye could see. And where was it going anyway?

After pap on that first day, we were marched down to the river bank to join other prisoners, milling in the mud. Long-hulled boats fitted with makeshift engines were tied up alongside and we were herded on, ten to a boat. We were squatting or half-sitting on the hull's rim and it was very pain-ful, but at least we weren't marching. A cloud of black smoke blew up behind us as we steered to midstream, the engine grinding against the current. We didn't know where we were going and for those few hours, we didn't care. The breeze was heaven and we were gliding past jungle that was actually beautiful. Carpets of deep green crept down to the water's edge and gnarled old tree trunks stood defiantly in the stream. All around us, and above the roar of the engines, the caco-phony of the jungle was deafening. God alone knows what was making all that row, but the place was clearly teeming with wildlife.

Cool, rested, almost relaxed, it came as a bit of a jolt when the boat slowed and we nosed towards the bank. This had to be Konyo, another camp much like the others. Attap huts were still being built here, by an army of barefooted Thai labourers in Jap-happies, as we learned to call the loincloths they wore, who hauled up bamboo uprights and lashed leaves together. Perhaps fifty POWs were there too, smashing into the hard clay of the ground with pickaxes and shovels. Beyond the huts, on high ground, the jungle stretched on for ever. Suddenly, it wasn't beautiful any more. It was obvious, even without any instruction or explanation, that it had to be cleared. The jungle was the enemy again.

Konyo was killing. Its atmosphere hit me like a rifle butt and I couldn't remember ever feeling so depressed before. Out there, somewhere to the west, far beyond those trees, was a world I once knew. A polite old soldier was still serving squaddies in his restaurant in Bombay. Sylvia Cohen was wandering her white beach at Cape Town, scanning the horizon for me, or perhaps for some other passing soldier. My dad would be sitting in the City Arms about now, come opening time, sipping his warm Ansells and wondering why Reggie hadn't written for a while. All the cheery bollocks we usually used, of putting a brave face on it, muddling through, keeping calm and carrying on; none of that counted now, because none of that worked. Nobody in the world knew where we were and there's something appallingly lonely about that.

We were pushed by the guards into a hut. It was A-framed, rectangular and its walls were made of bamboo and rattan. Each end was open to the elements and the roof, inevitably, was sheathed with attap. Welcome to Hotel Konyo. There were no chairs, no cupboards, just hard bamboo beds made of a single platform and raised from the damp earth floor, trodden flat by the men who had built it. We took a space each and marked our territory with our kit; in my case a towel, a razor and a rapidly disintegrating shaving brush. I was careful to keep my pipe and tobacco out of sight. Some of us slept. Some of the time.

The first day at the new camp the whole complement stood on parade in what the Japs called *tenko*, roll call. Later, we'd learn to count in Japanese – and I still can – *ichi, ni, san, shi, go*; the rhythm and the guttural growl have never left me. But that first morning was a pep talk from one of the most vicious of the 'little yellow bastards' I was ever to meet. He stood five feet tall in the sun of the parade ground, his face lean and dark, his eyes expressionless. He told us, in broken English, that his name was Lieutenant Usuki. That was before he became, to all of us, the 'Konyo Kid'. His boots gleamed, so did his sword's leather scabbard as it trailed behind him. *I* could look down physically on this man and the six footers probably found it difficult to keep a straight face. At least, that first morning they did.

Our task, he told us, was to clear the jungle and prepare the ground for a railway to be built, beginning on the rise beyond the camp's perimeter.

'All will work,' he spat as he strutted. 'Including officers.'

There was a stunned silence. Then a polite, typically civilized voice said, 'May I remind the camp commander, that under the Geneva Convention, officers do not have to work.' There was another silence. And he went on, 'And we will not do so.' I had to admire the man. The Geneva Convention! The Convention didn't come this far east. No convention in the world could hold a candle to bushido, the way of the warrior. This was the cult of the Samurai which still operated in Japan and to Western eyes was appallingly cruel. The niceties of the Geneva Convention were not remotely recognizable under bushido.

The warrior's eyes narrowed in the silence that followed. We learned that day, if we didn't know it already, that what bushido could not tolerate was a loss of face. And here was this chinless Englishman daring to challenge him. He walked straight up to the officer in question and yawped at him. He only came up to where the man's tie knot would have been in more formal circumstances, but that didn't matter. He bawled him out, screaming at him until the veins stood out on his forehead. There was no response, the officers standing to attention as if he wasn't there. Then the Kid slapped one.

Everybody flinched at that first blow but nobody moved. The slap became a punch, the open hand a tight bunch of knuckles and then the Kid called in the heavies. Two men had been picked out deliberately – the spokesman and his adjutant, I guessed. Rifle butts thudded into stomachs or sliced horizontally against jaws and temples. Boots crashed into the officers' prone bodies, dust flying on the parade ground. There were thuds and moans. And still we didn't move.

But we all felt like cheering when both men got up. They dusted themselves down and stood to attention again, bleeding and trembling with shock, but soldiers still. The Kid may have had other weapons in his arsenal, but for now he wasn't going to use them. He stepped back and screamed for the parade to move. Time to work. Despite the guards' best efforts to keep us quiet, we muttered about what had just happened as we fell out. Was it Britain 1, Japan 0? Or was it all rather more subtle than that? The officers knew, we knew and certainly the Kid knew that he could have machine-gunned us all there that morning, like the Chinese civilians had been machine-gunned at Keppel beach. But they needed us, for Christ's sake. We were expendable, yes, but we were the workforce they needed to build their bloody railway and they couldn't kill us all. Could they?

The officers stayed behind, 'at ease' on the now-deserted parade ground. You could, I suppose, say they'd won that round. But in the end, what had they achieved? Throughout my time in the camps, I rarely saw officers. Sometimes they appeared on parade with us but at other times merely oversaw the work we did and conferred, usually by means of an interpreter, with the Japs. I have no idea what these discussions were about, so I do not know whether the officers' negotiations made life any easier for us. I have read in other memoirs that sometimes officers worked alongside the men, but I never saw that.

Nobody had said that other ranks couldn't work. So work we did. The thickets of bamboo were yards across and the Japs only gave us blunted axes in case we were tempted to use sharp ones on them, I suppose. The dull blades bounced off the bamboo as if it was made of iron; by the end of the day they were useless. We had to sharpen them on a stone when the day's shift was over. We had hoes to break up the ground and shovels to move the soil. The problem was that this was virgin jungle and nobody had tilled it before. Below the top-soil, solid with bamboo and other roots, the yellow clay was unyielding, sticky and soul-destroying. I had no idea about how to build a railway and neither, it seemed, did the Japanese. The British had built the first railways in the world while the Japs still walked around in armour with their women ten paces behind them. But the navvies of my great-great-grandfather's time, who had built the Leicester–Rugby line that ran past my old house in Healey Street, were a breed apart. They would have used cross-cut saws to slice the clay into blocks. We had inferior tools and no idea. We dragged the tangle of weeds away in woven baskets and hauled at rocks with our bare hands, the skin of our fingers cut to ribbons. We worked in silence because the Japs allowed no talking. After an hour or two of effort, your back knotting and your legs giving way in that dreadful, endless humidity, you really had nothing to say to the bloke next to you, the bloke who was living in the same hell as you.

At first, you can't believe the pain. Your thumbs don't seem to belong to you any more and there is a constant tingling of your nerve-endings that shoots all the way up to your shoulders as your axe bounces uselessly off yet more bamboo before a couple of plants go down. None of this made sense. If the real intention was to build a railway, as some people suggested, all the way to British India, why not give us the tools to do it? Trucks and cranes and all the mechanization of the West. '*Speedo! Speedo!*' just wouldn't do it for men near breaking point. Rest periods and water were strictly limited and calluses and blisters simply had to be tolerated.

A piece of bamboo, ten to fifteen feet long, is bloody heavy. We had to carry two of these away at a time as we cleared the jungle. First you try one under each arm. That doesn't work. So you lay them across your shoulders like a yoke. Except that your shoulders are aching too much for that and you try something else, carrying the damn things like a baby across your chest. So I started to carry just one. I was prepared to make the extra journeys to spare my arms, but a Jap guard saw me and had, after all, a job to do. He came for me, screaming incomprehensibly, pointing at the bamboo length and raising two fingers. For a fleeting mischievous moment, I thought of returning the compliment. The symbol had no significance for these people and I doubt if even Churchill's reversed 'victory' sign meant a damned thing. So I just stared at him until he took those two fingers of his and jabbed them into my eyes. The pain was appalling and in my shock I dropped the bamboo and cursed him under my breath. He paused and half turned and I knew what to expect, so with wobbly vision and the mother of all headaches, I picked up the bamboo I had dropped and dashed back for another one. I never made that mistake again.

The guards watched us constantly. If we weren't *speedo* enough, they'd slap us around the face, three, four, five times. Punishment in the British Army was marching at the double in full pack. To be slapped was completely alien to us. It stings a lot and there's a little yellow bastard at the other end, snarling gibberish in your face. You don't know what he's saying so you try to react as he'd expect. Show defiance of any kind and the slaps become punches, to the stomach, the throat, the head. Swear – like I had under my breath – and the punches pummel you to the ground. Then the boots go in, to your ribs, your back, your head. You curl up on the clay-marbled ground, covering your head, protecting your face. So the boots crunch on your arms. And if your arms are broken, you can't work. And if you can't work . . . The rifle butts slam into your head and if you're lucky, you'll pass out. If you're not, it's back on your feet and back to work – '*Speedo! Speedo!*'

And around you, you watch men die. It was terrifying the first time I saw it but you can become hardened to anything in the end. Some bloke has offended a guard. He doesn't know what he's done or hasn't done. Neither do you. You watch the slapping, the punches, the kicks out of the corner of your eye because you can't believe it's happening and you can't look away. He's too weak to fight – and anyway, to fight would mean death. He's too weak to work. He should be in hospital. Except there isn't a hospital.

The flies, black and heavy, buzzed around us all the time and you knew a man was finished when he couldn't swat them any more. To them, he was carrion already and their grim egg-laying could commence. The Kid supervised it all and administered some beatings himself, just because he could. His dark, glittering eyes missed nothing and he strutted around like some sort of sadistic peacock, that bloody silly sword dragging in the dirt.

In the endless, grinding hours hacking order out of the

jungle, you have time to think. Some men thought of their wives, their girls, their kids. The younger ones probably thought of home and Mum and Dad. Some, and their numbers may have increased, thought of God. I thought, at first at least, of escape and we even talked this over from time to time. Instinctively, I suppose, you believe your side will win, not the Battle of Singapore, certainly, but the war. The men who lost that belief didn't make it. You'd see it in their eyes, the 'attap stare', as we all called it, of a man lying on his bamboo bed with his eyes fixed on the roof overhead. What did they actually see up there where the sunlight flashed between the leaves? Not victory, certainly. Not an end to everything they faced every day. What had lost us Singapore was a lack of air support and a lack of armour. You couldn't use tanks in the jungle, our top brass believed. But the Japs could. They arrived in numbers at Johore and they rumbled across the Causeway onto the island once they'd rebuilt it.

Escape, though. That was different. It depended, like all escape plans, on luck; but there were two unknowns. First and always was the jungle itself, alive with things that could kill you. Second were the locals. We were somewhere along the Burma–Thai border so the natives could be Burmese or Thai. That didn't matter. What mattered was how they'd react to an escaped Tommy running all but naked through their back yard. I know human nature. Not everybody is kind and not everybody is brave. The women who'd given me eggs and bananas, the old soup-seller; these were the exceptions, not the norm. They were under the yoke of the Japanese, like we were. What was to stop them selling us out?

By the end of the first week at Konyo, I'd come to a decision: I was going to survive. Escape was impossible, so stop worrying about it. You become hard, isolated. I suppose I'd always had that streak in me. Darwinists call it survival of the fittest, don't they? What that means is survival of the most selfish bastards imaginable. Was that me? Was that what the war and the Burma Railway made me become? I don't know.

What I do know is that once I'd made that decision, my depression, so acute and mind-numbing when I first saw Konyo, lifted. And I played mind games to keep that depression away. People had survived in this God-awful place for centuries. So could I. And I didn't need centuries. I just needed to hang on until the Japs were beaten. And I had no doubt they would be, one day.

I began to focus on the jungle, not as an enemy but as a fascinating new friend. The bamboo clumps we hacked at day after day were made up of ten or more stems, each one up to fourteen inches in diameter. When the Japs used explosives to blow them up or they finally fell to our saws, their shards were razor sharp and a cut from one could have been fatal, but they had a beauty of their own and a practical and multi-purpose use. All our huts were built from the stuff. We slept on it. And the locals made rafts from it, that they ferried up and down the river.

The jungle floor was alive. I'd known the frogs since before Jitra. They were the size of guinea pigs and struck up their interminable noise along the river bank as soon as night fell. Centipedes were six inches long, scurrying blindly over your boots as you hacked at the ground, annoyed, no doubt, to be disturbed. I never counted the types of snake I saw. Some, of course, were poisonous, especially the ones with bright colours, and you learned to watch out for them and keep away. I remember watching fascinated one day as a constrictor caught a frog, right in front of me. It didn't bother with the whole crushing action because I suppose the frog was too small. The snake just snapped it in mid-jump in the air and held it there, its legs twitching. Then it jerked back its jaws and swallowed the thing whole.

On Sundays, while most men slept or lounged about enjoying the day off, I took to wandering in that jungle. I was never stopped, nor even challenged as I left the camp. The guards knew I'd be back. And I found what I called the Silent Forest. Far enough away from the river for the frogs not to be a problem, there seemed to be no monkeys or even birds. To me, it was a special place, as magic as Great Glen, but more private. There was no Bob Hillier here; I was alone. I would sit on a dead tree stump and watch the red ants marching. If you weren't careful, they'd be over what was left of your boots and socks and crawling on your skin looking for food. Then there were the bats. They lived in caves darker than the night and resented my intrusion. The noise they made as they took off from their subterranean roofs was terrifying. Like something out of the Apocalypse, they swarmed in their vast numbers at sunset, swerving and diving in their erratic flight, snatching insects on the wing.

The river drew everybody like a magnet. In that rugged, wild, beautiful country of virgin jungle, it was a central highway, a means of getting from A to B and the quickest, usually the safest, option. The water was always brown and sluggish, carrying rich sediment and debris from further upstream. We'd soak in it after a gruelling day's work, chatting, easing away the aches and pains. Around us fish swam in light shoals; I was idly treading water one day when I felt a nibbling sensation, tickling my leg. I kicked out but it went on and when I looked down, there were half a dozen fish chewing a scab on my shin.

'Bloody hell!' and I was on my feet in seconds and up on the bank. We were part of the food chain. Actually, it was oddly therapeutic having this nibbling sensation. People pay a fortune today for such treatment at health spas.

Only in the monsoon season was the river a killer. The dark clouds rolled over the trees and the wind whipped the bamboo into a frenzy. The Kwai roared its anger as it pitched and rolled, tearing down its own banks and ripping trees from the ground. The water foamed and frothed, flooding the camp as we waded through a quagmire and slept in a swamp. Nobody ventured into the river when it was in this mood – the already-drowned jungle creepers could lash around your legs and drag you under. I could never forget how Albert Lockton had gone to eternity on the bridge south of Jitra.

The river became everything to us. We drank it, boiling it at first when we had the opportunity but afterwards not giving a damn about that. We bathed in it, peed in it, relaxed in it and cooked our pap rice with it. We lived alongside it, built bridges across it over the months ahead. And died alongside it, burying our dead along its banks.

I don't know how many weeks it was before my uniform rotted away. The itchy battledress, puttees, boots and Glengarry of Glen Parva were distant memories. I'd even forgotten how to handle a .303 or a mortar. Some of us still had shorts but a lot of men who did kept them for Sunday best. Like most of us, I wore a Jap-happy, which some of us knew as a bollock bag, and I became all but indistinguishable from the locals. My hair was crawling with lice and my skin had tanned to the colour of old leather. Because my boots had gone and my socks were a collection of holes, I had no choice but to go barefoot. It hurt like hell at first, stubbing your toe, treading on roots, rocks, ants, but my soles hardened and I realized now how every bloke in Singapore could play football barefooted. The real danger underfoot were the scorpions, little black buggers whose aggression made the Japs seem like choirboys. Their pincers would be splayed and their stings in the air long before you saw them. In all my time in the jungle I never trod on one but I knew men who did. They would scream with the pain; their foot would be swollen and black with poison within the hour. Not all of them survived it.

Slowly but surely, our health deteriorated. The pap wasn't enough to keep a kid alive, still less men who were supposed to be clearing a jungle. We sometimes had river fish to supplement it and at first I took to saving some scraps of this to keep with me (when I still had shorts with pockets) for the *yasumé* meal at midday. It was always the same. In this short time, the stuff was crawling with maggots and stank to high heaven. I picked off the maggots and ate it anyway. From time to time in the camps, I met men from the Leicesters and one of them was the bloke back in barracks at home who had taken exception to the caterpillars in his cauliflower.

'Bet you wish you had those caterpillars now!' I winked at him.

There was no smile. Barely a grunt. I didn't see him again. I often wonder if he made it back.

The weaker you are, the more susceptible you become to all manner of disease. Burma was a white man's grave anyway, even without building a railway. Men went to the MO and to the makeshift hut they'd set up as a hospital. There was almost nothing in the way of medicine, but the diagnosis was usually spot on and we all learned to recognize the symptoms – malaria, dysentery, beriberi. Each one just a name. Each one something that killed us in our thousands up and down the peninsula.

You get used to funerals. But you never forget that yours might be next. The Japs let us bury our dead and we did the best we could. We had no flag-draped coffin, no bugler to play the Last Post and sure as hell no shots fired over the grave. We just dug another pit in that yellow, unyielding clay and wrapped the poor bugger up in his half blanket if he had one or simply in his Jap-happy. There was no coffin, no real shroud and just a small, hand-made cross to mark the last resting place of a man. One of the officers said a few words over him but nobody sang a hymn. I always walked to that little cemetery on the edge of the jungle with Jackie Weston and if we started talking together in hushed tones, the reality of death soon stopped us. With each shovelful of earth we tipped onto the man who had yesterday been working alongside us, we made a vow, Jackie and me. We made a pact to stick together no matter what. And we'd beg, find or steal to do it. If we could help anybody else, that was to the good, but it wasn't likely. Helping yourself was paramount; helping a mate was risky; helping anybody else was a luxury nobody could afford.

Our working day ended abruptly about six o'clock when night fell. There'd be half an hour of livid, achingly beautiful sunset over the darkening jungle and then blackness. Escape may have seemed impossible but the Japs couldn't risk losing any of us under cover of night so we'd trudge back along the widened trails to the cookhouse for pap and fish. Food became an obsession with us all because we got so little of it. I kept my mess tin on me and joined the queue. There were two queues, the second known as the Leggie Queue. You ate your pap in a minute flat and then stood in the Leggie Queue hoping for any seconds that were going. Jackie and I hit upon a dodge. Not for us the lottery of the Leggie Queue. Hunger drives you on; you take chances, take short cuts, bugger your fellow man. So we'd sneak off the track on our way back to camp and slide down the slope to get to the cookhouse first. It was rough ground and we were both exhausted after hours of back-breaking slog in the sun. If we'd fallen, ripped our skin, broken a bone, that would have been it. But we made it and got to the Leggie Queue more often than most. I let the religious types stand around waiting for a miracle.

It must be said that the Jap guards didn't live high off the hog either. Their huts too were made of bamboo and attap and they had to slip and slide through the mud when the river flooded. Their food wasn't much better than ours, although they had far more of it. One day I heard a shot as we were coming back to camp. Immediately, you think – who's dead? Who's pissed off the guards enough for them to open fire? In fact, they'd shot a wild cat. Jungle, flat-headed, fishing – take your pick; all three species live in the jungle. So do leopards. To me, it looked like a cheetah, with spots, long legs and scrawny sides. It was hung up as a trophy that night, like an English gentleman of my dad's generation might have it stuffed in a glass case in his study. Then the Japs skinned it, cooked it and ate it. We weren't invited to the feast.

After a month at Konyo, my ignorance damn near killed me. The tropical ulcer the MO had diagnosed at Tarso was getting worse. I had seen these revolting things now in all their ghastliness, the black flesh, the grey bone, the flies endlessly swarming around other men who smelt of death. The ulcer covered the whole of my calf and I knew I was staring death in the face. So I went to the camp hospital. Konyo General was another attap hut. The only difference between the MO's 'consulting rooms' and the place I called home was that the hospital was swept and washed down every day. It didn't achieve much, but in that impossible world, we all of us conned ourselves that it was the height of hygienic sophistication.

The MO looked as exhausted as if he'd been working on jungle clearance too; perhaps more so, because *all* his patients were in God's waiting room and there was damn all he could do about it. 'You should have come to me earlier with this, Twigg,' he said grimly. 'Didn't you notice it?'

That was all I needed. A life-threatening condition *and* a ticking off. 'No, sir,' I told him. 'Well, I saw it at Tarso but didn't think too much of it then. It was small and . . .'

He told me that had it gone a day or so more the only solution would have been to amputate. That was done with what little chloroform the camp had, at speed and with only the most basic sterilization. He must have seen my expression. 'Look,' he said. 'All I can suggest is that you take your sugar and soap ration, mould it all together and use it as a poultice. I can let you have a bandage. If that doesn't work . . .'

If that didn't work, I'd lose my leg. And at very best spend the rest of my life hobbling on crutches or swinging some sort of artificial limb. On the other hand, if the Japs found no further use for me as a clearer of jungles, the rest of my life may just be a figure of speech. I felt sick. Nothing Jackie Weston could do would save me, pact or no pact. The rations the doctor suggested were little more than a serving suggestion. Our food ration included a dessert spoon of sugar and we were also given a little soap at Konyo. This was like soft putty in the heat so I moulded it with the next day's sugar and flattened it to make a sort of pancake. It hurt like hell but I wrapped the thing around my leg with the MO's bandage and did this for the next three days. Each time I took the poultice off I cleaned the rotting flesh away with boiled water, then added more sugar as before.

On the morning of the fifth day there was a small pinkish spot in the centre of the ulcer. A sign of healing, surely? I left the bandage off to let the air get to it and over the coming weeks, the ulceration lessened. It was painful and of course I had to keep working, but just before Christmas, it was gone – the best Christmas present I'd had since I was five and my dad came home from the war. I thanked Fate, I thanked the MO, I thanked a scrap of Lifebuoy and a handful of sugar crystals. Did I even thank God? I may have.

It was about a week after the ulcer went away that I passed my twenty-ninth birthday; I won't say 'celebrated' – that's hardly the word. The work was agonizing and grindingly slow because we'd reached a particularly rocky outcrop in the jungle and it was all shovel and spade and pickaxe. The Japs decided to speed everything up by blasting. A team of prisoners was chosen to drill firing holes while the Jap engineers prepared the charges. It was our sappers who lit the fuses but the rest of us had to move away from the blast and we wandered to the river's edge. It took for ever so I sat down and found myself alone. Jackie and the others were some yards away. Across the river I saw two rock pinnacles in the distance above the trees, lit by the dying sun. A soft wind rustled the bamboo leaves near me although I hadn't been aware of any wind until then. The sound seemed to fade, the murmuring of the lads, the jabber of the Japanese, and I felt a kind of peace I can't describe.

I've thought about this since. I'm not a religious person. I went to Sunday school as a kid for the treats. I pinched the vicar's apples and regarded him with the childish contempt I had for all authority. I'd seen too many men die around me along that bloody river to believe in a kind and caring God. And yet, as I sat on the banks of the Kwai waiting for that dynamite blast, *something* happened to me. Something intangible. Something I can't explain. But it was something that told me that I'd be all right; I was going to get out of this, somehow. I'm not a religious person. I don't believe in God.

And yet . . .

8

Hell Camps

Weeks had passed and we'd cleared a swathe through the jungle and levelled the ground. The rocks that we'd shifted by hand now had to be shattered with pickaxes to rubble that was scooped to form an embankment. With no wheelbarrows the only way of working was to load our baskets with these stones and hurl them onto the pile. As the pile took shape, we had to struggle up the slope, pebbles sliding and rolling under our leather-tough bare feet and dump yet more of them. Then we had to flatten the top and prepare it for the sleepers and track lengths to be laid down.

It was now taking us half an hour just to get to the end of the line we had created, so the Japs decided to build a new camp further north, so that we wasted less time in getting there. Thai labourers began this work, presumably on the grounds that they built attap huts better than we did. But in the end the work parties had to spend Sundays – that sacred day – and any other 'spare' time working alongside them. The only officers I ever saw at the new camp – which we dubbed Konyo 2 – were the two the Kid had picked on, on our first day downriver. They were present on parade each morning and evening, but other than that, they kept to themselves in their own hut.

The commandant at Konyo 2 was a *gunso*, a sergeant whose name I never knew. He was short and squat with the manners of a peasant and he seemed hell bent on impressing his boss, the Kid. This man took the art of sadism to a new level and the pace of work became impossible. Konyo was already underway when we arrived but Konyo 2 was ours – we built it. Just like we dug our own graves.

Men who couldn't stand for *tenko*, the morning parade, sat on their bamboo beds – if they could sit at all – and watched us go into the tracks to start work on this new stretch of jungle. I often wonder if they felt relief at not having to join us. The fact is I don't think they did. I don't think they felt anything. You knew by their eyes, they'd got nothing left. They were walking skeletons, blistered and ulcerated, their skin glistening with lesions and lacerations, their tongues thick in their mouths, their stares vacant.

We took turns to lay out the dead. In the villages of Leicestershire when my dad was a lad, there were people who did this out of habit and tradition. Old women who had seen it all would strip and wash the latest departed and wrap them in their winding sheet. We had no winding sheets and we had no time to wash the dead, despite the nearness of the river. We were hacking through clay all day, every day, so burials were no different. We were too exhausted to give a man his full traditional six feet and could only manage three or four before our bodies seized up entirely. The dead were often men younger than me, squaddies I'd come through Glen Parva with. We'd sat polishing buttons together, lain side by side in snowy fields on the Kibworth range, wondered at the stars and the sunsets on the deck of the *Duchess of York* and belted out Vera Lynn hits to further order. Now they were wizened, worn-out wrecks, worked to death by the sheer, blind inhumanity of the warriors of Nippon.

When we'd filled one cemetery space, we had to dig another. You know 'The Soldier', Rupert Brooke's poem from the Great War? 'That there's some corner of a foreign field that is forever England'? Well, there isn't. There's just a shallow pit by the side of a stinking river and nobody knows who's lying there now. Digging those graves made me harder, toughened my resolve. With every swing of that pick and every lunge of the spade I vowed I'd make it. And no one would be digging a grave for me. Not this side of the Andaman Sea. I'd survived Singapore. I'd survived that bloody awful train north. I'd survived Konyo. Now, I'd survive Konyo 2.

I started smoking again. My pipe still lay stashed with my little bundle of precious possessions under the bamboo of my bed, but the Walter Raleigh I'd got at Changi had long gone. The curious thing about being a prisoner of war of the Japanese was the fact that we were constantly being pestered by the local civilians. They came to the camp upriver on their bamboo rafts, loaded high with rotten mangoes to sell. Nobody had much money left but we traded what we could. Along with the mangoes the river traders had rough shag tobacco that grew wild in the jungle. According to those who tried it, it was pretty powerful stuff. My limited cash reserves wouldn't run to a deal; I needed to keep money for food.

On one of my jungle rambles I recognized the leaves of a tobacco plant and took some back; over the weeks I amassed quite a stash. God knows where I'd picked up the basics of curing the stuff, but I gave it a try. Ideally I should have soaked the leaves in molasses but that was a luxury too far, so I settled for sugar, now I didn't need it for a poultice any more. I dried the leaves in the sun and dissolved several days' sugar ration in a solution of weak tea. I added more leaves until all the liquid was soaked up, then chopped and moulded them. When I'd finished I'd got a mess tin's worth. I tied it tightly in cloth and hung it over my bed. One of the other curious things about being a prisoner of war of the Japanese is that nobody took much interest in what you did. The Japs themselves regarded us as completely expendable and weren't remotely interested in us as people. As far as the others were concerned, I could have hung stark naked from the rafters singing 'Rule Britannia' and I wouldn't have merited more than a glance; men were too wrapped up in themselves. Nobody so much as asked what I was doing.

I left the tobacco to ferment for a fortnight. It was moist and smelt sweet and fragrant, not unlike pipe tobacco, in fact! I broke a piece off, like I did all those years ago when I'd pinched Dad's pipe and made myself sick in that Leicester field. And after weeks without a smoke, I felt just as excited. I rolled it, packed it in the bowl and lit up. Perfect! Jackie and a couple of the lads shared it with me – a little taste of heaven at hell on the Kwai.

Ginger Hallam loved a pipe as much as I did. He was a Sherwood Forester from another part of the Midlands from me, but I didn't hold that against him. We'd sit outside the hut of an evening, a little fire keeping out the surprising cold of a winter's night, and Ginger would blow rings to the sky, rubbing his rice-bloated stomach. 'Just imagine, Twiggy,' he said one night, 'one day we'll be able to have a proper pipe of St Bruno. And a pint.' He smiled at the memory of it. 'And there'll be no bloody Japs kicking us around!'

'That's right, Ginger,' I said. 'Just got to keep going.' Kinfi-nobbleation-mira-moka-kid-comeday-mumday-all-a-mid – I didn't say it out loud in front of Ginger; he might have thought I'd gone mad. But it was precisely because I said it in my mind and all that it meant to me, that I didn't.

Christmas 1942. Unaccountably, the Japs gave us a couple of days off. In an ungrateful sort of way this only made things worse. It gave us all more time to think, become introspective, nostalgic and sentimental. These things don't matter in peacetime. They might not even matter in wartime if you're winning. But if you're losing – or worse, if like us you've already lost – such thoughts can become corrosive. You wrap yourself in memories, lose yourself in what was. And that can make it more difficult to cope with what is. In our minds we put up trimmings around the huts, holly wreaths on doors where there were no doors. We smelt the roasting cockerel and the plum pudding and we scoffed the lot. And after lunch, warm and full and happy, we all wandered down to the local for a couple of pints.

In all this I watched men's faces. Sheer exhaustion was written all over them and I could almost tell who was going to make it and who wasn't. I lay on the hard bamboo under my thin blanket that night. The whole hut was curiously silent – even the usual jungle chorus seemed far away. Suddenly, a single voice came from nowhere – a beautiful rich baritone singing 'Silent Night'. If anybody was already asleep, the strange, almost alien sound woke them up and everybody listened, some resting on one arm, others sitting up to catch every word. Nobody joined in – it seemed an insult to the soloist – and I expect many of us were too choked anyway. The sound drifted across the whole camp, over the Jap guard huts – I wonder what they made of it – and down the river, echoing eerily in the jungle night. Then . . . silence again.

And I woke up the next morning to the usual dawn chorus of the monkeys. I have treasured every Christmas since.

I don't know what they paid the Kid but early in the new year he was certainly earning it. He was forever up and down between the two Konyos and he hit upon the idea of Sunday sports. Yet again, the inexplicable, the peculiar, the odd. Here was a man who supervised an impossible work rate, who encouraged brutality in his guards and personally beat people to death. But that was the weekday Kid. On Sundays he turned into the most genial of prison governors, concerned for our welfare and hoping we wouldn't get bored. His real purpose, however, was to prove the superiority of the Japanese. When we were assembled at roll call, the Kid would strut between our rows, dragging his sword behind him in the dust, selecting individuals with a grunt and a tap on the shoulder. Then, as we formed a hollow square, the chosen men wrestled within it, with the guards. They'd strip off to loincloths like the Jap-happies most of us wore, but of course the guards were incomparably fitter than we were in our ill, weakened state. As unequal contests go, this was top of the list. Wrestling was a Japanese martial art; British blokes boxed. They knew all the moves and we didn't. And it wasn't really wise to give one of them a pasting even if anybody had the strength to do it.

It was all just to make a point as far as the Kid was concerned. After every bout, with some poor bugger lying trampled in the dust of the parade ground, he would get on his soapbox and extol the superiority of Nippon. They'd beaten us at Singapore and all points north; they were doing it still.

It may have been on a Monday – I no longer remember

because the days and weeks tended to merge into a sickening endlessness – that the Kid had something important to say. He stood in front of us on the parade ground, arms folded like some hideous goblin. 'You do not work hard enough,' he snapped in that harsh, guttural voice of his. 'You work harder or you will be punished. You have good treatment. This will change if you do not work harder.'

I've thought a lot about this over the years. It was a common theme that the Japs were treating us well. And I've come to the conclusion that it wasn't hypocrisy – they actually meant it. To them, warriors of bushido, a couple of handfuls of rice and occasional fish, together with a leaking hut and a rock-hard bed, *was* good treatment. At the time I just felt sick. Everybody did. How the hell could we do even more? The cemetery was full of men who had given their all, worked until the life drained out of them into that blood-soaked Thai soil. Was that their plan? To fill the jungle with our bodies until there weren't any of us left? A just enemy would have machine-gunned us there and then. But justice and the Konyo Kid weren't even passing acquaintances.

So we marched onto the tracks again, to carry on where we'd left off, to bend our backs and take our chances preparing the ground for the sleepers and track which were brought up by train. The guards were watching with a new intensity now, because the Kid had decreed it. If the Japs were bad, our Korean guards were worse. Being at the beck and call of the Japanese made them bitter, edgy. And they took it out on us. Years later I read it was the same in the European concentration camps. They were run by the SS but the day-to-day beatings were administered by the Kapos, hardline sadists who went cap-in-hand to the Aryan master race. So it was with the Koreans on the Railway. I never heard a Korean answer a Jap back or even hesitate before carrying out what was clearly an order.

'*Speedo! Speedo! Bugero.* All men no *yasumé!*' It was their mantra and they never tired of saying it. Later that day, I saw their zeal in action. I was working alongside George – I never knew his surname – and he was in trouble. He'd been in the sick bay the day before but had been forced out of there by the guards once they realized he could stand. I knew all the signs by now: the sunken eyes, the drawn face, that ghastly pallor that hung over men who were nearing the end. We were breaking rocks, our pickaxes striking sparks as the metal bounced off the surfaces and earth flew in all directions. George was just going through the motions, swinging his pick perhaps once to my four. I tried to slow down, hoping nobody would notice, but a Korean did and out of nowhere, he jumped down from his perch over the rocks and slammed his rifle butt into the small of George's back. God knows what state the man's kidneys were in already, but he wasn't getting up from that hit. His face lay against the rocks he couldn't break, twisted in pain. Finished. The guard kicked him, driving his steel-shod boot into George's ribs. '*Curru bugero!*' he yelled at him, '*Speedo! Speedo!*' standing over him as George dragged himself upright. I don't know how the man had the strength but he bent to scrape rocks into his basket.

For a while he managed a murderous speed, but we all knew he couldn't keep it up. I tried to position myself between him and the guard as the Korean wandered away to torture some other poor bastard. If I'd intervened, I'd have got a rifle butt and a boot too and two men would have been on their way to the cemetery. We were slaves. We had no rights, no honour, no sense of worth, no feelings. We were the beasts of burden who built the Burma Railway.

George was still upright – just – as darkness ended the day's work and he shambled back with the rest of us. The last time I saw him he was wandering like a zombie into his hut in the darkness. I never saw him again because he died two days later and became another of the silent crosses by the river.

I think it was George's death that brought out the worst in me. Or was it the best? I'd always lived on the edge, fronted up to authority, tried it on and bent the rules, even to the point of stealing. And if I could steal from a well-meaning soul like the vicar and a harmless old lady who kept a sweet shop, I could sure as hell steal from the Japanese. But now, it was all about extremes. I would steal to get food and stay alive. And if I was caught, it wouldn't be a clip round the ear and a stern sermon in Sunday school and my dad's belt. It would be a bayonet in the guts or it would be my head bouncing in the dust after one sweep of those bloody swords.

The key of course, the scene of crime, as it were, was the Jap cookhouse. Behind it, backing onto the jungle as it did at Konyo 2, was a metal container, a kind of skip. It was full of dried fish. It was about fifty yards from my hut and I noticed that at night, the place was deserted. There was no curfew and with the Japs relaxing in their own quarters and our blokes collapsed on their bamboo, I had the place to myself. Around the second or third week in January I took my chance. The night was warm and the stars studded a velvet sky, all of it totally at odds with what was happening down here on the ground. I could hear the hum of occasional conversation from the POW huts but nobody listened any more to the noises of the jungle night. I just had to be quiet. Just had to be careful. I was about twenty yards from the skip when my stomach knotted. I froze. It was adrenalin; that do-or-die, fight-or-flight moment when every sense is heightened and you've just got to get on with it. Nobody would know, of course. Only me. It wasn't like those planned escapes we all read about after the war, from places like Colditz, with committees and teams and underground tunnels. Out here, in this different war, it was every man for himself. I was that every man. If I didn't go through with this now, I may as well dig my own grave and lie in it.

Suddenly, I was at the skip. I lifted the rough matting over the top and grabbed two pieces of fish, shoving them down my Jap-happy with only a wince. And I retraced my steps, strolling slowly as if I was still taking the night air. Back in the hut I lay down on my bed. My heart was leaving my mouth by this time and I could breathe again. Jackie Weston was sitting up, looking at me. I grinned and ferreted in my loincloth, hauling out the fish. Neither of us said a word. We just lay there, giggling like two schoolboys who'd been looking up the girls' skirts at home.

I carried out the same nightly routine three times. And you know what they say – it gets easier each time. Jackie and I slipped the fish into our pap rations. It didn't make much difference and it wasn't worth dying for. But it wasn't about the fish or the protein in our diet. It was about survival. It was about putting one over on the 'monsters of Nippon' and getting away with it. With Jackie as my lookout, I lessened my chances of getting caught and it felt good to be part of a tiny team that was actually *doing* something.

I suppose the ease of all this made me cocky. The Kid had his own chickens in a yard at the back of the commandant's hut and no doubt he and his *gunso* had their fill of eggs. Whenever I could I'd walk past that compound with its flimsy wire, thinking – it would be so easy. There'd be eggs lying about all over the place in that straw. How difficult would it be to grab a hen, wring its neck before it flapped and squawked and have ourselves that Christmas dinner we'd missed last year? Then, reality kicked in. The smell of roasting chicken would be a little obvious in this back-of-beyond hellhole. And the Kid would probably have roasted me alongside it.

We'd always said that the railway line made no sense. It twisted and curved its way along the side of hills, across ravines and fast-flowing streams that became torrents in the wet season. Even so, thanks to our hard work – and our lives – the thing was coming together. I didn't lay much track myself; this looked like harder work than clearing the ground and I did my best to avoid it. The sleepers were huge slabs of dense, solid teak and the rails needed several men to lift them into position. Above and below us, we heard from the gossip of the river traders, the line was joining up and once it connected to the existing rail system, then there was no reason why troops and equipment shouldn't be sent up-country towards the Indian frontier; if that was, indeed, the Japanese master plan.

But nothing *quite* worked. The navvies who built the British network blasted their way through solid rock and smashed cuttings through mountains. The Japanese went around obstacles and at times the whole process seemed like a huge joke, as if our guards and we were operating in what today people call a parallel universe. The Jap engineers didn't seem to know what they were doing. We'd see them sometimes, Jap sappers with blueprints and theodolites, pointing, sketching, arguing. Our tools were useless. If they'd given us so much as a wheelbarrow, we could have got the job done in half the time. Mechanical cutters, bulldozers and tractors would have revolutionized the situation.

Probably the most ludicrous constructions were the viaducts that spanned the valleys and ravines. These were always made from timber; presumably importing enough quality stone or brick from elsewhere would have been too slow and expensive. But these always looked to me as if every sabotage king in the British Army had had a hand in the building of them. And early in 1943, I had proof of just how useless the viaducts were. An ancient locomotive, small, black and belching smoke, was tentatively trying out a new section, teetering high over a jungle-clad gorge. It looked like something George Stephenson might have built and it reminded me of a doddery old man trying to cross a stream via some stepping stones. The engine driver and his mate were hanging out of the cab as they inched their way forward, the locomotive snorting and wheezing with the effort. As we watched, leaning gratefully on our pick handles in a moment of *yasumé*, there was a series of loud cracks that echoed around the gorge. The upper portion lurched to one side and the struts gave way under the engine's weight. The first men out of there were the driver and his mate, who clearly had no intention of going down with the ship, and they leapt from the cab, shrieking hysterically. For a second, the locomotive and tender seemed to hang in mid-air over the chasm, then they rolled slowly off the track and twirled almost in slow motion before bouncing off the bottom of the hill, shattering trees and crashing into the foliage, steam bursting out of the fractured boiler. It was all we could do not to cheer, especially as the Japs ran in all directions in a panic. As far as I know, that locomotive is there still.

I think it was around March 1943 when the old Twigg luck seemed to have run out. I was working at the top, the most northerly section of the line that followed the river out of Konyo 2. My vision became blurred, then downright fuzzy. I'd had this before – the sting of sweat in your eyes, the buzz after a Jap slap around the head for not being *speedo* enough. But this, I knew, was different and it got worse as the day went on. So did the swelling in my legs. From the knees down the skin was tight as a drum and my pickaxe was clattering feebly on the rocks. When we got back to camp, I went straight to the MO.

We'd built a sort of field hospital at Konyo 2 in February at the insistence of the Japs. This wasn't for humanitarian reasons, of course; if the workforce plummeted any more, they realized there'd be no railway at all. The MOs were the unsung heroes of the Burma campaign but as far as I know, nobody ever got good news about what ailed them. Everybody came out of the hospital with a face like thunder. And I was no exception. The MO had pushed a finger into my calf and it disappeared! When he took it out, it left a hole behind.

'You've got beriberi, I'm afraid,' he said. 'You'll have to stay here until I can get you back to Tarso. There's not much I can do for you here. And you'll also have to wait until there are enough sick to make up a boatload; the Japs won't let us do it any other way.' This wasn't a problem. We both knew that a boatload would take a couple of days. So I didn't know whether to laugh or cry. I was going. Leaving this God-forgotten hole and I wouldn't be dragging myself through the jungle either. On the other hand . . .

The other hand was beriberi. You can look it up today in the medical dictionaries. There's no consensus where the name comes from but it was first diagnosed by a Dutchman in the seventeenth century. And it's endemic in South-East Asia. In other words, the locals got it too. It's caused by vitamin deficiency, specifically B1, and you can attribute it in my case to months of eating not much more than boiled white rice, day in and day out. The symptoms are lethargy, weight loss, pain in limbs and swelling of various bodily tissues. Severe cases lead to heart failure and death. I was, after all, lucky. I didn't have it that badly. I'd seen men who had, their skin lacerated by the constant and terrible itching and huge bulges in their Jap-happies when their balls became the size of things rugby players played with. What I couldn't understand was that I was being sent away to hospital when other beriberi cases were told to get over it and carry on working.

That night I said goodbye to Jackie. He muttered something about catching something too so that he could come with me. That wasn't how it worked. You had old mates; you made new ones. You hoped they'd all come through it, but you knew, deep down, that some of them wouldn't. The next day I slogged with the other walking wounded back down the trail to Konyo. And there I broke my back again for two days until there was, at last, a boatload. My vision was still blurred, my arms and legs felt like lead, but I was going. Out of the jungle. Away from the hell camps. And that last night my pap tasted of egg and chips and my boiled river water turned to pure Ansells Best Bitter.

The breeze along the river was heaven sent as we chugged downstream in the same sort of rickety Thai boat that had brought us to Konyo in the first place. And it was then I thanked whatever divine being there might be for my own situation. About half the blokes on board were dysentery cases. They were skeletons, drawn and pale with the sunken eyes that presage death. Most of them were stark naked because a Jap-happy is just a nuisance when you have to shit up to a dozen times a day. They just hung their arses over the side and shat as we steamed into mid-channel. Most of it was a stream of brown liquid but I was astonished to see the water seething where it landed. Hundreds of fish were gobbling it up, fighting each other for the morsels. We eat the fish; the fish eat our shit; we eat the fish. The rhythm of life in the jungles of Thailand. Two of the dysentery cases fell over the side on that river trip, too weak to hold on or save themselves. Some of the fitter of us tried to grab them, but we weren't that strong ourselves and the guttural snarling of our guard and his pointed rifle had us turning away in helpless despair. More food for the fish.

We'd been travelling for a couple of hours when the engine suddenly coughed and spluttered. Dead in the water, the boat began to drift towards the bank. The Jap guard screamed at the Thai boatman, pointing at the bank, the engine, the river, us. The Thai's face was a picture of indifference. Was there a war on? He hadn't noticed. It was as if he was saying, 'Engines die, mate. What am I supposed to do about it?' The guard grabbed the tiller and hauled it backwards and forwards, achieving nothing. He punctuated this with muttered asides and more accusatory screams at the Thai. Here it was again, the loss of face which all Japanese seemed to dread. He pointed at us, screaming, I suppose, for us all to stay put. Then he propped his rifle by the tiller, stripped off his cap, boots, tunic and trousers and slipped over the side in his underpants.

If this was a film and I'd have been Errol Flynn or John Wayne, I'd have grabbed that gun and shot the vicious little bastard dead before steering the boat to the coast and all the way across to the Thames, ready for a triumphal home-coming – 'now for Burma and a crack at those Japs'. As it was, none of us moved and we watched like the institutionalized idiots we'd become as the guard came up for air. Whatever problem he'd found below the waterline, he'd solved it because we were soon coughing and spluttering out into the current again and on our way south.

Talk about being left high and dry. At Tarso the guard disappeared and the boat chugged away upriver. Feeling like spare parts, we all wandered around looking for old faces. The dysentery cases made for the camp latrine. The hospital hut was packed with men with every ailment under the sun and I was told to report back tomorrow. The MO told me I was on sick leave and I could have kissed him. I wanted to tell him that just a few miles upriver, men were dying in the most appalling conditions while Tarso had the feel of a luxury hotel – at first.

My sick leave meant undemanding work rather than no work at all and my beriberi cure tasted disgusting. It was a supplement of rice husks, the bits they usually take away but which contain the all-important vitamins I needed. It had a bitter, almost sour taste but if it stopped me going blind through 'camp eyes' and reduced the aches in my joints, it was worth it. For the first time since leaving Changi, I was doing light duties around the camp and not slaving under the sun and the guns of the Japanese.

It sounds odd but only now, as my strength slowly returned, did I register toothache. In fact the damned thing had been niggling for about two months but what's a little throbbing by comparison with everything else we had to put up with? I've read since that the men in Gallipoli in the Great War had no dentists at all – and they were supposed to knock the Ottoman Empire out of the war. In truth, of course, I hadn't much choice. There was no effective medical aid at either of the Konyo camps so this was my first real opportunity to have it looked at. Everybody hates their dentist, don't they? I'd never been to one because dentists cost money and I didn't go to one now. I went to the MO.

'It's not going to get any better, Twigg,' he said, 'so the pain's not going to go away. I can take it out, but I'm afraid there's no anaesthetic.'

He wasn't half as afraid as I was, but I wasn't letting him know that. 'All right, sir,' I said. 'When shall I come back?'

'No need to come back,' he said and suddenly he was brandishing a pair of pliers. These weren't surgical instruments, they were the things you've got in your toolbox or kitchen drawer at home. You take bent nails out with them, not teeth. For a second, I was back in the Grace Road cinema with every mad sadistic doctor from Caligari to Frankenstein leering at me. My instinct was to run but he was fast and strong. Before I knew it he had my head in a vice-like grip and was working the tooth backwards and forwards. It made that ripping, cracking noise that sounds as if your jaw is coming off and then it was out. He didn't ruffle my hair as the hospital staff had when I had my stitches out as a kid. I expect he'd have felt a bit silly doing that. You've heard me say it before, but I'm not afraid to say it again – we owed those doctors a lot; they literally saved our lives.

And I should have needed their services again days later. The heat at night was unbearable by the end of March so I took to sleeping under my half blanket on the ground outside the hut. I was woken by a vicious stab in my hand and the pain was appalling. In all my months in the jungle I'd never stepped on one. And now I'd put my hand right on top of it – a little black scorpion. The next day I was numb nearly up to my elbow but I knew the MO couldn't help this time and that men had survived stings from much larger scorpions than the one that had got me. In four days, the swelling had gone. I was extra careful after that.

It was at Tarso they put the madmen, poor lost bastards who just couldn't take it any more. Mental illness is the polite term for it, but my generation knew of those places back home. They were lunatic asylums and if they didn't exactly chain people to the walls, it was the next best thing. Violent patients had to be restrained – that was the bottom line. I'd heard of cases – and seen a few, too – where men had cracked. Most of them just sank to the ground if they were working, crying for their mothers. Others hit out at anything, anyone. If it was a Jap, fine, but they died for that. If it was a mate, it was a sign of how desperate they were. Some, in many ways the saddest of all, just sat on the ground, playing with their fingers or with the ants that were eating them alive. They didn't know where they were or who they were any more.

Prisoners who'd been at Tarso before us were allowed to build several bamboo cages, six feet square. Surrounding them was a palisade so that no one could see in and no one could see out. The mad were given food and water but only the MOs went into their compound, and then only when they had time away from the endless exhausting work in what we laughingly called the operating theatre. You could hear those poor bastards, the inmates of the asylum, jabbering and giggling into the night. I kept away from the place as far as I could and even now as I write, I feel my hair crawling at their screams and laughter. They never came out and I never even saw one on a stretcher on his way to the cemetery. There were a lot of things the MOs couldn't cure, but somehow madness was the worst. It was the worst because you never knew whether you might join, tomorrow or the next day, the lunatics' unholy company.

Tarso was huge and I didn't see a single face I recognized other than the men who had come down from Konyo with me. 'If you want the old battalion . . .' Well, you won't find them at Tarso. I'd always been outgoing, so striking up new friendships wasn't a problem and I was chatting to a lad one day when he told me our kit from Singapore was here, in Tarso, in a store run by POWs. My Aussie Red Cross parcel! And even, if it hadn't melted into oblivion, some chocolate – something I'd almost forgotten the taste of. At Tarso, far more than either Konyo, some of the structure of the British Army still held sway. There was a corporal in charge of the stores – he still, amazingly, had the stripes to prove it – and he went out the back in search of my treasure. No, he told me, nothing with my name on it. Could I come back in about two weeks, after which there might have been a second delivery? Why not, I thought. I told him I had no other plans and I saw him again after a fortnight.

'No, mate,' the corporal said. 'There's only one kitbag left. Name of T. Wigg.'

I asked to see it. Like most corporals, the bloke was an idiot. The label read, very clearly, 'Pte Twigg, 1st Leicesters'. It couldn't have been more obvious. Neither could the fact that the bag was empty.

'Where's all my belongings gone?' I blurted out, furious.

'Dunno, son,' came the considered, helpful reply.

'Did it turn up like this?' I wanted to know.

'Dunno.' That corporal was a master of wit and repartee.

When I asked an officer about it, he looked at me sympathetically and said, 'Bad show, Twigg.' It was. It was possible, of course, that the Japs had rifled the bag, but they, surely, would have rifled them all and nobody else mentioned any losses. That meant that it was one of our own, a comrade-in-arms who had helped himself to my treasure. After all we'd gone through in the last four months, this was too much. These were the only times I visited the store and I wouldn't be going again. What was I going to do about it? Give up and join those sad bastards behind the bamboo? No, I was going to survive. Me, T. Wigg. The rest of them could go to hell. If they weren't there already.

It was shortly after this that I was given the opportunity of a lifetime. An officer told me to make coffee for the men after the 'gourmet dinners' we got at Tarso. I don't know what it was about me that made him see an entrepreneur, unless he knew a jack-the-lad when he saw one. He even told me how to make the stuff. He'd get me a two-gallon tin and some rice. I was to light a fire on the open ground between the huts and the river and burn the rice on a flat tin. I was then to collect river water in the two-gallon drum and boil any nasties crawling in it. The burned rice was then to be ground down and poured into the water. He also gave me a two-gallon tin of golden palm sugar paste called gula melaka to sweeten it. I was to hawk it round the camp at five ticals a mug. (The local currency was the baht, but we all used the pidgin word tical.)

One of the most bizarre things about being a prisoner of war of the Japanese was that they paid us. Having done their damnedest to kill us all week, they then proceeded to dole out cash. It was a pittance (the officers, of course, got more) but it did mean men could afford my outrageous prices. I was to give the cash to the officer the next day. And so, over the coming weeks, everybody got used to Reg 'Rosie Lee' Twigg staggering round the huts after evening pap. 'Hot Rosie Lee. Get your Rosie Lee here. Only five ticals a mug. Get it while it's hot.' It says a lot for the actual taste of the stuff and the long-suffering acceptance of POWs, that what I sold as tea was actually supposed to be coffee.

And, I'm afraid, I pulled a fast one. Apart from the MO the only time I ever dealt with an officer was when I handed over the Rosie Lee cash and I realized he had no idea how many cups I'd actually sold. So for every four, I kept one back. Was it theft? Yes. But who was making the bloody stuff, night after night, collecting water, lighting fires, grinding the mixture? And what did the officer do for his lion's share? Nothing. All right, he was the ideas man, I suppose, but for all I knew he could have been the man who nicked my chocolate and rifled my kitbag. All was fair in love and the Second World War.

On my rounds one night I heard a noise, half croak, half shuffle, above me in the trees. I was halfway between our huts and the ramshackle camp of the coolie workers, mostly Tamils and Javanese who were, in theory, paid voluntary workers on the Railway. We never mixed, even though we were all in the same hopeless boat, taking our lives in our hands on a daily basis. The shuffler overhead was a vulture, huge and vicious-beaked. I'd only seen these birds up close once before and it had unnerved me then. They circled high overhead most days over the Railway, knowing full well there'd be a chance, at least, of a meal, picking at the corpse of some poor bugger who'd fallen from the embankment or we'd been ordered to leave behind as we marched back to camp. Instinctively, I threw a stone at it, shouting at the murderous bastard to get the hell out of here. I must have hit it because it fell off the branch and floundered on the ground, its great wings spread to break its fall and to threaten me. The bloody thing must have been nearly eight feet from wing tip to wing tip and it was struggling, trying to get airborne. It didn't make it.

A handful of Javanese came scurrying out of their camp, shouting wildly and waving sticks. They beat the vulture until its hideous, terrified squawking stopped and its wings flapped for one last time. And the hunters carried their prey back to their huts. Pap the next day was supplemented in the coolie camp with meat soup and the sellers did a roaring trade.

It was food that brought us together. If I had any Rosie Lee left, I'd sell it to the Tamils and in return the Javanese made excellent peanut toffees using gula melaka. Whenever I had a few ticals spare, I'd get myself a little bag. Blue Bird they weren't, but they were very sweet, chewy and had a slightly burned flavour. And they were a welcome change to pap rice.

After a couple of weeks I was back on the track gang. But there was no return to Konyo or Konyo 2. Instead I stayed at Tarso, where groups of us went onto the railway to maintain the track. The guards were still there, of course; the beatings went on and men died. But the jungle had been cleared and there was no Konyo Kid here, nor his murderous *gunsos* to bring their own particular brand of psychosis to bear on the day's proceedings.

And as I hauled the sleepers into position one of the many memories I had was of Nappi, the brilliant barber who had shaved us all while we slept and while we were, briefly, still a battalion, back in Sungai Petani. Now my chin itched, so did my neck and cheeks. Like I said, the forties was a clean-shaven decade and too much hair in the jungle is the last thing you want. I'd long ago used up all the blades in the safety razor I'd liberated from that bus back in Singapore, so I decided to improvise. I stole an old knife from the cookhouse which we used to cut up any dried fish that didn't just fall apart from decay, and over a couple of weeks I surreptitiously sharpened the blade on the whetstone of leather belts or smooth stones alongside the track. The Japs didn't object to us having potential weapons like pickaxes and saws, but deliberately sharpening a blade until it had, literally, a razor's edge, might be misconstrued. I kept it to myself, just in case.

I don't recommend you try this at home unless you're used to a cut-throat. I boiled some water and, using my last bit of carbolic to get some sort of lather, scraped the dinner knife down my cheek. I had no mirror and it hurt a lot, but it worked. And it got noticed.

'How'd you get a shave, Twigg?' I was asked over and over again.

'Shave me, will you?' somebody asked.

And so I became the Barber of Tarso.

9

The Emperor's Murderers

I couldn't exactly hang out a shingle but word got around –
'All right, then, you lucky lot – line up at Reg's Barbers.
Something for the weekend, sir?'

I didn't charge, though I think I'd have made a small fortune if I had. It filled my time, gave me a purpose and the
little al fresco shop at the end of my hut became *the* place to
be at Tarso. I kept a tin of water bubbling over a fire and used
my fingers in lieu of a shaving brush. As long as you wet the
blade regularly, it works very well. And my fame spread even
beyond the camp. One day a Leicesters sergeant came to join
my queue. 'You the bloke doing shaves?' My face fell. In front
of me stood Blackbeard the Pirate, a huge growth halfway
down his chest. 'I'll have a go,' I told him, 'but you'd better
get something to wipe your eyes with, because this will sting
like mad.' He'd come down that day from somewhere up-
country and clearly had never heard of scissors. The only
bloke who had a pair was the MO and it seemed a bit infra dig
to ask him.

He sat bolt upright on an old gula melaka tin which
served as my Sweeney Todd chair and braced himself. 'Get
on with it,' he said. 'Never mind me.' The man may have
lost his stripes and he may have lost his platoon but he was
still a sergeant in the British Army. A crowd gathered, as
crowds always will to watch a show. The Romans would

have recognized those faces around my 'shop'. They winced and sucked in their breath for the sergeant but he made no sound at all. I felt the hair ripping out from his follicles where I hadn't cut cleanly enough and his face was red with lacerations. Even some of the Japs came to watch, carrying on a running commentary, presumably admiring the man's fortitude. Tears welled in his eyes and streaked his bloody face but he still didn't move.

'What's up, Sarge?' I asked as I dipped my knife for the last time. 'You look as though you've been crying!'

It wasn't until I finished the line that I remembered Private Daniels back at Penang and the leathering I nearly got from being flippant at his expense. I needn't have worried, though. The sergeant just said, 'Thanks,' through gritted teeth and walked away. I never saw him again.

It was some days later that a young lad came to see me. He couldn't have been more than nineteen and didn't look as if puberty had hit him yet, still less that he was in need of a shave.

'Reg,' he said, looking furtively from side to side. 'I've got a problem.'

I looked at him. 'I do shaves, mate,' I told him. 'I don't see how I can help you.' There was never a padre around when you needed one.

'Actually . . .' he saw his way in, 'I do need a shave, but it's . . . down there,' and he pointed to his Jap-happy. 'I've got crabs in my pubes. They're itching to buggery and somebody told me the only way is to shave them off.'

'Well, you can borrow the knife, I suppose,' I suggested, not liking to think of the alternative.

The lad was clearly terrified of cutting himself and without a mirror I had to agree the operation was tricky. He virtually begged me to do it for him and asked if we could go somewhere private. In the end, I cracked. I felt sorry for him. When I was his age I'd still been living with my dad and working at Snaith's and my greatest adventure was cycling to Wales. This lad was a veteran already and every bloody awful experience I'd had, he'd been through as well. There had to be rules, of course. Yes, it must be in private. But he must also tell people what I was doing, when and where. Otherwise, the prospect of me on my knees in front of a naked man . . . well, I don't have to paint you a picture.

And of course, when *that* news spread, I was called upon to run what they started calling long after the war, a 'special' clinic. I felt like a poulterer at Christmas time, plucking birds for the table. Except *these* turkeys had to move their own necks with no help from me!

I'd just come back from the Railway one day – time had become a blur by now – when I saw a group of men wandering up from the river. They'd just come from up-country and they looked like walking skeletons. I realized again what a relative life-saver Tarso was because these men were from Konyo and there, in the middle of them, was Jackie Weston. We didn't hug each other in those days. We shook hands and exchanged platitudes. I asked two particularly stupid questions – 'How are you, mate? What are you doing down here?'

He should have said, 'I'm staring death in the face, Reg. And I'm here because I've got absolutely no bloody choice.' Instead, the same old Jackie. 'Don't really know, Reg. They've just moved some of us down-country. Don't know where we're going, though.'

I saw he was carrying his haversack, so I said, 'Got any tobacco, Jackie?'

'No, Reg,' he said. 'It's all gone. Any down here?'

'I'll get you some,' I told him. 'Tide you over till you get sorted.'

That night we sat and talked. North of Konyo they'd been digging a cutting the Aussies called Hellfire Pass. It was a mountain of rock and far tougher than anything he and I had met together further south. It was so bad and the Japs had got so murderous that they had to work through the night by torchlight. Beatings had increased and Jackie had lost count of the men who died. Crosses and sleepers in the jungle.

I scrounged some tobacco from somewhere and gave three ounces to Jackie, watching over him until he fell asleep on my bed. The man had survived Hellfire Pass and even then, before the name had passed into the nation's psyche, I knew that was some achievement. What can you give to heroes like Jackie Weston? Three ounces of shag and a hard, bamboo bed. I slept on the ground outside and when I woke the next morning, Jackie had gone.

His name wasn't really Smiling Joe, of course. We never knew what their real names were, the guards in the camps. And most of us couldn't have pronounced them if we had known. He was just an average-looking bloke, younger than me, I'd say, in a shabby, ill-fitting uniform. And he was Korean.

The Koreans were browbeaten by the Japs and even though they were allies, it was obvious there was a 'them and us' situation going on. Politics; the camps were riddled with it. All the traditions and customs and hierarchy of a thousand years and we'd landed like idiots right in the middle. You didn't understand it, still less conform to it. You just kept your head down – or up if you were on the parade ground, well above the bastards' heads. You never made eye contact. You worked fast. Even in that stinking, crawling heat; you worked fast. '*Speedo! Speedo!*' It was a kind of insanity, where everything had to be done at the double.

And although the Koreans were worse than the Japs, Smiling Joe was different. He was the first human being I'd come across at Tarso and he got his nickname because whenever he was alone with us prisoners, he'd smile and try out his broken English. You get paranoid in the camps. Somehow, you got used to the physical brutality; even, after a while, expected it. The hysterical screaming in your ear; the swish of a bamboo cane hurtling through the air to rip and tear your flesh; the brain-loosening thud of a rifle butt jarring against your temple. But this was something else – a Korean guard who tried to communicate, perhaps even tried to help. Was this some sort of new torture? Something psychological the bastards were using to disorient us further?

We've all seen it now of course, hundreds of times. It's the nice cop, nasty cop routine of TV shows and bad novels. One bloke slaps you around in a police cell, the other one gives you a fag, a cup of tea and sympathy. You end up confessing to every crime in the book. Was this what Smiling Joe was – a nice policeman?

And it was policemen that Joe was talking about, the first time I learned to trust him. 'Kempei,' he whispered when the coast was clear enough, 'Kempei. They come search huts.' The Kempei were the military police, sour-faced men with armbands and attitude. The morning after Joe had passed the word, there they were, snarling and screaming, turfing us out of our beds and searching our belongings. Their bayonets jabbed through blankets and bamboo bed frames. They threw our shorts and boots – those of us who still had them – over the ground, shaking out haversacks and thrusting their sticks into the attap roof spaces. You weren't allowed to own anything in the camps. Personal possessions were confiscated. Anything hidden – family snapshots, letters, diaries, keepsakes – led to a beating. The Kempei were particularly hard on letters because they couldn't read them. And even if they could, they assumed they were in some sort of code. That's why so few prisoners kept diaries in the camps; they weren't worth a beating. Because in that climate and in those conditions, a beating meant death.

So why did Joe do it? I'd long ago learned, as we all had, not to let the Kempei find anything in our hut, but even so the man was risking his life. I'd seen it happen. Those deadly swords, the curved ones they call katanas, sweeping down from a clear blue sky to send a man's head bouncing in the dust. I'd seen it at Keppel Harbour and in every camp since. That was the risk Joe took and he knew it. Did he hate the Japs as much as we did? Was there some personal story we could only guess at which made him take the chances he did? Or was he just that all-too-rare thing anywhere in the world, really, a purely good human being?

I hope he made it home.

If there was another end of the spectrum from Smiling Joe, it was the Silver Bullet. He wasn't the Konyo Kid; he was the Konyo Kid's more psychotic big brother. Where did the name come from? His uniform shone with polished leather and metal buttons in an environment where even the guards found it difficult to keep clean and maintain parade-ground appearance. The man would kill without a second thought. He was Korean too, and by no means high-ranking, but he strutted the camp with all the megalomania that war and

prison camps bring out in some people. He might as well have
been a field marshal.

I first came across him during my first days at Tarso. I suppose you could say, in the topsy-turvy madness of the camps,
it was all my own fault. I remember we were on the parade
ground, all standing to attention as far as that was possible, a
ragged, forgotten army in sweat-stained vests, Jap-happies
and the occasional hat. Because I'd come from Konyo, I knew
the score. Keep your head up. Avoid eye contact. Don't get
yourself noticed. And I looked down at just the wrong
moment. He'd been striding past us, back ramrod straight,
eyes everywhere, and I half glanced to see if he'd gone. He
hadn't. I heard his boots crunch on the hard-baked mud as he
whirled and started screaming. Now a lot of us were looking
down. It's instinctive. To see who the target was, to see who'd
been singled out. It was me.

Your heart stops. You feel dizzy and sick. You think
you're going to piss yourself and then you feel the pain.
Something hit me in the spine and I knew it was a rifle butt.
I weighed about seven stone by this time and my bones
were jutting just below my skin. Then there was a second
thud as my legs gave way, a rifle butt to my head. My vision
was blurred, and if I actually saw twenty pairs of British
Army feet, I thought I could see forty. I could barely move
but instinct kicks in and you do. I curled up into a ball,
burying my battered head in my arms, feeling my heart
thudding like a piston-engine high in my throat. I was
waiting for more from the Bullet. Perhaps he had a reputation to uphold or a name to make on that parade ground.
Either way, a salutary lesson had been given to one of the
hopeless ones, the failures, the men who had surrendered
rather than gone down fighting in the tradition of bushido

those lunatics believed in. It could only enhance the Bullet's status.

But there was nothing else. Nobody broke ranks – that too was a beating offence. The Bullet moved on, haranguing somebody else in that high-pitched staccato rant. At the end of the parade – and God knows how long I lay there – some of the lads helped me up. After all, I had a railway to build.

How I got through that day I'll never know. It's all a blur now as one day has merged in my memory with all the others. Mud. Heat. Agonizing pain in my back and head. Dizziness and nausea. I should have gone to the hospital, but what for? The MO had nothing to give me by now but his best wishes. He would probably have recommended a lie down, but to do that, on the Railway, during a work day, I would have had to be dead.

I, at least, had learned my lesson. From that day on, at every roll call, in the presence of every guard, Jap or Korean, I kept my eyes a clear six feet from the ground, well over the head of any local I ever met in Burma or Thailand. Not everybody learned that lesson. Or perhaps they had and just couldn't take it any more. One day the Bullet was strutting his stuff as usual, looking for a hapless victim to pick on. He couldn't have been taller than four foot ten and I suppose, consciously or otherwise, it rankled that he had to look *up* into prisoners' faces, even mine. I didn't look at him, of course, but I knew he was goading us, jabbering in his alien tongue, watching every face for a sign of defiance. And then he found one.

It was as though he'd chosen the biggest man he could find; a massive, bearded Sherwood Forester stood in front of him and the Bullet suddenly smashed his fist into his face. I wanted to scream at him, 'Look, you vicious little bastard, this man is a member of one of the oldest, finest regiments in the British

Army, going back to 1741. He's probably got a wife and kids. He's certainly somebody's son. And at the very least, he's a human being. And you have no right to treat him like this at all.'

The Sherwood Forester might have been thinking broadly along those same lines, if he was thinking at all as he lost it. I saw his right fist come back and smash forwards into the Korean's face and the guard flew backwards to bounce like a rag doll in the dust of the parade ground. I've never heard silence like it. Nobody moved. Nobody spoke. I'd swear nobody even breathed. The Forester had just signed his own death warrant. He knew it. The guards knew it. We all knew it. He just stood to attention, back as straight as months on the Railway allowed it to be, staring ahead. It was quite magnificent in its way. He was saying in that one perfectly aimed punch, 'How's that for bushido, you yellow bastard?'

Then the Bullet was on his feet and the moment had gone. He was screaming at the Forester as the other guards batted our lines aside and closed in on him, clubbing him to the ground with their rifle butts. The rest of us stood to attention, backs straight, heads up, as though there was nothing more fascinating than the blue of the sky, as though a man was not being beaten to death at our feet. We all knew the score. A man was going to die because he'd loosened a few Korean teeth. If we'd all intervened at that moment, we'd all have died, along with the hospital cases and God knows how many more in other camps. That was how the system worked. The old biblical 'eye for an eye' couldn't hold a candle to these blokes.

The Forester lay curled up like I had been, until he was too far gone to defend himself. When he uncurled and just lay there, his body jumping inertly as each boot and cane and rifle butt thumped into him, I knew he was past saving. The guards hauled him upright, his head lolling backwards, his face a mask of blood. And they dragged him away.

I never saw the Forester again. I never knew his name. Just another poor bloody conscript who'd ended up in a war he never expected to have to fight. They would have dragged him, half dead, into the jungle as we still stood to attention on that bloodied parade ground. Perhaps they finished him off with bayonets and left his body for the jungle scavengers, the rats and the vultures. Perhaps they just rolled him into that God-awful, brown stinking river where he'd have been too weak to fight the current and somewhere downstream his bloated corpse would have been food for the fishes. I hope he died quickly, but I'm all too afraid he didn't. This was around the time I'd discovered my old friend Harry Barnett emaciated by dysentery but refusing to die until the Japs murdered him, the only other time I crossed the Silver Bullet. I'm afraid the Forester would have gone the same way. I suspect he probably went like Dobson's dog.

Dobson was one of those blokes you wish you'd met back in civvy street, before all this madness began. The sort of bloke you'd have gone to the football with and downed a pint with at the City Arms. He was as cheerful as you could be in a place like Tarso. Today there's a trend to write the Home Front slogan – 'Keep Calm and Carry On' – on everything from a tea-towel to a computer screensaver. Well, that's what Dobson did. Even on the day they took his dog away.

The dog was one of those mangy strays that wandered the river camps in Thailand. God knows what breed it was, if any, but the thing latched on to Dobson, perhaps sensing a kindred spirit. Dobson felt good about the animal, the way you do when a defenceless thing seems to put all its trust in you. It was a rare piece of affection in a loveless world and it slept at Dobson's feet in the hut, big brown eyes staring up at him as if Private Dobson was the most perfect thing in the world. I never spoke to Dobson about it. You didn't need to. The faithfulness said it all. The dog sat at the edge of the parade ground every morning and he was there again at night. He'd curl up at the edge of the jungle as we hammered away at the rails all day and he'd wag his tail gratefully whenever Dobson slipped him what he could spare of the day's pap rations.

The Japs, of course, didn't approve. Perhaps it was against their army regulations or their religion; I have no idea. One morning, the *gunso* told Dobson, in his broken English, to get rid of it. To be fair, Dobson tried. He shooed the thing away, threw things at it, even gave it a half-hearted kick on one occasion; but the damned thing still came back. He would creep into the hut after dark, muzzle near the ground, forelegs and shoulders hunched. The poor little bastard must have invented the word 'hangdog'. And maybe Dobson didn't try too hard to get rid of it once and for all.

So the Japs did it for him. One of the guards grabbed the dog, which cowered away from him in terror. I remember thinking, 'Go on, bite him. Get your own back.' But this was a camp dog. He'd been kicked around by humans since he was weaned off his mother's milk. Like most of us, he didn't have much fight left. The guards got into a huddle deciding what to do with the animal. After a minute or two, they broke up and one of them got a length of rope from somewhere, looping one end around the dog's chest and front legs and the other one over a tree branch. The cur just dangled there, its head hunched, its hind legs and tail trailing against the tree trunk. It struggled a little, but the rope made much movement impossible.

What happened next appals me still. The guards fixed bayonets if they hadn't already and formed an orderly queue. I couldn't look at Dobson and I knew he couldn't look away. One by one the guards charged the tree, like footballers taking penalty shots at goal. Each one of them was screaming some demented war cry, their eyes bright, their teeth gritted, their arms locked in the 'attack' position. The dog yelped the first three times the steel slid home, to be wrenched out with a deft flick of the wrist. Then it was silent, dangling there like a broken marionette. Its body was really only held together by the rope and blood was dripping down into a dark pool in the sand. When the laughing and cheering subsided and the guards had wiped their bayonets clean, I saw Dobson cross the parade ground. His eyes were brimming with tears and I thought for a moment he'd go for the guards. But that was not Dobson's way. He cradled the dog's head and loosened the rope, letting the ripped animal flop into his arms. Then he took his friend away and, with only his hands for a shovel, buried him.

People asked me when it was all over, when all this became common knowledge from the lips of those of us who came back – why didn't we fight? Why didn't you and Dobson and the others *do* something? We must have outnumbered the guards, dozens to one. It's difficult now to put into words. You're reading this in an armchair, in the comfort of your own home, and armchair soldiers for generations have pondered such things wrapped in the cotton wool of peacetime and freedom. For them it's all about statistics and logic. We in the camps didn't have those luxuries. Being a prisoner isn't just about vicious brutality, back-breaking labour, bad food and no medical facilities. It's a mindset. It saps your strength, it robs you of hope. There's nothing here but the guards, edgy, unpredictable, armed to the teeth. And there's nothing out there but the jungle, untold miles of bamboo and deadly swamp, where every other creature can kill you, if the exhausting, all-destroying heat doesn't get you first.

But of course, we did fight back. Some, like the Sherwood Forester, died for it. The rest of us carried on what today would be called civil disobedience. We dawdled if we could, made mistakes that would not be found out so that the Railway would never be finished. We swore under our breath from time to time, especially when we knew a guard couldn't understand us. 'You fucking murdering bastard, I'm going to skin you alive and stake you out over an ant hill,' and all of it in a flat, emotionless tone with a blank expression on your face. I had tried it once, and I don't actually recall what I said. I had frozen as the Japanese guard came over to me. Could he speak English? Had he understood everything I'd said or even part of it? He muttered something incomprehensible and walked away. I didn't do it again.

Then there was the monkey. There were millions of them in Burma and Thailand, all sorts of species screaming and screeching night and day. I'll swear they had day and night shifts just to make our lives even more miserable. But this one – and don't ask me what type it was – was different. It was the guards' pet. I have read since that monkeys were worshipped in old Japan so maybe this was some weird relic of that. The thing was horrible, standing two feet tall on its hind legs, its little black eyes watching everything. As soon as we'd left our hut for morning ablutions, roll call or work, it would be in there, moving like greased lightning from bunk to bunk, grabbing something and running away. It was almost as if the guards had trained the damned thing to steal. If we shooed it away, it would bare its yellow teeth and chatter, as if to say to its masters, 'Look at what these nasty white men are doing to me.' So tellings off were done sotto voce or with the odd flick of a half blanket, rather than a full-blown hue and cry.

One morning, however, the monkey appeared to have blotted his own copybook in some way and we never found out how. There was much hilarity from the guard huts and the door of one of them opened. Out strutted the monkey, harnessed to what I can only describe as a small cart, a sort of kid's toy. Had it crossed them somehow? Or was this just another example of Dobson's dog, the Japs proving their absolute power over every living creature they chose to dominate? I'm afraid we didn't have much sympathy. For days the monkey wandered the camp, chattering his complaint to all and sundry. Sometimes his cart was empty, sometimes loaded but he didn't have the know-how to undo the harness. Then one day, he didn't appear. And later we smelt the unaccustomed aroma of roast meat coming from the Jap cookhouse.

At Tarso I tried very hard to understand the mentality of the Japs and Koreans. I learned that, to Buddhists at least, the idea of reincarnation is crucial, but it depends on having lived a good and honourable life in the first place. What was good and honourable about people who killed for the sake of it, up close and personal? Many of us who fought at Singapore had killed, whatever the history books might tell you today, but that was relatively long distance, at the business end of a .303 or further, the range of a mortar or heavy gun. These men delighted in torture, of animals as well as people. What kind of culture was it that found honour and goodness in behaviour like that?

And yet. And yet. Nothing is ever black and white, is it? From time to time on the Burma Railway I personally witnessed acts of kindness and beauty that made no sense at the time and still don't make sense today. What happened on one Sunday afternoon, that God-given interlude, that day off from slavery which the Japs decided we could keep, didn't fit into any category, cruelty or kindness. It was just bizarre. This particular day we were sitting cross-legged outside our hut, the merciless sun beating down on our bare shoulders and legs and the sweat dripping from our hair. I saw him rolling towards us. He was one of the regular guards we knew well, but he was nondescript so we had no nickname for him. I couldn't quite believe it, but his careful, accentuated steps made it clear he was drunk as a lord. The problem with alcohol, of course, whatever nationality you are, is its unpredictability. There are happy drunks who will greet you like old chums and tell you their life stories. There are maudlin drunks who cry all over you while telling you their life stories. And there are dangerous, psychotic drunks who will beat you to a pulp because you are not actually listening to their life stories. We didn't expect a life story from this bloke, but a rifle butt, cane or bayonet was always on the cards.

To my horror – and that of the chap next to me – the guard made a meandering bee-line for us and grunted in broken English, 'You come me,' and he beckoned us over. We felt everyone's eyes on us as we got up and followed him towards the guard huts. No prisoner ever went near these without permission and we had no idea what was coming. He vanished inside and emerged moments later with a huge fishing net, the type you cast with weights on it for some serious fishing. 'We go,' he pointed to the river. 'We fish.'

We both looked across at our mates still sitting by the hut. In other situations, there'd have been whistles and cat-calls, cheering and attempts at witty comments. Instead, of course, there was total silence. Just rather a lot of raised eyebrows and open mouths. At the river bank, we were out of sight of the camp and there, tied to a post, was a little rowing boat. It had oars without rowlocks and was very small but the guard staggered somehow into it and we followed, the bloke with me wrestling with the mooring rope to cast us off. We wobbled like idiots for a few minutes then found our balance and the guard shouted at us. He didn't know the word for row but we couldn't make the boat move any other way so we went for it. Though the current was quite gentle we had to put our backs into it but with the lack of rowlocks and the inevitable toll of months on the Railway, we didn't exactly make much headway. The guard alternately stood or sat, shouting instructions until we were in midstream.

Then he stood up and hurled the net with all his strength, nearly losing his balance in the process. As it hit the water and the weights took it under, he reached into his back pocket and pulled out a small bottle, the Japanese equivalent of a hip flask. He uncorked it, took a swig and settled down to watch the net. Nothing. Just the endless rush of the brown water and the non-stop chorus of the jungle from each bank. Muttering what sounded pretty earthy even in a language we didn't understand, he hauled in the net and tried again. Again the net slapped the river's surface. Again he resorted to the bottle. How many times he did this I don't know, but he eventually decided this was the wrong part of the river, made rowing motions and pointed so that we tried out various other positions. When the net hit rocks or debris (the Kwai was always full of something floating) we were ordered over the side to sort it out. In fact, in that heat the water was heaven and we both made the most of it, careful to keep our mouths shut when we went under.

After about two hours of this, the great fisherman decided they weren't biting today and we rowed for shore. The guard staggered off the boat more blotto than when he'd got on. He rolled and swayed his way towards his own hut, falling over twice in the process before he waved us back to our own area.

The whole experience had been surreal. Why him? Why us? Why fish? The questions tumbled over and over in my head and they were still reeling there, unredressed, when I went to bed that night. It must have been the early hours when I woke up with a strange fluttering sensation across my stomach. I was about to look down in the half-light when a movement caught my eye and I was staring into the black, shining eyes of a rat, inches from my face. Anyone more poetic would have been reminded of the Sherlock Holmes untold story of the giant rat of Sumatra. Well, I saw the bugger and I'd be delighted to tell Mr Holmes all about it some day. As it was, I sat bolt upright, shouting and flailing my arms about. The rat was gone and the whole hut was silent. My heart travelled down from my mouth again and I decided to sleep, but with one eye open.

I survived the Railway for any number of reasons, but one of them was a stroke of luck. Don't ask me when it happened, still less why. We had no radios in the jungle, no watches, no calendars. On one particular day six of us were marched from roll call not out to the embankments and the usual back-breaking work, but to a long, low building we called the Tool Shed. We were general dogsbodies, labouring and tidying, but by contrast with the daily grind of the Railway, it was paradise. And it may have saved my life.

Not that it appeared much of a paradise at the time. Our *gunso* was a squat little Jap whose name I never knew. As with any new guard, we weren't sure what to expect. It turned out that he was old-school Japan – or was it new-school? It hardly mattered, because mindless thuggery was his religion. He was a shit, to put it in a nutshell, more obsessed than most of them with efficiency and speed. Though he spoke a little English, he didn't use it on us, not at first. He screamed and ranted if we moved too slowly, if our lines weren't straight, hitting one or all of us across the face until we'd done whatever it was he wanted.

On the second morning he lined us up and pointed to a tree about a hundred yards away. Then he astounded us by speaking English, albeit broken. 'You race there,' he said. 'Race back.' This was actually very painful, not just in a physical sense in that we were all pathetically thin and weak but because I'd always prided myself as a runner. Across the barrack square at Glen Parva, along the back streets of Leicester, in the inter-battalion sports with the Tigers, Reg Twigg was always somewhere out in front. It was little consolation that I came in the first six – there were only six of us! For three mornings we did this, shambling as best we could, touching the smooth bark and shambling back. On the fourth morning the *gunso* lined up the two worst runners and raced against them. He was back at the starting point before the lads had reached the tree. He then proceeded, I assume, to lecture us on the superiority of Japanese athleticism and, no doubt, culture; just like the Kid had after the wrestling matches at Konyo. What on earth was the point of that? Even if I could have beaten him, I wouldn't have dared because of the reprisals that would follow. What was it about their psyche, we wondered, that made them believe racing cripples was any kind of achievement at all?

Then came the morning of the terrapin. We jumped to as

usual when the *gunso* appeared outside the Tool Shed and lined up. But this morning there was no '*Curra bugero!*' In fact he ignored us. He walked across to the furnace, a small open-topped clay-and-brick charcoal oven that was kept permanently stoked, even in that sweltering heat. Under his arm he carried what looked like a terrapin, a beautiful animal with yellow and black markings. He popped it down alongside the oven and pumped the bellows like a thing possessed. The charcoal glowed red hot and the *gunso* filled a large metal bowl with water and slid it into place on a metal grille over the fire. Then he picked up the terrapin and plopped it into the water. None of us had moved and when he glanced in our direction we were all staring up at the sky. He beckoned us over. We crowded round, not quite sure what was going on. The terrapin was swimming around happily enough in the lukewarm water – it was more or less his natural habitat, after all. But as the bubbles burst on the surface and the steam rose in gusts, it was clear the terrapin was in terrible distress. It was flopping around trying to find a way out of its boiling cauldron, its mouth opening and closing in what I can only imagine were silent, agonized screams. The more it suffered, the more excited the *gunso* got. He kept up what must have been a running commentary, chattering away, pointing, jumping up and down. Then, quite suddenly, it was all over and the terrapin lay on its back, quite literally boiled alive. As though somebody had flicked a switch, the happy, smiling face of the *gunso* turned back to its usual scowl and we were shouted back to work.

But the *gunso* didn't just have it in for terrapins. He had it in for rats too. They were everywhere in the camps, scuttling through huts, rummaging around the kitchens and slop bins, nesting, I suspect, near the latrine pits. It's bred in the bone, I suppose. From the Black Death to the Piper of Hamelin to my dad's experiences in the trenches, rats hold a special terror for us. The *gunso* used to trap them in an ingenious little tunnel he'd made out of bamboo. It was a sort of cage with bait at one end – rice, of course – and as the rat scurried in through the tunnel, it dislodged a piece of wood which brought a flap down behind it. The animal couldn't get out. So far, so humane. It's more or less the sort of gadget you can buy in shops today so that the RSPCA don't get upset. Except that the *gunso* had never heard of the RSPCA and for him the fun had only just started.

One morning the trap contained the biggest rat I'd ever seen – the big brother of the one that had run across my stomach and sat on my chest a few nights earlier. It was so big its flanks were bulging between the trap's bamboo uprights. The *gunso* clapped his hands when he saw it, moving the cage about to view his catch from all angles. He disappeared into the Tool Shed and came out with a piece of bamboo, waving it in triumph and babbling in delight. We were working away in silence, ignoring him as far as possible as he whittled the bamboo to a needle sharpness with his army knife. He put the rat cage on one of the workbenches and talked to the rat, before poking it teasingly with the bamboo. The rat flinched and cowered backwards, baring its teeth. This was a great game for the *gunso* and he laughed each time he prodded, spattering the animal's fur with more and more blood. After about fifteen minutes the rat had squeezed itself into one corner of the trap and didn't seem to want to play any more. This appeared to annoy the *gunso*. Suddenly, he skewered the rat with the bamboo. It squealed so he did it again. And again. Once it was dead, he pulled it out of the cage and threw it at one of us, with instructions, presumably, to get rid of it.

Rat hunting was a sport at Tarso as it had been at Konyo. It was partly to alleviate boredom for the guards and partly to contain a real problem, the spread of disease. On certain Sundays and under the commandant's watchful eye, we all went out looking for rats. There was fierce competition involved in this as far as the guards were concerned. The *gunso* wanted to win and we were in his team, jogging along the river bank behind him to the best of our ability, looking for the horrible, black-brown things. They skulked particularly in rotten timbers; as I dislodged one, a huge rat shot out and disappeared into a gap in a hollow tree. The *gunso* at once saw the potential for torture and started grabbing handfuls of tinder and shouted at us to do the same. We stacked the stuff at the base of the tree and he set fire to it. As the tinder crackled and spat the *gunso* danced around, delighting in the flames until suddenly a smoking object came hurtling out of the tree's open top and landed at my feet. It was the rat, most of its fur burned off, and still twitching. The *gunso* knelt down, turning it over with a stick until it died. Again, he was talking to it, in low guttural tones, extolling no doubt the superiority of Japanese culture. I don't know who I felt more sorry for – the rat or the *gunso*.

In the midst of this pointless cruelty, some of us were able to find a kind of beauty and a kind of peace. If we hadn't, we'd have gone mad, joining those poor lost bastards in the compound at Tarso, who raved night and day, not knowing one from the other. I had been in the Tool Shed contingent for a few weeks and we were out collecting bamboo for firewood one day when I saw a fallen log. Most of the timber in Thailand rots if it lies on the ground long enough because of the appalling humidity but this had simply matured and it had a particularly beautiful grain. I couldn't help thinking that there should be a use for this, the possibility of making something even more beautiful out of what was beautiful already. The guard that day had a smattering of English, so I asked him if I could take the wood back to camp. He agreed, so I dragged it back (not easy when you weigh seven stone) and stashed it in the Tool Shed.

I'm no carpenter, but I'd done a bit of woodwork at school and you never forget these things, do you? I had the tools I needed and I decided to work on a chess set. I started with a pawn, one and a half inches high, whittling away in the half-light after work or whenever the *gunso* was away. In the weeks ahead I made an entire set, polishing each piece until it glowed with that beautiful grain. The tragedy was I couldn't use them. I'd always enjoyed a game of chess, but I had no board and that kind of marquetry was beyond me. One or two of the officers had them but we hardly ever saw them and anyway, in the British Army, privates didn't hobnob with the officer class in that way, so I never asked to borrow one.

With the spare wood, I made two pegboards for dominoes or crib. After the intricacies of the chessmen, this was a doddle and a little reminder of civilization that now seemed so far away and long ago.

I was working at my bench one afternoon in the Tool Shed when a Jap officer came in. We had little to do with these. Most camps were run by *gunsos* and we usually only saw officers on the parade ground when they had a speech to make. This gave me a problem. Knowing how pathological the Japanese were about respect and hierarchy, I knew I was supposed to stand up and salute; perhaps even bow. But we had also been told by the *gunso* and just about everybody else not to stop working for any reason. So I carried on. I felt him standing a little behind me, watching me work and he suddenly picked up the pegboard I'd recently finished which was on the bench next to me. I had no idea how he'd react to this. I'd made the thing with 'company' materials, using 'company' tools, more or less on the 'company' time. I'm sure there was something in Japanese Imperial Army regulations about that, let alone in the code of bushido.

'I speak English,' the officer suddenly said. And he spoke it well, too. So well in fact that I still didn't stand up. Or salute. Or bow. I just nodded.

'Did you make this?' he asked, still holding the pegboard.

'Yes, sir,' I replied.

He put the pegboard down and was thoughtful for a minute. I looked at him out of the corner of my eye. He was in his forties, I'd say, rather weather-beaten and experienced-looking, with an air of calm I'd never seen among the guards.

'Could you make an imitation of my sword?' he asked. The thing hung from his belt in a leather-covered scabbard. It was a symbol of rank and status in the Japanese Imperial Army, as it had been not so long before in the British. But I'd seen those things take heads off – they had a power and beauty of their own. Emotions poured through me. To do that would be one hell of a challenge. To do that would also be collaborating with the enemy, not in the usual daily sense of do it or you die, but almost as one friend might make something for another. Then again, why was he asking me this? And what would happen if I refused? Or if I couldn't, in the end, do a very good job?

All this came out in a single, guarded, 'I will try.'

'Good,' he said and pulled the sword out from the scabbard in one swift, deadly movement and laid it on the bench. Then he left.

Being alone with that sword gave me goose bumps. It was the most beautiful weapon I'd ever seen, designed to be gripped in both hands and the hilt was bound with brown cord pulled tightly over ivory-coloured fish skin. The blade had a curious 'wave' pattern all along its length that almost shimmered in the shed's half-light. I didn't know it at the time, but some of these wartime swords were very old, with sixteenth-century blades refitted in modern housings, carrying on an ancient Samurai tradition. I set to work in the evenings after the long days, measuring, making a template, rubbing down and lacquering until the blade was smooth. The hilt was a problem because I had to carve individual strands of cord and the stipple of the fish skin out of the solid wood. When I'd finished there was probably more work in that than in the original weapon. It wasn't a masterpiece but, given the circumstances in which I'd made it, I was proud of the thing.

At the appointed time I took it, along with the sword itself, to the officer's quarters. He came out to meet me at the door and examined my handiwork. He showed no expression. There was no smile. Neither was there any complaint. He thanked me courteously and went back inside. I waited for a while, stupidly and naively hoping for some sort of small reward. I didn't expect any ticals but a little extra dried fish would be good – we got that for catching rats. But he didn't come back out, so I left.

I often wonder if, somewhere in a Japanese home today, that wooden sword is hanging on a wall, a reminder of Grandad's service in the Japanese Imperial Army.

Men beaten to death on parade grounds, bayoneted in the jungle. Terrapins boiled alive, rats tortured with bamboo

skewers. Fishing expeditions with a drunken guard. Hours in
the half-dark whittling a copy of a sword that its owner could
use on me any second.

Welcome to the Burma Railway in the year of our Lord
1943.

10

The Flames at Tonchan

Food. It became an obsession with all of us along the Railway. It wasn't just that the endless pap rice was causing beriberi wherever you looked; it was the sheer monotony of the stuff and the tiny helpings. As I was passing the cookhouse one day I had a Damascus Road moment. Very rarely, we were given pumpkin or marrow and husks and seeds were thrown onto a heap behind the hut that had its edge to the jungle. It was just the debris that any camp throws out – at Glen Parva the slops were dumped in dustbins. But here, with the humidity and the searing sun, everything germinated and grew. So, sprouting up between the trees were pumpkin and marrow plants; the bizarre thing was that nobody else seemed to notice!

So I helped myself. Before, in the cases of the spuds at Glen Parva and the Blue Bird toffees at Aldershot, it was greed and bravado. Now it just might save my life. I took one or two, never enough to make it noticeable, and cooked them later in one of the two-gallon drums, sharing the stuff out with a few mates. I made my mind up that if they moved me on again to another camp, my first port of call would be the back of the cookhouse.

The rain, which we dreaded because it swelled the river, soaked our huts and made hacking through the clay all the more difficult, could be a godsend too. I'd long ago got into the habit of standing in it to cool off and now I collected it in a two-gallon drum and drank it rather than the boiled river water, where the taste of mud always lingered. Nobody else did this; just like nobody else cooled off in a rain shower. Maybe most people were just too British. At home you curse the rain and hide from it; you don't make it work for you.

If anybody from back home had seen me one particular evening at Tarso they wouldn't have said I'd gone native – they'd have said I'd gone mad. I was squatting at the edge of the jungle in my Jap-happy, watching a lizard. There were thousands of these in Thailand, scuttling through the under-growth with their little darting movements. They were all colours and all sizes – this one was about a foot long. But I wasn't admiring the creature's beautiful markings, bright eyes or quick movements; I was wondering how I could catch the thing and eat it. And I was still pondering this when I heard whispers in the trees. I squinted into the fast-darkening jun-gle and saw a Thai, in his fifties perhaps, wearing the flimsy clothes the locals wore. He squatted next to me, still whisper-ing and pointing at the lizard.

'Yes,' I whispered back, anxious not to frighten the liz-ard away or alert the guards to 'dinner'. I made the universal signs of hunger, licking my lips and rubbing my stomach. The Thai grinned his gappy smile, then got up. When he was in the safety of the trees, he beckoned me over. There was no one around so I followed him. He picked up some pieces of thin bamboo and stuck one in the ground, loop-ing a second piece over it. He was making a trap. With incredible speed, he hung a small string noose from one of the taut branches and started to point. His finger moved in one direction, then another. He was pointing out some-thing I'd never noticed before, for all my months in the jungle – lizard runs criss-crossing the ground. And his noose was right in the narrowest path.

He led me a few yards away and we squatted again, waiting in silence. Lizards are used to the howl of monkeys and the frog orchestra but they are wary of men. I don't know how long we stayed there and I was beginning to lose the feeling in my feet. Then there was a blur of metallic green and a large lizard hurtled along the run, straight for us. The bamboo trap snapped with a crack and the lizard was hanging in mid-air, struggling to free itself from the Thai's noose. The man grinned again, nodding with pride. Then he grabbed the spitting creature and broke its neck with a single twist. From nowhere, he produced a knife, freed the lizard from the trap and cut off its head. Then he slit its belly open and gutted it. Skinning took a little longer, but this man was a pro and it was a joy to watch his skill. By a series of signs he told me I mustn't eat this raw; it had to be cooked. I shook his hand and carried my prize back to the fire, being careful to take the bamboo trap with me.

Lizards, in case you're wondering, taste a little bit like chicken. It was marvellous that night, in the midst of all that horror, to sink my teeth into some real flesh for a change. The downside came immediately. There's not much meat on a lizard and as I licked out my own mess tin I realized I was hungrier than ever now. The meat had reawakened my sense of taste, after so long. Even so, over the months that followed I often used the Thai's trap to good effect. And if the ecologists today are aware of a sharp decline in the lizard population of Thailand in the 1940s, that will be because of me!

One thing I've learned in this vale of tears – you can't win 'em all. Trapping lizards was one thing; to bring down a fully grown steer was something else entirely. To be fair, the animal was already caught and for reasons known only to themselves the Japs gave it to our cookhouse. We'd never had fresh meat before and the news spread like wildfire. Some people were suspicious; what was this all about? Needless to say, Reg Twigg Inc. was down there before anybody else to see what I could scrounge. The animal was tied to a post, a scrawny, sorry-looking thing about the size of a donkey with huge, outsize horns and sad eyes. It had that look of resignation I'd seen on the faces of the men around me from time to time, especially the hospital cases. There was nowhere to run. No point in fighting. For the briefest of moments, I felt like one of those vultures who circled the Railway or fluttered, clicking, into the trees. Then I put the thought out of my mind and watched as one of the cooks swung a two-handed axe onto the cow's head. It grunted and slumped to the ground, eyes glazed. I wasn't certain one blow could do the job, but I suppose the cook knew what he was doing. The others were on it in seconds, slitting its throat and slicing open the stomach.

'Do you want this?' one of them asked me, holding up a piece of offal.

'I'll have it all right,' I said and grabbed it before the competition arrived. It smelt to high heaven so I dragged it to the river. It was black, bloody and slimy, about the size of a bin-liner. It wasn't until I got it to the bank I realized what it was. It was the cow's bladder, full of piss, and as I cut it open with my razor-knife, the smell was indescribable. I picked off the red maggots and rinsed the thing in that brown, muddy water. All I could think of was tripe, the off-white stuff that used to hang in butchers' shops and nobody eats any more. There had to be a way of converting this disgusting bag into food. I dragged it to the hut, sliced it up and cooked a piece in my two-gallon tin. It took about four hours and the smell, to men used to pap, wasn't bad. Even so, I noticed that nobody was circling my fire, licking their lips and jingling their ticals.

Anyway, I'd show them. If they didn't want to benefit from my culinary skills, that was their problem. I cut a piece off, blew on it, flipping it from hand to hand, and took a bite. Actually, I didn't. My teeth hit rubber. It was like chewing a tyre. I waited until nightfall, then dragged the rest to the latrine pit and threw it in.

But the latrines gave me another food source. It may have been the ammonia in the ground that made things grow there and this particular plant was a sort of large thistle with a purple flower, but no barbs. Its fruit was fleshy and in a moment of desperate hunger I picked it, boiled it and tried a bit. It was pretty tasteless, but it didn't kill me and I added it to the vegetable dish they served with dinner at the Hotel Tarso.

I don't know who arranged it or why the Japs allowed it but one day in late spring I noticed that a new clearing had appeared at one side of the camp. Blokes were sawing and hammering, building a platform out of the inevitable bamboo and bits of river driftwood.

'What's all this, then, Sarge?' I asked an NCO who had long ago lost his stripes.

'Not sure, Twigg. I think they're putting on a show.'

A show. Here, in the middle of the bloody jungle. Here, where men died slow, lingering deaths and there was never enough to eat and where vultures circled. Perhaps it was a British thing, I don't know. When we'd left home and still had the comfort of a wireless set, every Thursday night was compulsory listening. 'Can I do you now, sir?' Mrs Mopp would ask Flying Officer Kite and we all fell about with laughter. They said in 1940 that if Hitler was serious about invading us, the time to do it was half past seven on a Thursday night; the entire nation would be glued to their wirelesses. *ITMA – It's That Man Again* – was a national institution. And we'd all heard about ENSA – Every Night Something Awful – a unit which put on professional concerts for Tommies.

This was different, though. This was home grown and I didn't fancy it. I couldn't carry a tune in a bucket and of course we didn't have any instruments, not even paper and comb. I didn't do the best Robb Wilton in town, although we could all chew our fingers and mumble, 'The day war broke out, my Missus said to me . . .' And, let's be honest, I just didn't have the legs for a grass skirt. Not that that stopped some of the others. For weeks the chorus line worked on its routines, though how those blokes had the strength after work on the track all day, I didn't know. It was only slowly it dawned on me that this was *therapy*. I took refuge in ducking and diving, selling my Rosie Lee, shaving my regulars and hunting for food. These blokes put on attap skirts and high-kicked like something out of a rather strange Folies Bergère. That was their survival strategy.

Then it occurred to me. I could use this to my advantage, but I needed help. And this is where Howard Reast came in. We'd palled up some weeks earlier at Tarso and I had a plan. I'd noticed that the Japs and the Koreans were fascinated by the stage antics and wandered across to the homespun stage to lose themselves in the theatricals. A soliloquy from Hamlet didn't do much for them, but blokes in skirts with coconut shells strapped to their chests was a sure-fire winner.

'The Japs won't be about when the show's on, Howard,' I hissed out of the corner of my mouth, Changi-style. 'We can get down to the cookhouse and see what we can pinch.'

I hadn't realized that Howard might not be as keen on the

idea as I was. 'Bloody hell, Reggie,' he hissed back. 'You must be mad. If they catch us, we'll be shot.'

'Best not get caught, then.' I winked at him. I'd done this before, but a lookout wasn't a bad idea and I thought Howard was just the man. I didn't have a clue where poor old Jackie Weston was, but he wasn't here. Howard was. 'You don't have to go into the cookhouse yourself,' I told him by way of coercion. 'Just stand on the slope above it, between the huts, and whistle if anybody comes.'

Howard wasn't sure but I worked on him some more with tall tales of the goodies we might find in the cookhouse and he finally cracked. 'All right,' he said. 'But that's as close as I go, Reg. You'll get us all killed.'

And of course, he was right. Retaliate against a Jap beating; try to escape; steal anything, anything at all – those offences in particular merited the downward sweep of those bloody swords, not just for the man concerned, but for a whole load more, picked in some insane random lottery by the Japs.

What do they say in the theatre? It'll be all right on the night? Well, that night there was a bloody full moon and it lit the camp's pathways like day. Sharp shadows of the attap huts stood stark against the ground, pale in the moon's beams. But Howard and I had no time for romantic views. We had a job to do and we had to get our timing just right. The show's director – I can't remember who that was now – hadn't seen fit to give me a programme, so I had to play it, literally, by ear.

'We'll Meet Again' didn't sound right in a tenor key, and it didn't get the audience reaction we needed. I'm sure Corporal So-and-So gave it his all and there probably wasn't a dry eye in the house, but we wanted *noise*. And we wanted every Jap and Korean in the place down by that stage. 'Bless 'Em All' was more like it, especially the version the Tarso Glee Club belted out. By the time the chorus line gave their curiously convincing falsetto rendering of 'The Bells of St Mary's', we saw our moment.

I kept to the shadows as far as I could, Howard scampering in my wake. Having no boots at all was a godsend during this sort of work and we padded noiselessly to the cookhouse.

'The balls of Sarn't Major are wrinkled and crinkled,' we heard from the theatre, to the cackling delight of the whooping audience. 'Capacious and spacious as the dome of St Paul's.'

I smiled at Howard. They didn't write them like that any more.

> The crowds they do muster,
> To gaze at the cluster,
> They stop and they stare,
> At that glorious pair
> Of Sarn't Major's balls.

The roaring chorus was taken up by everybody. I wouldn't be surprised if half the Japs weren't roaring it out too.

'Balls, balls, balls / Balls, balls, balls,' ringing out on the Tarso night and echoing along the Kwai.

We backtracked past the hospital hut, careful not to be seen by the poor sick bastards who were lying there, too ill to cross to the stage and getting the fun second-hand. I left Howard on the high ground, standing on tiptoe against the dark of the trees, keeping what I hoped was an eagle eye out. There was nobody at the back of the cookhouse. A couple of Jap cooks lounged at the front, but they were looking across the parade ground at the show and didn't notice me. And they didn't notice me again when I snatched handfuls of soya beans and dried fish. Like the Blue Bird toffees, like the spuds at Kibworth – enough for your needs; not so much it would be noticed. I don't think Howard was so glad to have got anything over with for the rest of his life and we scurried into the shadows again. Just as well, because the whole camp had fallen silent now and a solitary baritone voice was singing, 'For a moon is shining on Malaya, stars are twinkling down from up above. Girls in their sarongs and kebayas, in their *kampongs* sing their songs of love.'

Both Howard and I knew that it wasn't Malay girls the lads were thinking about, but their own girls back home. The song was very sad and there'd be a lot of blokes sitting cross-legged on the ground in front of that stage who a minute ago were rocking with laughter, but would now be choking back tears. I don't know who the impresario was that night, but his timing was perfect.

I'm afraid we didn't share our spoils of war. Howard and I were the only ones with extra rations that night. How far, among all those men, could those beans and fish have gone? And after all – and, call me petty, but I couldn't forget it – one of those bastards had helped himself to the contents of my kitbag. He wasn't getting any more out of me. So it became a regular thing. Whenever there was a show on, it became for me ENSA – Every Night Something Acquired. And it worked like a dream. It wasn't always Howard with me – our paths only crossed from time to time – but he, with his Puritan streak and his terror of being caught – he was the bravest and the best.

I wasn't the bravest or the best when I cleared out the huts but I did it anyway. Whenever a unit was moved on, upriver or elsewhere, I'd be first under the attap, checking in corners, under the bamboo beds, anywhere the Kempei may have missed. Anyway, they were looking for diaries, letters, anything that might be a radio part, none of which had a street value at Tarso. A glittering cap badge might. I've no idea which unit it came from but part of it was a thistle so it had to be a Scots regiment. None of us had any rank or regimental badges left so this must have been somebody's treasure, stashed away to remind him of better days. Maybe he thought wherever he was going, he wouldn't need it. It was brass, of course, but I polished it to buggery so that it shone like gold and waited for the river traders to arrive. Usually the Japs watched our transactions like hawks; for all they knew we were trading information and in our cut-off state we were desperate for news of the 'outside'.

While negotiating for a few ropey-looking mangoes, I flashed the thistle.

'Gold,' I said.

The trader looked at it. And looked at me. I knew that in that humidity the gleam would disappear soon enough and the game would be up. He held up five fingers, one per tical. I shook my head, holding up both hands. 'Ten,' I said.

These blokes bartered for a living. And they'd been doing it since they could stand. He held up seven fingers and I had no time to argue. Any minute, a Jap guard could come our way. So I took his seven ticals and he took 'my' badge. Was it a fair trade? I don't know, but every day for the next week or so I expected the trader to come looking for me, having discovered he'd bought fool's gold. He never did. And the seven ticals? They kept me in Javanese toffee for a fortnight.

There wasn't much to laugh at at Tarso, if you don't count the shows. But you find your fun where you can because the human spirit needs it. Stop laughing and you stop living. You become a cross alongside a railway track. And there was one incident that kept us going round the campfires for days. The camp, by the summer of 1943, had become an important railway junction with four tracks running off the main line and a reception hut, a sort of waiting room, at the intersection. We were working there one day, hauling large logs into place which would be used for fuel and hut repairs. The Japs were using those little diesel trolleys I remembered seeing in silent black-and-whites at the Grace Road pictures when I was a kid, when half the New York police force seemed to be forever chasing Charlie Chaplin. On this particular day one of these came chugging down from the north manned by a single officer. He stopped the thing and went inside the hut.

We worked on, oblivious, until a terrified shout made us look up from our logs. A huge water wagon, the size of a locomotive, was rattling along the gentle gradient from the south. We got used to seeing these; they brought fresh water for the guards, though of course not for us. But this one was different. It was a runaway, rattling and bouncing on the rails with a Thai driver on the top, screaming his head off and waving his arms.

I've never seen so many skeletal, exhausted and overworked men move so fast in all my life and I was one of them. On that single track, the outcome was inevitable and we threw ourselves flat as, with a tremendous crash and roar, the water wagon ploughed into the officer's trolley and slowed slightly with the impact before carrying it on up the line. Somehow, the water-wagon driver stayed on, his legs in the air, gripping the wagon's rim like grim death. Simultaneously the Jap officer came barrelling out of the hut like a scalded cat. He stopped dead and watched as the wagon lurched on round a bend, bits of his trolley dropping with a loud clattering onto the track and the driver's hysterical screaming fading into the distance. Charlie Chaplin couldn't have done it better; the Jap officer actually took off his cap and scratched his head. If he'd twirled a little stick and waddled away, I wouldn't have been at all surprised.

As it was, forty or fifty soldiers of the king became blind and deaf. With completely straight faces, we carried on hauling the logs, until somebody couldn't bear the moment any longer and muttered, 'Nice work, you yellow bastard.' This may even have been me.

Tilley had been a huge man once, with the build of a bear. The Nippon Slimming Club, to which we all belonged, had cut him down to size, but he was oversized in a number of other ways. He had a gravel voice and his body was covered in tattoos. I remember particularly the coiling snakes writhing on his chest and curling down his arms. Around the campfire of a night he had tales to tell; he would reminisce about the girls he'd had in every port from Liverpool to Shanghai. We took it all with a pinch of salt, but one day I saw him in action – almost.

We were soaking away the cares of the day in the river stark naked when we caught sight of a Thai boat moored on the far bank. The traders came and went all the time, of course, but most families ignored us and we only ever did business with the men. In the prow of this boat was a gorgeous girl, probably late teens, and she was watching us. She seemed to be alone and Tilley had stopped talking. I looked across at him and he was standing up, the waters of the Kwai around his knees, with a pretty impressive erection in his fist.

'Aye up, Tilley,' I laughed. 'What's all that, then?'

'Just look at her, though, Twiggy.'

I did. Maybe three's a crowd or I had the evil eye, because she turned and disappeared into the small hut the families used for living quarters on the boats.

'Never mind, mate,' I said. 'Maybe that nasty swelling will go down now.'

It didn't. In fact, it got even bigger because the girl came back. This time she'd taken off her top and stood there, her beautiful breasts naked to the sky. I stood there, speechless, but Tilley was making the most of her keenness.

'Come on, then!' he shouted at her, his whole body shaking as he jerked himself.

'What are you going to do with that now?' I asked him, and, as if to compound the embarrassment of the situation, lost my footing and landed flat on my back in the shallow water. The girl was still watching Tilley's antics as she slowly buttoned her top and disappeared again. Tilley threw himself face down in the water quivering with frustration and left millions of little Tilleys in the mud of the River Kwai, muttering, 'Cock teaser.' Did I embarrass him further by re-telling the story around the campfire? Of course. And Tilley would just sit and shake his head despairingly.

It occurred to me how far we'd fallen by the summer of 1943. At home, Tilley would have gone up to the girl, bought her a drink, even – horror of horrors – asked her to dance, got to know her. Would it have ended in a roll in the hay? Quite possibly. But along the Kwai that summer, this girl was untouchable. At least it proved one thing. We were, despite everything the Japs had put us through, still men.

There was another incident, though, that was not one for the campfire. In the summer of 1943 my oppo on those bloody hard bamboo beds was Corporal Roger Curtis, a thoroughly nice bloke with a boyish face and a smooth body. Across the

aisle from us was a Liverpudlian called Basil. I'll skip his surname because these were different days and some things we
just didn't talk about. Basil was a wreck. He never joined the
queue for Reg's Barbers and seemed to love the life of a tramp.
He was just one of those blokes you have around. You nod.
He nods. Nothing more.

But one night, Basil was in an expansive mood.

'You all right, Twiggy?'

'Not bad, Basil,' I said, enjoying the nuances of his conversation.

'Wondered if you'd fancy doing me a favour?'

Ah. There had to be a reason for his sudden bonhomie.
'What's that, then?' I asked him.

'Swap beds with me,' he smirked.

'What for?' I asked, wondering whether the north-facing
aspect of his own was somehow displeasing to him.

He nudged me in the ribs. 'You know,' he grinned.

'Er . . . no,' I said, green as the jungle. 'My bed's much the
same as yours.'

He paused for a second. 'No,' he said. 'It's not that. It's . . .
you know . . . Roger.'

I happened to know that Roger was as straight as a die. He
had a wife and kids back home to prove it. *And* Roger was a
corporal. *And* homosexuality in the army was still called buggery. Come to think of it, so it was in civvy street too. They
put you in prison for that. Call me prejudiced. Call me a
bigot. I was a child of my class and my time.

'Piss off, you dirty bastard!'

Basil's face fell and he wandered away. He never spoke to
me after that.

And he never propositioned me either.

Concert parties. Men in grass skirts. Sex rearing its ugly

head. It could be a holiday camp. Except it wasn't a holiday camp. Men still died. Faces vanished. The crosses increased in number. The yelling and the rattan canes, boots and rifle butts were a daily reminder of where we were and what had happened. The Japs had won. And they were going to remind us of this every single day.

In accounts I've since read, written by men who survived the Railway, you have this strange compulsion to carry on, to pretend you're still living a half-civilized life. One example in particular sums up all the camps I knew. An Aussie artist called Ray Parkin who was a prisoner at Bandoeng wrote an illustrated book based on what he and his mates went through.

'When your ship takes you home,' he wrote, 'what will you think about? 'Twill be of the things we did; you did; they did. Things which kept us smiling, busy and kept us bearable to our fellows.'

That was what the concerts were all about. *That* was what Tilley was doing in the river. *That* was even what Basil wanted to do by changing beds with me. All part of the human condition. All a reminder that there had once been life before the Railway. And, when our ship took us home, there would be life again.

By June 1943 Tarso was overcrowded. I didn't have the same freedom to move about as I once had and the pickings were getting scarcer. So I wished for a move. A change. Some fresh challenge. And, almost immediately, I wished I hadn't.

A large group of us were moved upriver and then through the jungle to a place I think was Tonchan. You have to remember that these camps were hacked out of the undergrowth by us, the British, the Aussies and the Dutch. They had no names before we got there because they had no existence and you won't find them on any map today because they've been demolished. We were extra labour and within days we knew why we'd been sent. The death rate at Tonchan was higher than anywhere I'd been before and a basic problem was that it was not on the river. So there'd be no gentle soaking in the Kwai after a day's work and we had to haul large rusty drums of water from the river to drink and cook with. The one good memory I have of my first days at Tonchan was the little colony of weaver birds that nested along the trackway we used. Their nests hung like inverted beehives from the branches and they flew in and out through holes in the side. As always, I was looking for the angle. Beautiful birds they were, but they laid eggs in the spring and eggs were food. You never forget things like that.

In the hut near me was a bald, middle-aged bloke who looked far too old for the army game.

'Are you a regular?' I asked him.

'No,' he said, straight-faced. 'I volunteered to get away from my nagging wife and moaning kids.' He was 'Chalky' White and I'd barely got to know him when the MO paid him a visit. I woke one morning to find Chalky sitting on his bed and he had that look on his face. The attap stare. It had come on so quickly, his face drawn and pale, like a death mask. The MO took him away. It was cholera and it may have come from the coolie camp nearby, where conditions were even worse than ours.

The symptoms are grim. You throw up watery vomit, pints of the stuff. And your shit is the same consistency as the Kwai and pretty well the same colour. You can't stand because you're too weak and you can't lie down because the cramps in your stomach are appalling. Your eyes stare out of your head and you get washerwoman's hands, your skin pale and wrinkled. Even the MO has difficulty finding your pulse and pretty soon you can't speak (that's after your words are croaked and barely audible). You breathe rapidly, trying to cope with everything your body is going through, trying to make sense of it all. Your breath is icy on the warm night and there is a roaring in your ears that blocks all other sound. Worst of all, for those of us looking on helplessly, is cholera sleep. You lie with your eyes open and the eyeballs rolled up and everybody thinks you're dead but you're not. This is how Chalky went before he died two days later.

Fear hit Tonchan that day. Chalky wouldn't be the only one and we were all looking out for the symptoms. Most of us handled it with a shrug. This wasn't indifference and it wasn't 'being British'. It was resignation. If your number's up with cholera, it's up, and there's damn all you can do about it. We'd heard of cholera in other camps up and down the river and some of us had seen it. In a way, we'd all grown up with it. Every army that left the shores of Britain got it at some point. And in my great-grandad's time, there were epidemics at home, too. Even so, we had to take precautions. A corporal told me and another bloke to burn Chalky's bedding and belongings and to do so far away from the camp.

The Japs were terrified of cholera. They kept away from us and made us sprinkle a white powder between their huts and ours. God knows what this was; some sort of hysterical mumbo-jumbo, I suppose. While the epidemic raged, all of us were confined to camp except parties sent out to fetch more bamboo for the cremations of those who'd died. Of all the work I carried out along the Railway, fanning those flames at Tonchan was the worst. The MO ran things because the Japs were happy to keep away. A gang of us dug a deep, wide trench as far away from the huts as we could and we

made a grid across it of bamboo and bits of iron we were able
to salvage from the Railway. I had no idea how infectious
cholera was but since we were all drinking the same revolting
water that caused it, actually carrying a dead man wasn't
going to make a blind bit of difference. We carried the victims in their half blankets. Most of the corpses were skeletal
and didn't weigh much, but then, neither did we. I guessed
that after a month or so at Tonchan, my weight had dropped
to about six and a half stone.

We laid the dead down until the grid was full and set the
bamboo alight, while the MO or another officer said a few
words. I've never seen anything so horrible in my life. The
smell was unbelievable as what little fat was left on the bodies
spat and crackled, dropping into the trench pit. Hair frizzled
and shrank and as the bodies multiplied and we threw another
one on, arms and legs moved as the flesh dried out and tendons curled. Watching a dead man sit up in the middle of an
inferno is something not even Dante could imagine, but I saw
it; we all saw it in those trenches.

Much of my time was spent fetching more bamboo, which
I was grateful for because it got me away from the smell and
the unbearable heat and the sight of mates melting and disintegrating. I didn't count, but I know we burned more than
two hundred men at Tonchan in the space of a week.

There was no rhyme or reason to survival at Tonchan. A
bloke I'd seen in the hospital with beriberi so bad that his balls
were the size of a football made it, but the bloke I'd burned
Chalky White's bedding with ended up on the pyre.

Eventually, the outbreak subsided, as these things do. We
had no effective treatment and we still drank the same water
– although, to be fair, we were extra careful when boiling it
– but the number of cases dwindled. I still collected roof

run-off water as a better bet than the river stuff in those filthy drums.

And then, they moved us on again.

It must have been late August when we got to Rin Tin. We were back on the river now but the work was relatively light. There was no track laying, no bridge building, just mainten-ance of the line. As the Jap quarters were far away from ours, the risk of raiding their cookhouse was too great so Howard could breathe a sigh of relief. I settled for lizard trapping and even tried snakes. They made good soup; I don't recommend you barbecue them. Too many bones. When Shakespeare wrote 'Fillet of a fenny snake' in Macbeth he didn't know what he was talking about! And of course the back of our cookhouse had the usual crop of fast-growing pumpkins and marrows.

As in other camps, the Korean guards here were a breed apart. For sheer savagery I'd met nothing like them. They didn't seem to have a guiding light, a hard bastard like the Kid or the Silver Bullet, goading them on. They just did it any-way. The stinging slaps, bamboo canes that raised weals and caused tropical ulcers later, boots that broke ribs, the rifle butts that shattered skulls and loosened brains. I kept my head down.

It was at Rin Tin that we first saw signs that something was going wrong for the Japs. Lying on my bamboo at night, I began to hear the drone of distant aircraft. This didn't mean much, because it could easily have been their own Zeros. The day told a different story. We were marched up-country through the steaming jungle to what I can only describe as a train wreck. But this was no accident. There were bomb cra-ters everywhere – huge mounds of earth and rock piled up with trees shattered to matchwood. The train had been carrying Japs and POWs – we knew those God-awful cattle trucks too well. The bodies had gone by the time we arrived, but there was blood, dark and dried on twisted metal. It took us two days to drag it all away and repair the track.

I suppose we all felt it; a mixture of exhilaration and fear. Your heart thumps but your mouth is dry. You feel like pissing yourself but you've got to hold on. It was pay-back time for the Japs. The bastards who had driven us out of Jitra and Singapore, who had bayoneted nurses in hospitals and tortured so many of us to death on the Railway, were on the receiving end at last. But this, we quickly realized, would be a two-way street. Who would be at the receiving end of the reprisals if the Allies got too close and did too much damage? Us, the forgotten army.

So the morning after we'd cleared the track, it did my heart no good when the *gunso* picked me and another bloke out on the parade ground and marched us to the Jap huts. There was a shrieking sound from the yard at the back and the hairs stood up on my neck. A huge pig was panicking, charging around its pen while a couple of guards wrestled with it. As we watched, one of them drew his bayonet and cut the animal's throat. Blood spurted; the guard wasn't very good at this, unless his aim was, after all, to make the pig suffer. Its squeals were almost human and must have gone on for nearly two minutes before the blade severed its windpipe and it died. Tortured to death.

'Get bamboo for fire,' was the *gunso*'s order to us.

What this was all about I don't know. A little sign of barbarity to encourage the others? Don't forget, we can slit Englishmen's throats too? After all this time and umpteen camps, I'd stopped trying to work it out. It was November by

37. Konkuita, where the railway lines from Burma and Thailand met. 'This bend in the river was a beautiful place. I worked in a cutting near here and swam in the river. However, it was a very tough place and the guards were vicious.'

38. 'The bamboo bridge at Konkuita where I worked on the cutting in 1945. The land was waterlogged here. When the track was "upneck" in water it moved with the weight of the trains and engines sometimes jumped the lines.'

39. Train on the bridge at Tamarkan, 1945. 'We worked on this bridge. We were in the water all day long and it came up to our chest or worse. Towards the end of the war I saw it being bombed.'

40. 'Bridge over the River Kwai, 1943' by Leo Rawlings. 'This is exactly what it was like.'
(IWM ART LD 6035)

41. 'The Blondinis' by Murray Griffin. The title reference is to the famous tightrope walker. 'One slip and you were dead, though I never saw anyone fall. You could grip better in bare feet.'

42. 'Journey by Train' by Leo Rawlings. 'To start with it was closed wagons, and then the open ones towards the end. I went to Uttaradit in wagons like this. Along the track the Thais tried to flog stuff – sometimes it was allowed, sometimes not, depending on the Japs' mood.' *(IWM ART LD 6031)*

43. Bomb damage to the Kwai bridge at Tamarkan, 1945.
'I worked on the wooden bridge behind.'

44. POWs on
Liberation Day,
14 August 1945.
'We too were
laughing that day.
The men are
carrying a stretcher.
We made them out
of branches cut out
of the jungle and
any old sacking.
We used them for
all sorts of things.'

45. Free men, Rangoon, May 1945. Major McLeod, the Canadian doctor, inspects the stump of one of his patients whose leg he had to amputate.

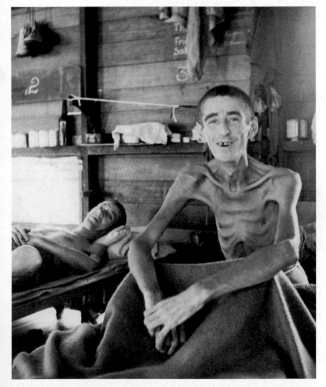

46. 'This is Jack Sharpe, who was also with the Leicesters. I never looked as bad as him. I didn't see him in the camps but we met sometime after the war and discovered that, amazingly, he only lived half a mile away.'

47. The Twiggs and the Hilliers go camping at Miller's Field, Great Glen, 1948. Cleaning up after breakfast: I am leaning over the fire next to Bob Hillier's son Bobby; Bob is shaving, with the tent behind him; my half-sisters Denise and Sheila and Bob's daughter, baby Susan, are standing in front of Bob, helping with the drying-up.

48. Me and my girlfriend Kathleen, Welsh Borders, 1949.

49. At the annual POW dinner dance, 1957: (*left to right*) my scavenging buddy Howard Reast, my wife Kathleen, Howard's wife Laura, me.

50. Albert Wingell, a friend who didn't make it back.

51. The track along the edge of the Kwai, 1944.

52. Return in 2006. 'I never wanted to see the river again after the war. I'm glad now that I went back to show my family where I'd been and say hello to some of the lads I found in the cemeteries. Life wasn't fair to them.'

53. Konyo cemetery, 1945. 'I was nearly buried there but I fought it off. If I hadn't moved down country – or downriver – when I got beriberi I would have been there. Instead I buried others before their time.'

54. 'This is the old Konyo and Hellfire Pass area. I slaved on parts of the line. Now it is 2006, but my mind sees other things.'

then and the bamboo leaves had turned to a dry, brittle yellow from their vibrant green. It was warm and I felt strangely elated. Bombed rail tracks meant they knew about us. Somebody out there had seen the Railway, knew it was Japanese and maybe who had built it. And, after all, it was a pig lying back in that pen with its throat cut, not me. So we returned with the bamboo and lit the fire and smelt the delicious, heart-aching aroma of roast pork. Did we get any, my oppo and me, for all our hard work and the huge risks we took? Of course not. There was a war on.

It was at Rin Tin that I learned to supplement my food ration another way. Sometimes the Japs fished the river using dynamite. The little explosion would stun the local fish population and we'd be sent out, swimming against the current, to collect them. The reward was one solitary fish, but it was fresh and tasted good to men still on starvation rations. Where there's a system of course, there's what today they'd call a scam, and Howard and I lit upon it soon enough. We'd wait in the bushes downstream, knowing the fishermen couldn't collect all the fish. I tied a makeshift belt around my waist with hooks I'd made from twisted wire and dipped into the water, careful to keep out of sight of the Japs upstream. I'd grab as many floating fish as I could and hang them on the hooks before Howard dragged me back up the bank. Then we lit a fire in the trees and baked away.

I suppose I was pretty cocky after all this. I was catching my fish and scrounging, when I could, my pumpkins. As wide boys go, they didn't come much wider. Actually, they did and I met one at Kinsaiyok, along the river. This was a large camp made up mostly of Australians and we'd gone, with our guards, to collect stores from there. I was just sitting on a log minding my own business during *yasumé* – actually, that's not quite true; I'd nearly shat myself because I almost landed on a scorpion again – when I heard a voice.

'G'day, Pommie, how you getting on?' He was sitting on a crate under a tree, an Aussie about my own age but in a bush hat, clean shirt and shorts, like he'd just stepped off a boat. He also looked as if he'd never missed a square meal in his life.

'About the same as anybody else who's starving,' I said.

'Like some sugar?'

My jaw dropped and I asked him if he was serious. As it turned out, he was. He took me across to his hut and hauled out a large sack from under his bed.

'How do you get away with that?' I asked him, mightily impressed. 'Don't the Kempei come and search?'

'Nah,' he shrugged. 'They've been sent up to the front to try and hold our blokes back. Heard the latest?'

I'd heard nothing for weeks. Years later, I read the accounts of other Railway survivors,who write of radios and accurate gossip. We got none of this. And if we did, how could we rely on it? 'What's that?' I asked him. 'Mafeking been relieved?'

He laughed. 'Italy's surrendered.'

I barely remember him doling the sugar into my mess tin or me packing it tight with bark and attap leaves. But I do remember looking into the man's eyes and shaking his hand. He could have passed me by. He didn't have to share his sugar and he could have demanded ticals for it. And he sure as hell didn't have to tell me about Italy. But he did. He gave me a little comfort; far more importantly he gave me hope.

II

The First Mosquito

Christmas Eve 1943. The Japs let us light larger fires than usual and we had our two days off. There was no extra food but there was, as always over Christmas, too much time to think. I'd passed my thirtieth birthday days earlier and I began to wonder if I'd see my thirty-first. Alexander the Great had conquered half the world by that age. I had some way to go! The rumours about Italy had spread like wildfire around Rin Tin when we got back from Kinsaiyok, but in a way it made things worse rather than better. On my first night back in camp, I went for a walk along a moonlit jungle trail and came face to face with a massive snake uncoiling itself across my path. I knew from experience and the thing's markings that this one was venomous and I stood stock still until it had slithered away. It makes you vulnerable, good news; you get cocksure, euphoric. I realized then that one slip, one careless move and all the good news in the world isn't going to keep you out of that hospital, from melting on a bamboo grid or rotting in the jungle leaf-mould.

Maybe that was why I went with Howard on Christmas morning to the Rin Tin cemetery. We bowed our heads and Howard said a few words. He may have been talking to God, but I wasn't. I was just remembering all the good men we'd said goodbye to over the months. It gets you like that, Christmas.

The winter nights were colder and the sun went down earlier. That meant work got a little easier and the death toll seemed to be dropping. A thick mist hung over the river until mid-morning, the lianas and tree fronds hanging limp in an eerie quiet. There is no silence in the jungle, just degrees of sound. And the place I called the Silent Forest seemed miles away and years ago. But winter mornings on the Kwai were the quietest of all. I don't know what the date was but I do remember I was sitting on my bed in the morning when I started to shiver. The weather was warm so I couldn't understand this at first. Then it dawned. It was something I'd seen so often in the past year I don't know why it came as such a surprise to me. It was malaria. One of the crosses Howard and I had stood by days ago was the one that marked the grave of a fellow Leicester, Jack Clayton. He'd had the cerebral sort of malaria, the one you don't come back from. When we turned out for roll call and a sergeant shouted, 'Any sick?' I put my hand up. Thinking about it, we should all have joined the sick parade because none of us were remotely fit. The Jap MO took one look at me and sent me back to the hut. My shakes were obviously so bad that the others noticed and laid me down, covering me with their blankets and anything else they could find.

The shakes pass. The chill goes. Then you sweat and it seems ungrateful but I was throwing off the kindly lent blankets in all directions. Every muscle in my body was aching to buggery. If you've had flu – *real* flu, not the sort you ring in sick with – you'll know a little bit of what malaria feels like. I remember thinking, I'm not going like Jack Clayton. With a bit of Kinfi-nobbleation-mira-moka-kid-comeday-mumday-all-a-mid I'm not going at all. All our MO had was quinine. Whether he knew the stuff was impure out here and could do

more harm than good, I don't know. But if he did he didn't
pass on the information to me, so, yet again, blissfully ignor-
ant in medical terms I took the two doses and got over it. The
Jap view was that a walking man was a working man, so, still
sweating buckets, I was soon back on railway maintenance
again.

Isn't it funny the things you keep with you even through the
most ghastly times? For me, it was my pipe. For an Aussie
called Joe, it was his football. How he'd kept this in an unpunc-
tured state over what must have been months, I don't know.
It wasn't exactly round any more and the leather was as dry
and cracked as our feet were. At Rin Tin we rigged up a
makeshift goal of bamboo. We only had the strength for 'penalty shoot-outs'; the thought of actually dribbling and
tackling around a field was beyond us. The Japs didn't object
to this but stood and sneered at our feeble attempts. I'm glad
we entertained them.

Joe was a brash cobber. He was itching to escape and stick
it to the Japs. We mulled it over often in the still of a Rin Tin
night, but we knew neither of us was serious. Italy may have
surrendered. *Somebody* was bombing Jap trains. But in the
jungle, the endless, singing, forbidding jungle, life went on as
it had for thousands of years. Joe invited me over to Australia,
when our ship came for us and the war was over. But I never
went. I hope he got home all right.

They moved us in groups out of Rin Tin in the January of
1944. We rode the rails we had built, praying that our slip-
shod, sub-standard work would hold at least while *we* were
on board. I'd temporarily forgotten the cattle trucks, those
steel-roofed coffins that in the summer would be too hot to

touch. The stench, the jolting, the lack of water. Everybody pissing over the side and shitting in the corner. We'd all been here before.

We had no idea where we were but the train finally squealed to a halt in one of the blackest nights I could remember. No moon. No stars. Just blackness. We were told to sleep on the ground. And in the morning we knew why. I had wrapped myself in two half blankets and some old sacks I'd liberated and tied up with a rope. When I woke, I realized what the appalling smell was that had been with us all night. We were lying in a pit of human shit, not a camp latrine because there was no bamboo grid and no trench. And the guards must have known this when they told us to lie down. Just a little friendly welcome, no doubt. We had no time to wash it off because it was '*Speedo! Speedo!*' as usual and we were off again, marching through the jungle. It could only have been a few hundred yards and we were in a clearing with several attap huts.

'When's breakfast?' some wag asked. Nobody laughed, but it was good the man still had the balls for a crack like that. There was no time for rice, the *gunso* told us. It was straight to work. Howard Reast was already there. He'd been moved up the previous day and we whispered together as we shuffled along yet another trail in some sort of semblance of a march. It crossed my mind that I couldn't even manage 'General Monckton', the Leicesters' slow march now, let alone 'Romaika' that we'd thudded out on the docks in Keppel Harbour . . . how long ago was that?

They marched us on for about a quarter of a mile and we came to a cliff face, a sheer drop down to the river where the trees grew at crazy angles on the jutting rocks. Here the Railway jutted out into nothingness, the viaduct that had once held it up now a smoking ruin. We stood open-mouthed.

Our job was to fix that. As if it was a matchbox model we could knock up before *yasumé*. And for the next few weeks, we did nothing else.

Fit men and good engineers could probably have done the work in about a week. But we had neither. What we did have – and this was the first time I'd seen them in action – was elephants. They were huge and smelly, but we all got to love them because of their size and strength. These were Indian elephants, of course, with their small, flapping ears and tiny eyes. Their hides were scarred and scabbed and tufts of hair sprouted on their bony heads. Mahouts sat on their necks like monkeys, wearing Jap-happies like us and shouting incomprehensible words of command to the great swaying beasts as they tore up virgin trees with their trunks and hauled them with chains and grappling hooks into place. These trees became the uprights of the new viaduct and God knows how elephant and man could work on those sloping rocks. Our job was to tie the crosspieces to each upright, making the kind of trestle bridge I'd seen in black-and-white westerns before the war. Photos of those very bridges were taken soon after the war and you can't believe they even stood, never mind bore the weight of a train crammed with ammo and troops.

There were no walkways or safety rails and we clung on as best we could, our soles tougher by now than any boot ever invented and with better grip. Even so, one slip and you could kiss your arse goodbye. But in all my weeks on this godforsaken venture, I never saw anyone fall.

Anybody with the vaguest knowledge of the building trade knew that this structure couldn't last. The wood was untreated and it would be a race to see whether the termites or the bombs of the Allies would get it first. We dragged huge rocks, with the elephants' help, to pack tightly around the uprights' bases and we cemented them together to form a rough platform. Even the Japs realized that this work had to be undertaken by relays of teams because in the fierce sun the cement dried so fast that your hands were cut to pieces and you needed a day doing other work to recuperate. Just opening and closing your fingers was agony and making a fist impossible.

The seating plan for *yasumé* was limited. You either sat on the blinding rocks in the full glare of the sun or you crouched in the entrance to a cave at one end of the viaduct. It was cooler here but, like every cave in South-East Asia, it was home to a bat colony. I'd come across them before, of course, and they held no particular terrors for me. Even so, disturbed by the constant noise we were making and now us slurping our rice at their lair entrance, the black bastards dived and swarmed around us as we ate. Whoever said those things only hunt at night? Probably the same battalion smartarse who once told us the Japs couldn't hit a barn door at a hundred paces. We could only take bats shitting on us buggers below for so long, and I wandered away and found a cool spot by the river. It was a bit of a climb down and would be worse getting back up, but it was worth it.

A handful of coolies had the same idea and a couple of days later we were all down there, no doubt counting the blessings we all had in life when a couple of ducks swam gabbling into view near the water's edge. Two ducks, green and brown, just asking to be popped on a spit and done to a turn.

We were all exhausted. We were all starving but one Javanese coolie was faster than me and he hit the water like a torpedo and swam for the ducks. They squawked and swam away. He was working against the current and I could see his legs and arms stop moving after a while. He'd had it and made his way back. The ducks, however, remained tantalizingly within reach, veering towards me at my lower vantage point. Now it was my turn and I was thrashing through the Kwai like a thing possessed. No doubt the ducks' strategy was divide and get away, so they did but they made the mistake of not using their wings. The one I was after flapped and floundered in the reeds by the water's edge and I lunged and grabbed it. I wrung its neck as I had with so many lizards and snakes and knelt there, wringing wet and looking forward to a real meal for the first time in God knows how long.

The bushes crashed aside and I found myself looking at the business end of an Arisaka, aiming at a point roughly between my eyes. The muzzle wavered a little as its owner extended his left hand and shouted at me. I passed the duck over. The guard grinned. 'Present tonight,' he said. And whether that meant I would get a present later or whether the duck was my present to him, I wasn't exactly sure.

But you can probably guess how that turned out.

I was lying on my bed the next day. A Sunday. One of the guards came in and asked, in rough English, for volunteers. This wasn't a usual request on the Railway and, not surprisingly, nobody moved. So he chose six, including me, and ordered us to follow him. I'd been here before, with that curious and pointless fishing expedition at Tarso. Then the guard had clearly been drunk. This one wasn't, but he was certainly behaving oddly. Wherever we were going, it wasn't an extra work detail because he led us along the narrowest jungle trails with attap leaves slapping our faces as we struggled on. He was jabbering away, to himself rather than to us, and bursting out laughing from time to time. We were climbing higher with the sun until we could look down on the viaduct, the track and the Kwai, sparkling in the morning.

'All rest,' he said and squatted down with his rifle across his knees. Because we knew he had a smattering of English, we didn't discuss the situation much and in twenty minutes we were off again. We'd reached some sort of plateau and the rocky ground was hard going, even with feet as tough as ours. Suddenly, the guard stopped, crouching and pointing to a split in a rock. It looked small at first but before we knew what was going on, the Jap had squeezed himself inside like some bloody kid following the Pied Piper. More out of curiosity than anything else, we followed too.

I've never seen anything like it, before or since. The fissure opened into a huge cave, but not the batshit-encrusted sort we all knew quite well. It wouldn't have surprised me if Aladdin had lived there once. From ground to roof, the whole place shimmered with a kaleidoscope of colour, walls of crystal reflected over and over again by myriad water droplets dripping from overhead. We all just stood there, our mouths open. None of us could find any words at all. Neither could the guard. His giggling and joking had stopped now and he beamed broadly, spreading his arms wide as if to say, 'What about that, then?'

Then we went back along the trail back to the camp. I don't even know where to start on this one. Why a Japanese soldier, whose job it was to work us to death on a railway, would want to share this quartz brilliance with us, I have no idea. I'm glad he did, but in the end it was just another moment in these lost years of madness.

This camp was called Arrow Hill, and for sheer beauty I'd seen nothing to match it in South-East Asia. The Kwai ran, foaming and roaring, through a gorge carpeted with wild orchids, and thousands of monkeys chattered in the tree canopy. There was other wildlife too and I'd have appreciated it all rather more if it hadn't always been bound up in our minds with food. One evening we'd just got back from the viaduct and the elephants were being tied up on the edge of the coolie camp when I was aware of a rush of speed beyond the huts. The guards had seen it too because half a dozen of them were suddenly on the parade ground, rifles levelled. It was a deer, maybe a sambar, and it had gone before a single shot could be fired. Venison would have been lovely but we wouldn't have seen a morsel of that and I was pleased it got away. Perhaps escape was impossible for us but it worked for the sambar and that was one victim the Japs didn't get.

The koala bear wasn't so lucky. It wasn't a koala, of course; they only have those in Australia. I've tried to find a picture of this animal since and I reckon it was a sun bear. They're black with white throats and a big adult can stand nearly as tall as me. The Japs had seen one sitting in a tree near the camp, minding its own business, and they were clearly excited about it. Even so, nobody was aiming a rifle or sharpening a bayonet. They just told us to chop the tree down. The bear looked at us as his whole world shook and echoed to our axe swings. As the tree toppled, it calmly passed along a branch to the next one and looked at us again. I didn't like the look of the thing's murderous claws and little beady eyes but you couldn't call it aggressive. On Jap orders, we took down the second tree and again, it quietly crossed to a third. Now, though, there was nowhere else to go. And as the third tree creaked and crashed, the bear just held on until it could reach the ground. We expected bayonet thrusts, throat-slittings and the smell of roasting bear.

What happened to it? The Japs put the bear in a cage and fed it bananas.

It was still the dry season and the Kwai was at the lowest I'd seen it. This was handy for teaching Howard to swim because he had a natural fear of water and being able to put his foot to the bottom, like a nervous stork, was the making of him. It also revealed a food source even I hadn't thought of: clams. We hauled them out and we cooked them in the ubiquitous two-gallon tins. Everybody knew about the risk of eating this sort of thing, even with the exotic stuff I was putting away, so Howard volunteered to try one first. Up for anything was Howard – except for raiding Jap cookhouses and deep-water swimming. He popped the off-white clam in his mouth and chewed and chewed. Minutes went by and he was still wrestling with it. In the end he gave up and pulled it out. 'I think we've managed to make rubber, Reggie!'

The green chilli bushes offered a challenge too. The peppers made your hair curl and your eyes swim. Having tried one, I was running for river water, whether it had been boiled or not. As at Rin Tin, the Jap supplies and cookhouse at Arrow Hill were too far away to raid and I was thrown back on more difficult techniques. Until you've done without salt, you haven't lived. People are paranoid about it today, claiming that we use too much of it. But people today are not building a railway in tropical temperatures. I scrounged some rock salt from a local and kept it for as long as I could, sprinkling some on the pap and licking the rest. It eases your aching joints and brings back the feeling to your exhausted muscles. After that, it was down to lizard traps and snake skinning.

I couldn't lose the memory of that Jap and the crystal cave. Something was going on and it was shredding the Japs' nerves.

This showed itself in a number of ways and, looking back, the cave experience might have been the first. The second wasn't nearly as pleasant. One of the Korean guards seemed friendlier than most and I took him to be another Smiling Joe, who had warned us all about Kempei raids back at Tarso. I'd noticed him looking at me from time to time around the camp and on the viaduct and he seemed to be pointing me out to his oppos. One day he stopped me and started talking in broken English. He gave me a fag, which I took even though I didn't smoke the things because they were currency in a camp like Arrow Hill. I said, 'Thank you,' and may even have bowed, which was his custom, not mine.

'I like you,' he said, looking me straight in the eye. 'You have good body.'

My good body weighed about six stone by now, burned to a deep mahogany by the sun and covered with sores and scabs, but I don't think the guard was congratulating me on my aesthetic appearance. Panic. Red mist. All the prejudices of my class and my upbringing. Nancy boy. Poof. All the Leicester words for men-not-as-other-men whirled in my brain. This was Basil translated into Korean. And this man had the power of life and death over me. I played dumb, bowed again and went back to work, keeping my eyes open for the guard from that moment on. I read many years later of a Highlander who was almost beaten to death for refusing sex with a Korean, so I reckon I got off lightly. And he never bothered me again. Would he have propositioned me six months earlier? Perhaps. But little examples like that made me believe that the iron grip of Nippon might just be slipping a little.

And that idea was reinforced a few days later. It was quite late and there were no lights in the camps once the fires were out so it was very dark. A lone tenor voice began to sing

'Land of Hope and Glory'. We were used to this sort of thing, especially at Christmas. But they were carols, the earliest songs most of us could remember, and they tugged at your heart strings, driving you in on yourself and inducing in the end a profound silence. This was different. It was stirring stuff. Whether you listen to the words – 'Mother of the free' – or you just react with your dinosaur brain to the tune, it's the sound of defiance. One or two joined the singer and then we all joined in, the attap reverberating with the dangerous rallying cry as if a wounded animal was about to turn.

There was a thud of running boots and screams and shouts as the *gunso* and a handful of guards crashed through the huts one by one, slapping heads and kicking lying men. 'England finished!' the *gunso* shouted. 'England finished!' And anyone still singing would be shot. It all seemed a rather hysterical reaction to a nation that was no more. But of course, the Japs being the Japs, it didn't end there, with all of us whispering the last lines under our breath. The next day, as we collapsed onto our beds after another agonizing shift, the *gunso* was there, barking in his guttural staccato that we were responsible for the singing and that someone would be punished. We were on our feet again in an instant, standing as though on parade. *Tenko*. The bastard knew how to make us sweat. He walked up and down the hut, from one end to the other and back again, looking at each of us as we stood there. Nobody returned the glance. Everybody's eyes were fixed on the attap.

'You come with me,' he suddenly growled. And he had stopped by Howard's bed. We all followed him to the hut entrance. In a film, we'd have gone out there onto that parade ground and taken the same punishment they were going to dole out to Howard. But we weren't heroes. There were some of us who couldn't even remember we were soldiers.

The guards gathered round in a cluster, blocking our view of Howard and laughing and jeering with the *gunso*. He wasn't wearing a sword so I knew that wasn't how Howard would go. But we all knew the little yellow bastards had a thousand other tricks up their sleeves.

'You will march between huts until I say stop,' barked the *gunso*. 'Go!'

Now I knew that Howard could march for England – which was in a way what he was doing now. But this wasn't Glen Parva. And he had no boots, army, for the use of. Neither, of course, did he have a rifle and pack, which in that heat, even in the evening, would have killed him. The guards' taunts and jeers turned to a stony, sour-faced silence as Howard went through his paces. He got into his stride, about-turning with a slickness I doubt the Japs had seen before. And this from a man who'd just done a twelve-hour shift on the Railway and was marching in bare feet!

After half an hour the *gunso* stopped him and Howard snapped smartly to attention, his eyes fixed somewhere above the man's head, his shoulders back and ramrod straight. Any more singing, the *gunso* said, and the punishment would be continued. We said nothing, of course, but the moral victory was ours and Howard was all but carried shoulder high around the hut.

Whatever was going on up-country from us or far out to sea, we saw it translated into action at some time during the spring of 1944. The bat cave at the far end of the viaduct became a hive of activity one day with a swarm of Japs around it. With only minimal help from us they were putting up a huge iron bar across the cave's black mouth. At first, I couldn't work this out. It looked like a rather bizarre permanent high-jump bar. Then, when one of them bashed it with his rifle butt, we all understood. The thing echoed and re-echoed through the cave and down along the river. It was a makeshift air-raid warning, doing the same job as those wailing sirens back home. The meaning was clear. The Japs expected the bombers back.

I suppose I had been at Arrow Hill for about eight weeks. The trains rattled past us every day now that the viaduct was complete and I guessed they'd move us on somewhere else soon. It was morning, hot as hell, and the sweat was dripping off my eyebrows as I hacked away next to Howard at yet another stand of bamboo. We were high on the hill under that burning sun with the Kwai slow and lazy far below us. I don't know who heard it first. I looked at Howard. He looked at me. It was an aircraft, there was no doubt about it. The drone was unmistakable and it was getting louder. 'Aircraft. Drop!' I heard myself shouting and Howard and I flattened ourselves. That probably made us larger targets for anybody in the sky, but you don't think like that. There was no jungle up here to shield us and we both knew what flying bamboo shards were like.

I couldn't make it out at first as I peered up. The sun blocked my view and I couldn't see a damned thing. Then, there it was, a twin-engined plane flying low and level along the Kwai's course. I'd never seen speed like it. Come to think of it, I'd never seen a plane like it. As it screamed overhead and banked steeply to miss the jungle-clad hills I saw the pale blue undercart and the unmistakable roundels in red, white and blue. It was the RAF. I hadn't the first clue where the buggers had been at Singapore, but they were back now. I grabbed

Howard. He grabbed me. We wanted to shout and cheer and jump up and down. There had been no gunfire from the ground. I would learn a lot later that the plane I had seen was a fighter-bomber called a Mosquito – Howard and I christened it 'Charlie' – and that pilot had flown right up the Kwai and through Arrow Hill like he owned the place.

Now, there was no mistaking the mood. The next day, a Sunday, there was a special parade and we all stood in our Jap-happies with secret smirks on our faces. The commandant wasn't so amused.

'Your British soldiers are cutting off the heads of Japanese soldiers,' he told us. 'If this continues, this is what will happen to you. Now, you will run around the camp perimeter ten times then stand on parade until you are dismissed.'

So that was our Sunday mapped out. The 'run' was a shambling walk; starving, pap-swollen men with God knows what wrong with us stumbling like the cripples we were before those of us who could still stand did so, for a full hour under that bloody sun. What kept us going, what drove dying men to go the extra mile, was what we now knew. Nobody believed the beheading story. That was propaganda bollocks. I'd seen the heads of the looters at Keppel Harbour. That was Japanese 'justice', not ours. But our British soldiers were reportedly doing it. That meant, somewhere, along those jungle trails, up that God-awful river, beyond those mountains, there was an army, a British army. And it was looking for us. We were forgotten no more.

Things always seemed to happen on Sundays. I was up to my waist in the river on that *yasumé* day, with Howard splashing desperately across, trying to stay afloat, when we heard that eerie metallic echo from the cave. Air raid! We flattened ourselves on the Kwai mud but this time 'Charlie' was so high we could barely see him and there was no chance he could see us. And two days later all hell reached Arrow Hill and Nemesis came to the Kwai. We were working at the far end of the viaduct, making everything secure. The bar clanged again and this time we all hit the earth, guard and prisoner cheek by jowl as the red soil flew in all directions. I scrambled upright and got up the scree slope as best I could. I wanted to get to higher ground because I reckoned the bridge would be the target and I'd be safer above it. And anyway, I wanted to see those beautiful roundels again. I crouched behind a rock. Below me, scattered over a wide area and in every nook and cranny the ground possessed, lay the nut-brown bodies of my oppos and a scattering of the khaki-green of the guards. The railway line gleamed like a silver snake until it vanished into the jungle's green and the river sparkled in its greasy slide to the sea.

I hadn't heard noise like this since Singapore. It started as a whine far, far away. Then it deepened to a drone and then a thunder in the skies. My heart pounded, my throat had all but seized up. For an instant, I was back in the inter-battalion races again, legs pumping through the Leicester clay, lungs threatening to burst. Then I saw them. And they weren't Mosquitoes this time. There were six of them, flying in tight formation, and they were the most beautiful sight I've ever seen. I wasn't thinking about Sylvia Cohen just then, but if I had been, I'd have honestly preferred their sleek, green-brown fuselages and soaring wings. I couldn't put a name to them then and that made them all the more deadly. They were actually Liberators, heavy, four-engined bombers, and their payload was devastating.

Like the Mosquito that had come as an advance guard days

ago, this main army followed the course of the Kwai, roaring their defiance at the useless defence on the ground. The Japs had no ack-ack guns at Arrow Hill, and they were scuttling around like ants far below me, desperately trying to turn their machine guns on the raiders. It was like pissing into the wind for all the good it did. I saw the stick of bombs tumble downwards, silent against the roar of the Liberators. One by one they hit home, splashing into the river, churning the placid water. They shattered rocks and felled trees. They smashed the viaduct — *our* viaduct — like matchwood. And each one *hurt*. You don't just hear a bomb with your ears, you feel it in your chest. The ground shakes with the thunder and you don't think you'll hear anything ever again. Your body convulses like an electric shock has shot through you, even though the craters and debris are yards away. Imagine crumbs on a table that somebody has thumped with all their force, slamming their fists down on it. That was me, being bounced along the ground as though some invisible giant was rocking the land around me.

Twice the six planes came back, banking in a wide arc and soaring into the bomb run again. And again I bounced and again my lungs felt like bursting and the viaduct went down.

We'd lost nobody. Not a single casualty. But the viaduct had had it. Now we'd find out about retaliation. If they forced Howard to march non-stop in the blazing sun just for singing a song, what the hell would they do to us now? In the event, they made us work. *Our* planes had destroyed the bridge — most of it had floated away down the Kwai. So *we* had to make good the damage. There was no *yasumé* now. Everything was '*Speedo! Speedo!*' with barked orders, hysterical screaming, slaps and kicks. We barely had six hours' sleep now before we frantically started again, the elephants ripping up more jungle and nut-brown men scampering all over the bamboo scaffolding like demented ants.

It was back-breaking and many men died in those last weeks before the new viaduct was complete. Did that matter? Of course it did. The death of a man always mattered. But it mattered slightly less – or the sense of loss was less – because somewhere up there, his shadow silhouetted on the jungle, was 'Charlie'. The first of many Mosquitoes to come.

12

The River Gypsy

Chungkai, my next enforced port of call, was a different world. As always, I had no idea why they moved us. The place was huge, with about 80 per cent British and the rest Aussies and Dutch. It was also a base hospital. Up-country we'd had to make do with a single hospital hut with beriberi cases lying alongside malaria victims. Only cholera patients, because of the Japs' fear of it, were quarantined elsewhere. At Chungkai there were different huts for different complaints, like wards in a real hospital. Much of this, I learned, was the work of a remarkable Australian MO known as 'Weary' Dunlop. He'd gone by the time I got to Chungkai but the Aussies still there might as well have built a shrine to him. You could say the huge, reeking, disinfectant-smelling water supply *was* his shrine. It smelt awful, but it was probably the safest water I drank in South-East Asia.

The river itself was hopelessly polluted. In the second half of 1944 it was very low, with all kinds of rubbish and animal carcasses rotting along its banks. A flock of vultures came every day, flapping noisily, hopping from half-drowned branch to half-drowned branch, pecking at whatever caught their eye.

Chungkai was only about a hundred miles from Bangkok, and altogether more civilized than any of the camps upriver, where the work was hardest and the guards most psychotic.

To an extent, this explains the huge variety of accounts of Railway survivors. In the diary he kept during these years, Weary Dunlop writes of amputations and an appalling daily death rate. At the same time, at Chungkai, he took part in 'sports days' and went to Schubert concerts. That was because we all found our own methods of salvation, our own ways to cope. The men who never went further up-country than Chungkai were lucky. But luck is a relative term. And for all its veneer of sophistication Chungkai was still a prison camp run by people who had no concept of humanity as we understand it.

Above all, I couldn't work on my own survival dodges down here. The size of the place was against me and without Howard (he stayed behind at Arrow Hill) I didn't have a lookout for my cookhouse raids. Even lizards were scarce – the sheer number of humans scared them away.

I was astonished, in the first couple of days I was there, to run into two survivors of Sixteen Platoon, my old unit that had fallen apart at Jitra. One of them was a lad called Thompson and he was keeping a diary. This was a dangerous thing to do. On the one hand it was vital first-hand evidence of our treatment for possible use after this madness was over; but on the other, it was not something the Japs would have tolerated. The Kempei were real bastards here, all of them Konyo Kids or Silver Bullets, and there was no Smiling Joe to warn us. One morning three of them burst into our hut, shouting and throwing our stuff in all directions as we stood to attention, focusing on the attap. I don't know what they found in one bloke's gear but it was the equivalent of a death sentence. They slapped him to the ground and hit him with their rifle butts until he was senseless. Then they dragged him out and we didn't see him again. Another disappearance in the jungle.

This was how Thompson would have gone if they'd found his diary. As it was, malaria found him first, some tiny, vicious, disease-filled mosquito. He died quickly and his diary died with him.

Another face I knew was Wiggy, the bloke I'd eaten those stolen spuds with on the Kibworth range what seemed like an eternity ago. He had malaria too, a shivering wreck with the attap stare, and I thought he didn't have long. I tried to cheer him up with Glen Parva stories and what a miserable old sod Sergeant Moore had been and Porky Crane. He couldn't eat the meat of the lizard I'd trapped so I boiled it up into a sort of broth and fed him as best I could. I doubt whether it was enough.

And I was walking by the river after maintenance work one day when I heard a voice I recognized. 'Hello, Twigg. How are you?' We both knew it was a bloody silly question but the old civilities kick in. It was Lieutenant Savage of the First Leicesters. I'd been his batman at Changi and we stood to attention to salute each other as if we'd been on the parade ground at Glen Parva. In fact, we were both skeletons with barely a stitch of uniform left and we chatted like old friends. He didn't know the Konyo Kid personally but he'd heard of him from other POWs coming downriver. 'Don't worry,' he said. 'He's had it once the war is over.' And there was a quiet confidence in the way he said it that made me believe he was right.

After a few weeks at Chungkai I was off again, this time ferried north, back to Tarso. It had been over a year, I reckoned, since I'd been here and the first thing you do is try to find your old mates. One of these was Harry Foley – I hadn't seen him since Havelock Road. He'd been downriver for most of the time and nearer to civilization and news than most of us. Under the attap that first night, he told me in hushed whispers what he knew. The Yank navy was wiping out the Japs at sea. He didn't have an accurate picture of Midway or Leyte Gulf but, with the Americans, we both knew we were talking about a new force to be reckoned with, a military and industrial giant the Japanese must have been mad to attack at Pearl Harbor. Harry had also heard that somewhere far to the north, General Slim and his Fourteenth Army were coming south through the jungle, pushing the Japs back.

All this was music to my ears, but we also knew the downside; Harry had a hundred stories about worsening Jap atrocities now that they were panicking, on the receiving end at last. We were still wrestling with this problem – 'Would the bastards just machine gun us all on the parade ground one morning?' – when somebody tapped me on the shoulder. 'I managed to worm my way into the cookhouse, Reggie. I'll meet you by the river tomorrow night. Bring you something to eat.' It was Howard Reast. The old bugger had adopted my thieving ways after all. In fact, I felt a little upstaged the next night as we sat by the Kwai in the moonlight munching the duvar, the rice and coconut-oil pancake Howard had liberated. It was good to see him again.

Howard and I chewed over old times along with the rice. And not all of it made pleasant listening. Benny Watkins, who had taught us bayonet drill and how to use a 2-inch mortar, had dug in with his company somewhere south of Jitra as the Japs advanced up-country. They were outnumbered and virtually surrounded and Benny went for them, shouting, 'Come on, then, you yellow bastards!' I chuckled. I could just hear him saying it. A sniper got him. And 'Paddy' Daniels, the big Irishman I'd so upset at Penang that he tried to rearrange my features, had gone down fighting too. At Singapore he'd gone on a recce with an officer and they hadn't come back. A patrol had found them both the next day, Daniels's body ripped with bullets. But his hands were locked around the throat of a Jap and rigor mortis still held them together in that deadly embrace.

Good men. Sold down the river by a top brass who didn't seem to know what day it was.

Places like Tarso have a timeless quality about them. Seen one, seen them all. The square, the cookhouse, the hospital, the attap huts, the foul, stinking latrines. And, gliding by for ever, that bloody, killing river. Even so, things had changed. Nobody sold Rosie Lee around the huts of an evening and the courteous officer whose sword I'd once whittled had moved on. So had the Silver Bullet and I wasn't sorry about that. In my meaner moments I imagined him pacing around in a cramped cage made of bamboo while a giant rat poked at him through the bars, just like the treatment meted out to the rodent by the Tool Shed *gunso*. Only the cemetery was different. It was probably three times the size, the crosses already rotting in the hell-heat we now took for granted along the Kwai.

I took stock, of myself and my situation. You're an entrepreneur, Reg. Get a grip, man. *Do* something. So I became the Barber of Tarso again. Nobody had any soap by now so my coconut-oil lather, my attempt to replicate Nappi's magic method, was welcome and I soon had quite a queue of an evening, chin and groin. Even so, the heart had gone out of all of us at Tarso. Maybe it was the fact that the place was still here, that despite war and rumours of war, nothing had really altered. Could this all actually go on for ever?

It was one night towards the end of the monsoon season

and the whole camp was one huge quagmire, the duckboards useless in the sucking, clinging mud. I was actually asleep despite the machine-gun raindrops hitting the attap and spattering down onto us. I suddenly heard shouts and peered out. At first I couldn't see anything but the driving sheets of rain, as though somebody was pouring a bucket from the roof. The shouts were coming from the latrine trench and somebody was in trouble. The latrines in every camp were the same and in every camp the MO put in official complaints about them. And in every camp, nothing was done. We knew all about these latrines because we'd dug them; trenches four feet deep and twenty feet long. Across the top were bamboo slats and you'd stand or crouch on these and piss and shit for England. If you could, with the various medical problems we all had. At Tarso, there were no lights other than in the Jap quarters, so I was floundering on my way, absolutely drenched, in total darkness. When I reached the edge of the trench, my blood ran cold. A bloke was half-lying up to his neck in the contents of the trench. Only when it was full were we allowed to cover it with soil and start a new trench and this one had a way to go. I can't describe the smell. The dysentery cases visited this place a dozen times a night and had nothing to wipe themselves with. Harry Barnett, who had died the year before, had been one of them. Others, too exhausted to climb out, had simply slipped into the trench and drowned.

I edged closer on my hands and knees and reached out my hand. He caught it, his whole arm covered in slimy shit and white with crawling maggots. Then he slipped and fell back. 'Hang on,' I whispered to him. 'Hang on,' and I grabbed him again, with both hands this time. I pulled, throwing myself backwards and dragging him up with me. He was covered in the stuff from head to foot and, too ill or shocked to speak, turned to walk away.

'No, no,' I told him. 'Stand in the rain. Wash it off.'

He stood there, shivering, retching and spitting to clear his mouth and nose. I held him upright, calming him as far as I could and letting that blessed rain do the work for both of us. He never spoke. I doubt he really registered what had happened. And he staggered back to his own hut. I don't even know who he was.

I spent my third Christmas as a prisoner of war at Tarso. We attended a church service and the padre led us in carols. We also set up a football pitch and anybody with any energy went through the motions. Wembley, it was not! With the introspection that season brings to men lost and far from home, I realized I had not received one single letter from my family in three years. And I hadn't written one either. It was the most miserable Christmas of my life and I lay on my bamboo listening to the festive calls of the alien jungle.

And after Christmas, they moved us on again. To Tamarkan. Other survivors whose accounts I've read say this camp was more hygienic than most, but all we saw was work and plenty of it. There were two bridges across the Kwai, one wooden, one steel, and they had both clearly been bombed. Our job was to rebuild them and so there was no break. Just '*Speedo!*' and off we went, all hands to the pumps, the halt and the lame doing their level best to keep up.

It was February 1945 and the river was low. I know because I was up to my waist in it every day, the brackish brown of the water swirling around us as we hauled on the Monkey. We were organized in gangs of fourteen pulling a rope that was attached to what looked like a maypole. This in turn was fastened to a 500-pound weight which had a hole in the centre – the Monkey. At the top of the pole a Jap guard screamed out orders at us, arms flying in all directions as he urged us on. As the Monkey screeched its way up the metal pole, the guard chanted a rhythmic counting song – '*Ichi, ni, san, shi, go.*' Once it was there it would slide downwards to thud onto a massive tree trunk that was forming a pile for the bridge's superstructure. There were dozens of these out into the river and the noise was pure bedlam with the grunting, sweating men, the croaked chanting of the guards and the thud and splash of the Monkeys. By midday, the guards were so hoarse they had to be replaced. There was, of course, no relief shift for us. We even had to shit in the river and let it float away.

The little disinfected water they gave us wasn't nearly enough, so we drank freely from the Kwai we stood in, past caring about what its contents would do to our guts. Tamarkan was alive with lizards and because the jungle had been cleared they were easier to spot. I spent hours squatting on my haunches, Thai-style, waiting, and as the bamboo sprung I'd grab the wriggling things and twist their necks or smash their heads on rocks. It actually took several to make the equivalent of a chicken drumstick but most of the blokes in my hut had a taste from time to time to relieve the monotony of the pap.

By now I was an old hand. And the most valuable – and difficult – lesson you learn is not to get too close to anybody; because they may not be around for long. With Harry Barnett and Albert Lockton it had taken its toll. When a mate dies, especially out here in the unforgiving jungle, a little bit of you dies too. So I shouldn't have palled up with a sergeant in the Norfolk Regiment. Time has robbed me of his name but he was a thoughtful, helpful soul who would probably be some sort of counsellor today. He listened for England, sympathizing, commiserating, even though he was going through the same purgatory as everybody else. The malaria got him and he died in front of me and he wasn't there to listen any more. I shouldn't have got friendly with Pickering either. He was in the Manchesters and had been a professional moaner before the war. If you'd given him a ticket home he would have complained what a long way it was to go. One of the most consistent phrases you heard in our hut, on the sighed outward breath of men looking at the ends of their tethers, was 'For pity's sake, Pick, stop moaning.' And one day, he did. Because malaria had come calling.

Sunday. *Yasumé*. The day of rest. But on this particular one we were marched to Kanchanaburi with a couple of guards to fetch supplies. We were dragging ropey old carts which, even empty, weighed a ton over the ruts of the unmade roads and our route was fringed with waist-high sugar cane. As we crossed a field of the stuff, the guard at the head of the column stopped, pointed at the cane and made a drinking motion with his hand. We couldn't understand this sudden gesture of kindness; this particular guard had never seemed friendly before. At first we hesitated, but thirst kicked in and we started snapping the stems, sucking the sweet juice from the cane. It could only have been minutes before a terrible new thirst hit us. Your mouth seizes up and your throat blisters. You can't talk except in grunts and that's how our curses came out. There was no water, just endless fields of that damned cane that had caused the thirst in the first place. The Jap guards took hefty swigs from their water bottles and laughed.

On again to *yasumé* and we threw ourselves down at the

base of an old mango tree in the middle of a field of groundnuts. I checked, but it had been stripped of fruit long ago and
the groundnuts weren't ripe yet. '*Bugero! Speedo!*' The Japs
were on their feet after a fag break and we were on the march
again. I'd promised myself I'd never risk swearing at a guard
again after the near misses of the past, but this time I lost it.
Even so, my croaked 'Bollocks!' was so inaudible that I got
away with it. I could hear the terrifying Porky Crane back at
Glen Parva and had to paraphrase for him because then we
were thinking of an altogether different enemy. 'Speak up,
lad. We don't want the Nips thinking we've gone soft now,
do we?'

There were supplies at Kanchanaburi but no water and we
trudged back even more parched than we had been on the
way out, our lips swollen and our tongues stuck to the roofs
of our mouths. All in all, just another average Sunday on the
Kwai.

We'd nearly completed the repairs to the bombed bridge
and as I was resting at *yasumé* one day I looked at it. What
the hell was the point of it all? It was obvious to both us and
the Japs that the RAF could now take out any bridge, any
stretch of line, they wanted to. Just as we had been left wondering at Singapore where the RAF had gone, so there must
be a hell of a lot of worried, exhausted Japanese soldiers
who were wondering the same thing about their air force.
And I was still sitting there, among the near-silence of
exhausted men stretched out on the ground, when I heard
that magic sound again, the distant whine of Merlin engines
somewhere in the sky. Then suddenly – and none of us had
seen him coming – 'Charlie' was there again, reconnoitring
with an awesome speed, noting the bridge and the position

of the Jap ack-ack batteries. And he was gone without so much as a rifle raised against him.

Every day as dawn crept over the jungle and the sun dappled the waters below the bridge, I'd find myself looking down the river valley wondering if it would be today. And one day, it was. We'd just finished the pap breakfast and were lined up prepared to move off for the day's labours when the hysterical clanging of the air-raid warning saw us all scatter to the trenches, to the trees, the low ground. I couldn't reach the heights from here as I had at Arrow Hill so I knew I'd be in the firing line. Keyhole technology, precision bombing, smart bombs – all that lay in the future. We all knew that once that bomb-aimer had pressed his button, it was every man for himself and the devil take the hindmost.

Craning up in the trench I could see six dots on the horizon, skimming the trees from the north. Across the river the Japs were rushing in all directions, swivelling the ack-ack guns into position and screaming at each other. 'You can kiss your arse goodbye,' I heard myself growling, even though at this range it could be my arse too. The ack-acks opened up, spitting fire into the sky, the gun crews bouncing around on the other end because those things had kicks like mules. The bombers swooped down like steel Valkyrie but they weren't collecting the souls of the dead to take to Valhalla, they were sending the Japs to whatever hell the yellow bastards believed in. Explosions rocked the jungle and flak burst in black clouds around the planes as they soared in for the kill. Machine-gun fire ripped up the ground as if some demented giant was unzipping the earth and the ack-ack fire stopped.

My face had been pressed down in the soil while all this was going on, my hands over my head. It gives you no protection at all, of course, doing that; it's just instinctive. The ack-ack batteries were smouldering wrecks, twisted smoking metal against the dark backdrop of the trees. There were bodies everywhere, Japs blown to kingdom come by the explosions and the shrapnel. For a moment there was no sound apart from the crackle of the flames. Then the bombers came back.

The first run had been to knock out the opposition and now there was none. We all knew what to expect and we were, all of us, Jap and prisoner, pressing ourselves into the ground, doing our best to become invisible. The drone of the planes was eclipsed by the roar and thud of the explosives and the earth jumped and us with it. My head and ears were throbbing with the impact, the whole of the camp and the bridge and the line trembling and collapsing as the bombs hit home.

Then . . . silence. There was no all-clear, because no one was steady enough to sound one. One by one, men clambered out of their foxholes, staring at the devastation and not quite believing it. This was worse than Arrow Hill because the casualty rate was far higher and not one, but *two* bridges had been hit. One of the spans of the steel bridge had gone completely and the wooden bridge was nothing but matchwood floating down the Kwai and two shattered stumps, one on each bank, to mark where it had been.

Of course we had to rebuild it. The demented shrieking from the Japs began at once. There were bodies to move, comrades to bury, scattered arms, legs and heads to be reunited with their original owners. It would be '*Speedo! Speedo!*' as it had been at Arrow Hill and slaps and fists and rifle butts. But as we stood there at Tamarkan that morning, with the sun not yet high in the sky, we *knew* now, rather than hoped, that there was, somewhere, an end in sight.

We just had to hope we'd be there to see it.

13

'You are now free men'

They moved us on after that bombing raid, something that became standard practice. Whether they thought we'd be provoked into some kind of revolt by what we'd seen, I don't know. But they moved us anyway.

I had never been this far south along the river system. A party of us were chosen at random to take a boat to a 'go-down' camp close to Bangkok. We all thought the name 'go-down' derived from the fact we had to go down to it, but in fact in Malay *godong* means a warehouse. Which came first? I don't know. I don't know why I was chosen either. Why did the drunk guard take me fishing? Why did the peculiar one show me his cave? Why did I survive when so many died? Since all such questions lead to this one, I'd rather not start to try to answer them.

The warehouse was one of several built along the steep banks of the river, its twentieth-century brick and tin looking odd after so much timeless bamboo and attap. The 'beds' were actually worse – hard concrete rather than a bamboo platform which at least had some spring in it. I used my battered old kitbag as a pillow and there were no rats scampering over me in the night. You can't imagine the bliss the next morning. The place had taps and I hadn't seen one of those in three years. God knows if the water came from anywhere but the river, but it looked and smelt clean and we drank it anyway.

In the warehouse, I thought I'd died and gone to heaven. There were mosquito nets by the hundred, too late for too many poor buggers who'd already gone from malaria. And there was soap. Cuticura soap. I helped myself to a couple of bars because my tiny scrap had long gone. It was impossible to reach the river because of the steep banks and concrete reinforcements but there was a pond behind the warehouse. The second afternoon I tried it out, using the soap to lather up and then lay on the grass to dry off. God, it was marvellous! Just to feel and smell clean for the first time since 1941.

A day or so later we were back on the boat again, chugging through the sluggish river for Bangkok. For nights on end now aircraft had droned over us and we'd heard the telltale thud of distant explosions. I suppose I expected to see a smoking wreck like Singapore or even the centre of Leicester, but there was no sign of damage at all. It was a heady experience, gliding between those buildings, the breeze fresh in our faces. Singapore was a cosmopolitan place with colonial Britain written all over it. Bangkok was pure Orient. The locals call it Krung Thep and it means, roughly, the city of angels. Well, I didn't see any of them but I saw practically everything else. Along the waterfront, on both sides of the river they called the Chao Phraya, rickety wooden houses, packed tightly and teeming with people, stood on stilts in the water. Sinewy boatmen, like the rickshaw coolies who took us to Lavender Street an eternity ago, plied their trade here, calling out to each other. The noise was deafening – the jungle chorus replaced by the urban. The tall, gilded galleys of some grandee slid silently past dirty diesel tugs, belching smoke and trailing barges carrying the world and his wife. Beyond the waterfront, the houses were high and graceful, scattered with pagodas painted every colour of the rainbow. Saffron-robed monks with their shaven heads and their look of peace wandered together, talking quietly. As if there was no war. As if the Burma–Thailand Railway was just the deranged nightmare of a madman and had no place in reality.

As we reached the quay I stiffened. On a patch of open ground stood a group of Japanese officers, maybe as many as fifty of them. Most wore boots and glasses and carried swords. But these weren't cadets from the Jap Sandhurst; these men looked battle-weary, as if they'd just come the way we had, from up-country. A couple of soldiers were demonstrating flame throwers, the jets of fire arcing across the space to sear and burn some hapless bales of straw. But they weren't bales of straw; they were hapless British soldiers, to me and to them. I wanted to grab that flame thrower and turn it on them, watch them writhe and disintegrate in fire. For all they'd done to us. For all they were planning to do. I wouldn't, of course, have got ten yards. A six-stone wreck in a Jap-happy. I'd have become just more flotsam in the river.

They ignored us as we started hauling logs onto handcarts before taking them the half-mile to the camp. After the Railway, this was a walk in the park. It was while we were working here that we noticed the guard's attention drift to a beautiful Thai woman. She called him over, standing tall and statuesque in her Western clothes, and they chatted. I noticed she turned her back to us, which encouraged him to do the same. Suddenly I heard a voice whisper in my ear: 'America winning the war.' It was a Thai man who carried on walking as if he hadn't seen us. The woman's chat with the guard came to an abrupt end and the pair disappeared behind the nearest building.

And we whistled as we worked, taking the logs back to camp. It wasn't 'Colonel Bogey' yet. It might only have been

Flanagan and Allen's 'Run, Rabbit, Run,' but it was *ours*. We
hadn't felt that in a long time; that sense that you still belonged
to a culture that was alive as long as you were alive. The Jap
guard glanced at the bloke who'd started it. Last year, last
month, last week, he'd have screamed at him, slapped him with
a cane or broken his jaw with a rifle butt. Now he just muttered
and turned away. Something wonderful had just happened.

There were several trips into Bangkok and several chances
to escape. We talked about it out of the corners of our mouths
as we lay on our concrete beds. We were still going through
the motions. Standing to attention morning, noon and night
on what passed for a parade ground, calling out the alien
numbers with the old precision – '*Ichi, ni, san, shi, go.*' Carrying logs on our carts. Stacking them into neat piles. But we
watched the faces of the guards by the dim lights in the evening. They were tired, edgy, scared. Yes, we could have
escaped. Perhaps. But where would we have gone? Slap-bang
into a Jap street patrol in Bangkok? Run into our old friends
the Kempei on a sightseeing tour? Despite the risks run by
the Thai couple with their exhilarating news, how could we
trust these people not to betray us? No, better to stay put
with the devil we knew.

Soon we were back on the river again, picking up more prisoners, including Howard Reast at Tarso, and chugging
further north than we'd ever been, to Konkuita. God knows
how many camps we passed or how long the journey took us.
I was still a river gypsy, a piece of flotsam after all, carried
upstream rather than down.

Konkuita was the meeting place of the railway that came
down through Burma from Three Pagodas Pass. As soon as I
saw it – and smelt it – the terrible old fears came back and

Bangkok might as well have been on the far side of the moon. The coolie camp that backed onto the jungle carried all the memories of the fires at Tonchan. Had we come so close to what we thought was freedom, only to be thrown back into all this? Our job here was to keep open a cutting that had a tendency to flood. The clay was waterlogged and the daily rains ran off the higher ground so the track was often deep in debris and water. Heavy rains distorted or sank the line completely and in teams of twelve we had to shore it up using crowbars and packing it with rock and rubble. We were hacking at the ground with what was left of our strength, carving drainage trenches and praying that the rocks above us wouldn't work loose and crash down on us. Two elephants stood swaying and tethered nearby to be used in the event of a landslip.

That was when we saw them. As a train slowed to negotiate the narrowest part of the track, we saw what it was carrying in its trucks. They were girls, some of them barely teenagers, and they giggled together when they saw us. The picks fell silent and the shovels stopped. We stared at them in stunned amazement. They were sitting in cages just like the circus animals I remembered from home, rattling their way along dusty summer roads in Leicestershire to entertain another rapt audience in yet another town. We all knew where these girls were going – up-country to the Jap front-line troops; the most rapt audience of all. Then it was '*Speedo! Speedo!*' and rifle butts thudding against aching shoulders. As the train moved off, the girls giggled again and blew us kisses.

With the monsoon in late April I could scrounge my marrow and pumpkin plants again and Howard and I used the old fish/dynamite technique we'd worked before. Konkuita was, like Arrow Hill, a place of beauty. And like Arrow

Hill, the contrast with death and ugliness was almost painful. The thought of not seeing that sky again, those trees,
the fluttering of birds in the green canopy, was a constant
torment. The mosquitoes in that killing season were appalling, whining and biting with deadly effect. And there were
many men at Konkuita who never saw the sky again or the
birds or their canopy. It was about now that I saw one of
those sights that jolts you out of yourself. Four little words,
that was all. Inconsequential, really. Four years ago, three
even, I wouldn't have given them a second thought. Abandoned in a ditch on one stretch of the line we hadn't been to
before was a small steamroller. Presumably other POWs had
managed to get hold of it to build the line and it was now
useless, rusted to a deep brown and shattered beyond repair.
The four words were hammered onto a trade plate on its
side – 'Ruston Bucyrus, Lincoln, England'. It had come a
long way from the cathedral city rising out of the fenlands.
It had come the same way I had. Was this how I was going
to end up, broken and forgotten in a ditch and far from
home?

Konkuita was the last place where the Barber of Tarso held
court. I'd kept my knife in my kitbag and was honing it one
day on a flat stone when a guard came from nowhere. He
snatched it, examined it, grunted something and gave it
back. Which was just as well for Private Frederick Worrell of
the Manchester Regiment. Fred had the old crabs problem
and I went to work on him one night by the river. I'd long
ago lost my awkwardness at doing this job but Fred was particularly hairy and maybe the guard interrupting my
sharpening had left the blade's edge not quite so sharp. Whatever the reason, Fred was sore for days afterwards and took

on a mincing gait as he went about the camp. I wasn't one of those cruel enough to wolf whistle at him.

The other thing I carried in my knapsack was my chess set – the one I'd never had a chance to use. I was passing another hut one evening when I saw two blokes playing. I stood there for a while watching and told them the story of my set. We often played after that. It's a bit like St Bruno, really. A calming sense of reality and peace. I've never understood why people think of chess as a game of war.

The guards at Konkuita were just like everywhere else. But not quite. 'Abe' was different. He was barely five feet tall, with a hooked nose, and seemed rather nervous. Maybe the Jap cause was so lost by now that they were forcing schoolboys through the ranks. Howard and I teased him mercilessly, which would literally have meant death at Konyo. He couldn't speak English, so whenever he came within earshot, we'd break into the old love song, 'A-be, A-be, A-be, my boy, what are you waiting for now? You promised to marry me some day in June. It's never too late, and it's never too soon. A-be, A-be, A-be, my boy, what are you waiting for now?'

Abe gave us a sickly grin and wandered away.

Someone else who wandered away was the Silver Bullet. He'd turned up like the proverbial bad penny and I had a nasty feeling that I'd been fated to run into this bastard again. I knew his drill of old and was careful to stand to attention on the parade ground and fix my gaze far above his head. Somebody who didn't know him so well fell for it, however. He must have looked at the Bullet funny because the next thing we all knew was shouting and a rifle butt slammed into the side of his head. The prisoner went down, heavy and dazed, in the dust. And the kicking started. Rifles were levelled at us, almost as if the other guards expected some reaction from us now. There wasn't any. And the forgotten army still stood there stock still. We'd bide our time.

I then saw something I'd never seen before and never would again. A Jap *gunso* strode over to the kicking, screaming Bullet and said something to him. The Bullet stepped back with bowed head, staring at the ground. He was clearly getting a dressing down. A little miracle along the Kwai.

June 1945 saw us back in Tarso. We were still completely cut off from the outside world and had no idea that the war in Europe had finished. VE Day was celebrated on 13 May, with political broadcasts, flag-waving and thousands of deliriously happy people dancing in war-torn streets. On the Railway it was business as usual, although the heart seemed to have gone out of the Japs. It was still '*Speedo! Speedo!*' but they were just going through the motions now. Men, of course, still died. From neglect, from dysentery, from exhaustion; that endless cycle was all part of a war that, in the end, the Japs couldn't possibly have won. I was working near a couple of guards one day and their muttered conversation and grim faces said it all. As if to explain, one of them looked at me and said, 'America very strong.' There was no emotion, just the blank expression we'd seen on the yellow bastards' faces for so long. Would it be now? Would it be today they'd line us up on the parade ground as target practice for their machine guns? Or would that be tomorrow?

We might find out at Takanun. I'd lost track of my meanderings now, up and down that bloody river. We'd only been at Tarso for a fortnight and then we were chugging north again. I had the sense here, maybe for the first time, that I wasn't going to make it. The work was maintenance but it was hard and almost pointless, as if the guards were deliberately finding ways to prolong our slavery. The lethargy I'd seen at Tarso was missing here and the guards, exclusively Korean, took a positive delight in the beatings and the intimidation.

When a sergeant told me and Howard that we were on the train the next morning with our kit, I felt a weight lift from me. The sergeant was a Leicester called Burrell and in the absence of any officers, he was our senior man. We followed him onto the cattle trucks, parched and exhausted, and rattled and swayed south-east through Konyo, Tarso and Kanchanaburi, where we met the Thai rail network. Now we were travelling north-east, but away from the river, away from the camps.

Better the devil you know. For three and a half years we'd slaved in that jungle, built and lived and died in camps at its edge, dotted along the Kwai. Now we were in open country, peering over the hot steel truck rims. Coolies laboured up to their knees in paddy fields and there were terraces of cultivated land. This was the civilized face of Thailand and very glad I was to see it. At one station where we took on water, an officer was walking a grey horse up and down the platform, and turned in the saddle to look at us. But the uniform he wore wasn't Japanese. It wasn't even Korean. It was Thai – and that, although I didn't know it at the time – was a sign of the future.

My lips were thick and swollen with lack of water but we took heart from the hamlets we rattled through where locals came out to stare at us and kids waved.

'You no wave back!' our guard snapped.

And so we rolled into Uttaradit.

It was dark as we stumbled off those trucks, dehydrated and shambling. After hours standing in those steel-roofed coffins you've almost forgotten how to walk, still less march. They walked us along a road by a river I discovered was the Nan and through a set of double gates. The place had been commandeered, like half of Thailand, by the Japs, but it had clearly once been a school. Under a lean-to to one side an old Thai man was cooking rice in a huge pot and there were jugs of the purest water I'd ever tasted. If this was Nan water, it put the stuff from the Kwai well and truly in the shade. The rice too was real; not the pap we'd barely lived on for three years, but delicious Thai-fragrant, complete with vegetables. I had seconds! Feeling like Oliver Twist and weighing about the same, I held out my bowl. 'Mr Bumble' didn't lecture me and lock me up in the cellar. He just smiled and refilled my bowl. As for the cool, wooden floor of the school that was the best sleep I'd had since January 1942.

Uttaradit was what they called in western films a one-horse town. It had a single main street lined with ramshackle wooden houses with peeling paint. It had a barber's too and I wondered whether my Tarso sideline was well and truly over. The banks of the river were too steep for us to slip into to bathe and the only time we went into town was with guards marching with fixed bayonets. Local women watched us shambling past, muttering to each other, chewing betel nuts and spitting out the juice.

One day a corporal and I were sent with a message to the local head man. We were struck by the smiling locals and even more so when, behind the Jap guard's back, they put up their fingers in the by now universal V-sign. Victory. Was that, after all we'd been through, still possible?

Much of the work was digging trenches. Shouts of '*Speedo!*' were rare here and the pace was almost leisurely. It would certainly never have done for Tarso or either of the Konyos only a few months back. Even so, the trenches were beginning to take on a sinister significance. They were more like pits, wider than any slit trench and so random in their positions that they appeared to have no strategic defence purpose at all. I started counting how many blokes we had and wondering whether all our bodies would fit into these would-be graves.

I didn't know the date at the time, but it was 14 August 1945. And I didn't know either that eight days earlier Colonel Paul W. Tibbets aboard the *Enola Gay*, a B-29 Superfortress, had dropped a uranium fission bomb nicknamed 'Little Boy' on the Japanese city of Hiroshima. 'Little Boy' packed the punch of 20,000 tons of TNT and in the appalling firestorm on the ground, 80,000 people were incinerated in minutes. The mushroom cloud had become the destroyer of worlds. All I knew was that a Japanese army unit came through Uttaradit's only street. They walked in single file, their shoulders down, their faces worn with the exhaustion of defeat. I'd seen it before – on our own faces after Jitra and again at Singapore. It was unmistakable, but it was also far too dangerous to gloat. We kept our eyes on the ground and so did they. One question was uppermost in my mind: who would fill those pits first, us or them?

The next day we'd just finished our breakfast pap when we heard a plane droning out of the morning. We all dashed for the trenches, throwing ourselves flat and covering our heads. But there were no bombs. No thuds. No explosions. No thunder in the ground that jars you to the core. I looked up. Everybody was looking up. It was raining paper; thousands and thousands of leaflets were fluttering down out of the sky, turning Uttaradit into a ticker-tape parade route. I grabbed one and read, 'The Japanese have surrendered. You are now free men and we will get in touch with you as soon as possible.'

All around me men were standing like statues, reading their bit of paper, trying to take in exactly what those prosaic words meant. There was an eerie silence. Then it was as though somebody flicked a switch. Men dropped to their knees, praying. Men laughed. Men cried. We hugged each other and danced around like madmen.

'Where's the Japs?' somebody shouted. And the hunt was on. Bare feet thudded across the old schoolroom floor; office doors were wrenched open; furniture overturned.

'They've gone,' one voice called out. Then another, 'Gone.'

Like a bad dream, like a nightmare you've lived with through the longest night. The bogeymen had gone. But in all the back-slapping, the hugging, the very British handshaking, not all of me could believe it. And for days I watched out for the hidden machine gun. And for days – or was it for years? – I heard the shout '*Speedo! Speedo!*'

I didn't envy Sergeant Burrell. The poor bugger had somehow to keep the lid on the hysteria in that camp and it can't have been easy. He said we could go into town but pointed out, as only sergeants can, the very sensible advice on the back of the dropped leaflets, which warned us not to eat or drink too much because our bodies couldn't take it. Did we take any notice? The hell we did. We ransacked the Japs' quarters, but they must have sneaked out during the night and the place was deserted.

By mid-afternoon we were as ready as we'd ever be. Most

of us had got hold of cloth scraps and had converted our Jap-happies into short kilts that would become the height of fashion – on girls, of course – twenty years later at home. Home. It was there at the back of our minds all the time but few of us talked about it. We'd lived for the moment for three and a half years, because that moment might have been our last. We couldn't – daren't – think too far into the future. Take each moment as it comes. So we walked down the main street the Japs had retreated along the day before and tried to remember how to march. Heads came up, shoulders back and arms swinging at our sides. There was a hell of a queue for the barber's and I didn't see him take any money for his work. He chattered away nineteen to the dozen as hair flew in all directions and his razor flashed through the lather. I thought I was pretty good at Tarso, but I stood outside that man's shop, stroking my smooth chin and knowing I'd just met a real master. We couldn't help sniggering – wild men of the woods were transformed by the short back and sides so beloved of the British Army. I could almost see Sergeant Major Porky Crane nodding and smiling in approval.

The food and drink we'd been specifically warned against was everywhere, even though it was obvious that most of these people were dirt poor and didn't have much for themselves. A couple of saki cups of the local toddy and most of us were rolling helpless. Howard was a case in point – at least it *looked* like Howard through my rather blurred vision. As we wandered back to the schoolhouse, he was swaying to a waltz tune and dancing with an invisible partner all the way. Nightingales were singing in Howard's head – as well as Berkeley Square – by the time we got back. In his head too, he wore a carnation in the button hole of his blazer and his Oxford bags wafted in the evening breeze. The Thai women watched him in their frozen silence, chewing the nuts, spitting the juice. Nearly time for us all to go home.

A couple of days later we were all invited to a banquet by the headman, to be held at what at home we'd call the town hall. By this time Sergeant Burrell had scrounged us some uniforms. They weren't regulation, they weren't even British, but I hadn't worn a shirt, shorts and boots for so long that they all felt very strange. Like those first days at Glen Parva, with a pile of gear taller than I was. At the veranda, the headman welcomed us and asked us, in faltering English, if we could leave our boots outside as a token of respect. 'Eat all you want,' he said, beaming with pride at the spread. In the centre of the floor was a huge rectangular cloth laden with bowls of every Eastern delicacy, including – and I knew it so well – snake. There were no courses as such, just an endless gorging as Thai women bobbed around us, helping us to bowls and filling them again as they emptied. Sergeant Burrell made a brief speech of thanks after a couple of hours and we left.

The hum of chat ended at the veranda and we all stood there in silence. Our boots had gone. Every single pair had disappeared. The headman was appallingly embarrassed, screaming and shouting at his underlings who ran around in circles looking for the boots or the people who had taken them. Nothing. So we walked back that night in our bare feet. Some things never change.

Come the day. The day we left Uttaradit and the camps and the Kwai for ever. It's impossible to try to recreate the feelings of that morning. We were shadows of ourselves. Some of us would carry the physical and mental scars of the Railway all our lives, however long they would be. And the gaps in our ranks told their own story. Of the men, *our* men, who didn't make it this far.

I snatched up what few belongings I still had and stood by the schoolhouse – our last camp. Then I did something on an impulse I have regretted ever since. I took my chess pieces and my Tarso razor out of my bag and threw them into a trench. I never looked back.

The whole of Uttaradit was there to see us off. The sarge had got us more boots from somewhere and somebody had scrounged some cloth scraps from the locals to make a rough-and-ready Union Jack to tie to the first of the two motorized railway trolleys that were going to take us south. As we climbed aboard, gabbling like kids on a school outing, a Jap unit came marching along the platform. The silence actually hurt. We couldn't believe it. Had we tasted freedom only to have it snatched away now? Was this all some sort of ghastly sick joke they were having at our expense? Then we realized they had no weapons. There was no swaggering *gunso* with a beheading katana or a Konyo Kid with a bamboo cane or rifle butt. These men were *our* prisoners now. They were herded to the back of one of the trolleys, heads down, avoiding eye contact.

I suppose we could have killed them, weighed in with fists and boots and all the hatred the years had built up. It happened elsewhere. You heard stories and you knew they were true. Men who had taken too much, minds that had snapped. And the red mist. It's a primeval thing, revenge.

But us, we were too euphoric for that. We cheered as we set off, the Union Jack flapping in the wind. We thought of home and the rest of our lives, not quite believing we had made it. The humiliation on our guards' faces said it all.

Bushido. Contempt for the vanquished. And *they* were the vanquished now. Ranged against them was the full might of whatever was left of the British Empire, the United States, the USSR and the terrible, appalling certainty of a bomb that had changed the world in a few seconds. *Now* we whistled 'Colonel Bogey'. *Now* we belted out 'Hope and Glory'. We were like victorious football fans today, drunk on winning, euphoric just to feel the wind in our faces.

How long we rattled south I don't know, but journey's end came at a place called Lopburi. On the platform an officer met us, possibly a Chindit. His uniform was sweat stained and he had a full beard. His .38 was strapped to his thigh like a gunslinger in the movies and he drew it, pointing it at the Japs. Nobody on that platform had any doubt that he'd pull the trigger if any one of the yellow bastards so much as batted an eyelid. To us he said, 'Welcome, chaps. Follow this gentleman here and he'll take you to have some food and drink and somewhere to kip down for the night.' Then he grinned. 'You're on your way home and the best of luck.'

The fairy tale went on and on. We were told to help ourselves from a table groaning with Thai food and cakes. We took our time, eating slowly and relishing every flavour, discovering all over again what real food tasted like. Days ago we'd been eating pap rice in a prison camp, still wondering whether the Japs intended us to fill those pits. Now . . .

There was a party that night. For a while we stood like idiots, wondering whose permission we had to get. The bearded officer had gone. I don't even remember seeing Sergeant Burrell but he must have been around somewhere. Howard and I wandered the rundown town as the sunset darkened into night. The strains of music, Thai and British, wafted on the warm breeze and a sound we hadn't heard for so long – laughter. Everything was going to be all right after all.

As we passed a restaurant, a little Thai man came to the door and beckoned us in. There was nobody else there and we hadn't seen tablecloths since Singapore. The Thai man spoke no English but gabbled away in his native dialect and disappeared. When he came back he was carrying two plates – of egg and chips! Not only that, but a bottle of brown sauce with HP on the label! We couldn't believe it. A little taste of England so far away. The Thai restaurateur watched us putting the meal away with a beam of satisfaction on his face. At the end I asked him, by the usual series of hand signals, for a business card. He wrote his name on the back – Hwong Sisiwan – and because he knew we had no money, the egg and chips were on the house.

I have that card still. It's battered and faded, but it's a memento of another world and a memory of one man's kindness.

14

The Road Home

The route from Lopburi to Bangkok looked like one vast ref-
ugee camp. Hundreds at first, then perhaps thousands came in
by train and boat from the up-country camps. Men who were
actually dying were staggering around, laughing and joking.
They would never see home, but the thought of it may have
been enough for them. The British Army was back, with its
red tape and its by-the-book. We were kitted out in regulation shirt, shorts and boots. The underpants felt strange after
so long in a Jap-happy and it would be weeks before I got
used to the warm comfort of socks. We could shave and
shower whenever we wanted to. The bliss of hot water on
scarred and scabby skin, yellow under beards. The end of lice,
the end of crabs. The food got more plentiful every day as the
supplies increased and nobody minded queuing up if bangers
and mash was waiting at the end of the line.

Slowly, your strength builds up. Your bones don't show
through your clothes any more and the sores on your lips,
hands and feet disappear. We weren't subject to the usual
army routines – we could come and go as we liked. And we
wrote home. A motherly corporal gave us pencils and paper.
I wrote to Dad. What I said to him I don't remember. Just
that I was alive and well, I suppose. That's all he needed to
know for now. And I expect I sent my love to Cyril, Ken,
Evelyn and the girls, the people I'd left behind. *My* people.

It was in these insane days in Bangkok with its teeming waterfront and its saffron monks and its gorgeous, unreal pagodas that I realized the world was still turning and for those who hadn't gone through the camps, nothing had changed. It was just like those fleeting visits to Bombay and Cape Town on our way out to this godforsaken place. Whenever we left the camp on the city's edge, we were mobbed by kids, boys mostly, jabbering in Thai, grinning, holding out their hands for money, trinkets, *anything*. Didn't they know what we'd been through? With our scrawny bodies, hair still scabby and bellies only now returning to normal size: did we *look* like British squaddies just off the boat from home? That didn't matter a damn to them. One of them stole my bamboo pipe, the one I'd bartered from another POW nearly a year ago. I'd lost two before that, one in the shallows as we retreated from Jitra and its replacement somewhere along the Kwai during the umpteen moves I'd made. What would the little bastard have done with it? Sold it for a pittance? Dumped it? It's little things like that that rankle. Like my Red Cross parcel. 'Bad show, Twigg.' I still heard the officer's unconcerned comment in my head. More than the cane and boots of the Konyo Kid, the loss of that pipe hurt like hell.

Over the next few days I tried to resurrect my old ball skills. I only played one game and that didn't go to the whistle. My lungs felt like broken bellows as I wheezed and hissed all over the field, missing tackles and passing like an idiot, my legs turned to jelly. I suspect the local Thai team we played against were taking it easy on us but they ran rings around us with their bare feet and we lost 5–0! I didn't play again.

In the evenings we sat around campfires in early September, talking and re-telling tales of the camps and our experiences. Tales we couldn't tell later. Tales it became too painful to recount at home. Tales that a tiny minority would commit to paper in their memoirs years later. The attap huts, the latrine trenches, the crosses and sleepers in the Silent Forest, the screaming guards and the deaths. Above all, the deaths. Men you'd never heard of became your friends because they had been the friends of the men you were listening to now. They were dead, marked by some rotting cross in the jungle, but they were there with us during those nights outside Bangkok, all the Alberts, Jackies, Jacks and Harrys, all fused into one sad ghost who would be forever at my elbow.

For us, Reveille was a nightmare of the past. No Sergeant Moore turfed out late risers from their beds. No bugle shattered the morning. And I never heard the word *speedo* again. Even so, it was hard to break the habit and I was often up at dawn as I'd always been and I'd walk the flat grounds of the camp as I'd once walked the banks of the Kwai. One morning I was wandering back when I saw everybody milling round on the parade ground. There was an excited atmosphere, chattering and laughing. There was no barking sergeant major, no ranks standing to attention with rifles at the slope. But somebody important was arriving and we were the audience. I didn't expect General Slim – although by now I knew what the man looked like with his slouch hat and lantern jaw. I didn't expect Winston Churchill either, complete with cigar and V-sign. In my heart of hearts I hoped we'd been assembled to watch the hanging of the Konyo Kid. I'd have given a year's pay to see that. Hell, I'd have acted as hangman.

A jeep growled its way through the gates with a flag floating from its bonnet. Most of us hadn't seen a white woman since Singapore and there hadn't been many of them there. And here was one, tall and elegant in a modified army uniform, standing up alongside the driver. The officers were holding us back, forming a space between us and the jeep. Her clipped accent was full of confidence. She'd done this before. I'm not sure any of us heard what she said. We were all just staring at her, open-mouthed.

'Cheerio!' she called, assuring us we'd soon be back in Blighty, and then she was gone.

'Who was that, then?' I asked, like the village idiot.

'Lady Mountbatten,' somebody said, his voice full of reverence as if she was the Virgin Mary herself.

'Right,' I said. I was none the wiser. And that in itself was a mark of just how forgotten we had been. Her husband, Lord Louis Mountbatten, was Supreme Allied Commander in the East and on 12 September he accepted the Japanese surrender in Singapore. Eight days earlier, while we all began the start of the rest of our lives, the Jap General Seishiro Itagaki had signed surrender papers on board HMS *Sussex* in Keppel Harbour, which I had last seen as a bomb site together with the lopped heads of Tamil looters on bamboo poles. But the old arrogance hadn't gone. When the British generals arrived, a cocky Jap bastard told them they were two hours late. One of them turned to him and said levelly, 'We don't keep Tokyo time here.' I couldn't help smiling when I read that years later. If the shoe had been on the other foot, the Japs would have cut the general's head off for a crack like that.

On the night before the lorries came for us, Howard and I sat around a campfire with the others for one last time. We stared into those flames, with their ghastly memories of Tonchan and the writhing cholera corpses on the bamboo spits. Then we shook ourselves free of it and took up the chorus of 'Moon Over Malaya':

You can hear Trombolini and old Serena,
Songs their mothers sang in days gone by,
From Penang to Ipoh and old Malacca
You can hear those enchanting lullabies.

The moon was bright. The night was warm. I looked at the faces around the fire. We were the lucky ones. The ones who'd made it.

'Right, lads!' I'd know a corporal's voice anywhere and I heard it the next morning. He called out a handful of names including mine. 'Get your kit together. You're off today. Get down to the gate for eleven. Good luck.'

I still didn't have much to pack. Spare shorts, shirts, socks, underpants. My new mess tin. I said goodbye to Howard. We smiled at each other and shook hands. We were it. The last two to stand together under that Eastern sun, still there by some random chance that made no sense to either of us. And then the lorry came and I was bouncing along those God-awful roads to the airport. Army lorries. I hadn't appreciated them before. Ugly, green, rattling trucks which jolted over the Thai roads and jarred every bone in your body. But as they took us out of Bangkok that September day, it was like floating on a cloud.

I'd never been close to a plane before, still less got on board one. For the record, this was a Douglas C-47 Skytrain, waiting on the tarmac with its props standing tall. Everybody called it a Dakota and while we were in the camps it had been used by the Allies to ferry men and supplies from A to B. It looked pretty battered, as though the Jap ack-ack batteries had used it for target practice from time to time, and I couldn't help noticing that a few of the windows along its fuselage were cracked. We climbed a short ladder and were on board. There were no seats, no safety harness, no pretty airline stewardess passing among us with drinks, food and duty-free goodies. It was just a naked metal tube, dark at the tail end and lit by the fuselage windows along its length. The co-pilot hauled the door closed and the engine coughed and the props roared to life as we wobbled our way along the runway.

'Welcome aboard, lads!' the pilot was shouting back over his shoulder. He was Canadian by his accent. 'You'll soon be home now. It'll be a few hours and don't worry if the old string bag bounces a bit. It'll be fine.'

The old string bag. I didn't like the sound of that and liked it even less as we gathered speed across the tarmac. It felt as if the thing was going to shake to pieces and I momentarily wondered if my brother Cyril did this for a living, in his branch of His Majesty's Armed Forces. Then my stomach hit the floor and we were airborne, the runway, the paddy fields, the jungle a hazy, misty patchwork at crazy angles below us.

I don't know how long we flew for. One bloke had his eyes shut tight virtually the whole time. What made it worse probably was that we were only flying at a couple of thousand feet – close enough to see the ground but far enough away to realize the impact on the old string bag if we dropped. And drop we did, hitting air pockets like they were going out of fashion. 'Hang on to something!' the intensely cheerful pilot would call every now and again and we scrabbled at the fuselage frame, trusting to God that he knew what he was doing.

We'd all been so keyed up about getting – and staying – airborne that we hadn't given getting back down again a thought. 'Hold your breath, lads,' the pilot shouted. 'We're going to land.' And the Dakota banked, just like I'd watched 'Charlie' do along the Kwai. Then it had seemed as if the pilot was waving his plane at us, letting us know he knew we were there. Now it seemed like *this* pilot was trying to kill us. I suddenly felt sick. Fear? Tension? You name it. The Dakota hit the ground with a bump and the wheels squealed across the tarmac, burning rubber as they went. We slowed and the fuselage tail bounced to the ground moments later.

The pilot turned, still cheerful, still grinning. 'Take care, lads. Have a safe journey.' Please God, most of us thought, let the rest of it be safer than the one we've had so far. As we crossed the tarmac, girls came tumbling out of a low brick building ahead of us. White girls, laughing in bright summer dresses. They made a fuss of us, linking our arms with theirs.

'Hello, boys. I'm Gloria.' 'I'm Jane.' 'I'm Ethel.' There was a rush of names we hadn't heard in so long. Names of our wives, our sweethearts, our mothers and sisters. They were asking us questions – our names, where we came from, how we were. They didn't ask specifically about the camps and I doubt many of us could have answered them if they had. It was light and happy and undemanding and the whole moment became a blur of colour and movement and the scent of perfume and the swaying of bodies. Just to have my arm round a girl felt good, a girl who wasn't going to negotiate a price in some dingy knocking shop along Lavender Street. These girls weren't offering sex, they were offering us the first glimpse of a normal life we'd missed for so long.

You could say I'd been a caveman for three years, living with nature, hunting in the jungle, swimming naked in the river, standing in the thunder of the monsoon rain beating on my body. I was completely tongue-tied and God knows what nonsense I must have finally babbled on that tarmac. It was like starting life again, the brick wall of civilization standing in front of me and I had to remember how to climb it.

They took us to a room where the tables were set for tea. There were tablecloths, there was bread and butter and tins of peaches and pears. English tea time. I'd almost forgotten there was such a thing. That there were green fields in the Leicestershire uplands, the magic of Great Glen and the dark comforting waters of the Cut where the heavy horses once trailed. It was overwhelming, but I wasn't there yet. Not yet.

'Where are we?' I asked one of the girls.

'Rangoon,' she smiled.

I didn't know it at the time but it was fitting we'd come here; Rangoon, in Burmese, means end of conflict. The British had been driven out of the city by the Japs in March 1942 and we'd taken it back again in May 1945. Days before we'd arrived, Jap envoys had signed the bit of paper they called the instrument of surrender of all their forces in Burma.

After a couple of hours we were off again, to smiles and 'good lucks' and back into army trucks that took us to what must have been a hospital, though there was no sign outside. I remembered those frustrating days in the Alexandra Hospital in Singapore, how they'd kept us there after the retreat from Jitra when there had been nothing wrong with us. Now, there was everything wrong with us. Nobody could pass for fit. It was just a matter of degree.

There were POWs here from all over South-East Asia, the battered remnants of an army Churchill had said was an army no more. Yet here we were, still standing. There were Leicesters there I hadn't seen for years. We shook hands, perhaps two, to emphasize our delight at seeing each other again. Nobody cried, nobody threw their arms round each other. We all came from the stiff-upper-lip generation after all and we were British. Crying, as all the men who were boys when I was a boy would say, is for girls. Ginger Hallam was there and the last time I'd seen him we were smoking Reg Twigg's Own Tobacco in a bamboo pipe at Konyo, dreaming of St Bruno. His rice-bloated belly had gone now and we had our pipes again. I'd been able to replace the one nicked by the Thai lad and we sat in the hospital grounds that night, blowing smoke rings to the unbelievable sunset and talking about the men who were no longer with us.

On an impulse we went to the pictures, in a clapped-out old building on the edge of town. I'd forgotten what this was like. Even though there was no gold-braided commissionaire and the one-and-ninepenny seats weren't as comfortable as I remembered them, this too was a reminder of civilization. Ginger and I fell about at the antics of Cary Grant, his dotty old aunts and the cousin who thought he was President Roosevelt in *Arsenic and Old Lace*.

After the show Sergeant King joined us and as we walked back to the hospital barracks he asked me if I'd heard the latest song from Blighty. It was called 'Yours', and even though the sarge wasn't exactly Vera Lynn, he gave it a fair old bash on that balmy Rangoon night:

> Yours 'til the stars lose their glory!
> Yours 'til the birds fail to sing!
> Yours 'til the end of life's story,
> This pledge to you, dear, I bring.

I loved this. I had no girl to pledge anything to, but the tune and the lyrics were so right I asked King to write the words down for me. And he did. 'The end of life's story'. For Sergeant King, for Ginger Hallam and for me, that wouldn't be just yet.

We weren't allowed into the heart of the city. As so often happens when a hard regime is overthrown, the new freedoms get out of hand and the place was swarming with pick-pockets, criminal gangs and political agitators who would probably make short work of underweight ex-prisoners of war who had forgotten which end of a rifle was which.

I wrote home, to my brother Ken in Leicester, and hoped to hear something back from him, Dad, *somebody*. Nothing came. It must have been two weeks later that we set off in lorries again, rattling to the docks. We'd got money in our pockets – pounds, shillings and pence rather than the ticals of the camps – and they put us on board a Dutch liner, the SS *Boissevain*. Like many wartime transports, this one had seen better days, but it was very like the *Duchess* we'd come out on. The difference – and it was a big one – was the routine. There wasn't one. On the *Duchess* it had been PT, Swedish drill, jumping up and down in readiness for whoever we'd be fighting wherever it was we were going. That and being hosed down by the navy as we slept up on deck, unaccustomed to the new heat. Now we lounged on the decks all the time, feet up on the rails while a string band played for us. 'Yours' featured prominently. There was a bit of Hutch and a scattering of Gracie Fields. Everything else seemed to be Glenn Miller and none of us knew that the man himself had become a casualty of this long war when his plane disappeared over the Channel in December 1944. We had good food, good tobacco (I hoarded quite a bit for later – the jungle ways died hard), cheap beer and even tots of navy rum. We sat on the decks after supper belting out 'Dad Smoked a Pipe' and after a couple of rums, it all sounded pretty good.

This time there was no threat of German U-boats in the Med, so we took the short route home via the Suez Canal. I can still see that weird geographical thing now – an ocean liner sliding, as it must have looked from the banks, through the sands of the desert. This was a bit of a blow for me. Throughout my time in the camps I had kept at the back of my mind my memories of Sylvia Cohen, the beautiful girl from Cape Town who had been so kind to a squaddie far from home. We wouldn't be passing that incredible mountain again, one of the little sorrows in an ocean of sorrows.

At Port Said we knew we were nearly home because they issued winter clothing. Shorts and open-necked shirts had felt odd enough after the Jap-happies, but the itchiness and weight of a Leicesters battledress was horrible and we all walked around scratching and squirming. We didn't notice Biscay on the way back; it was almost as if the waves were being kind to us, knowing what had been. When we reached the dark waters of the Mersey – *so* different from the Kwai – and the port of Liverpool, the cold hit us like a sledgehammer. It was early October but it might as well have been Siberia in January. We trudged down the gangplank with our greatcoat collars turned up and our kitbags over our shoulders. I'm not an emotional man, but when I saw those crowds waving Union Jacks, and heard the band playing 'Romaika/A Hunting Call' and all the other tunes of glory of all the other regiments on board, I felt an iron-hard lump in my throat. We hadn't been forgotten, after all. Here were wives, sweethearts, mums and dads waiting for their loved ones. Here were people who didn't know us and we didn't know them. But they'd read their papers, heard their wireless bulletins as Alvar Lidell told them all about Burma and the unfathomable engineering feat they were already calling the Railway of Death. We felt pride, we felt gratitude, we felt special. And as we marched through that crowd, who were slapping us on the back, shaking our hands, blowing kisses, I felt Albert marching beside me and Jackie and Harry. They *should* have been there, *deserved* to be there. And, just for an hour on that cold Liverpool dock, they were.

That night we slept in a transit camp outside the city. Britain had been full of these things for years, especially in the south, as the build-up to D-Day began and the Yanks arrived. Schools, hospitals, libraries, colleges – you name it, any building big enough had come under the umbrella of the War Office, guarded by policemen or snot-nosed kids in uniforms too big for them; like I had been four years ago. Nobody checked our kit as we came through customs, so I kept my tobacco stash. The two army blankets we were given that night were nowhere near enough in an unheated dormitory so I asked for more. Oliver Twist all over again. And this time I did get the Dickensian response.

'*Two*, lad?' the stores sergeant said. 'Where d'you think you are, man? This is the British Army.'

So I slept in my greatcoat.

The next day was a Saturday. It's funny how, when you've lost track of time for so long, the days take on a new significance. There was one phone at the camp and we queued with that endless resignation of the British to use it. We'd queued in the camps for food, for water, for haircuts and shaves; it was the way of things. Nobody owned a phone in those days so you'd ring a workplace, a pub, maybe even the local vicar. I knew my dad worked half days on Saturdays at Snaith's – if he was still there, if Snaith's was still standing. By the time I got to the front of the queue, Snaith's would have been closed, so, in the end, no one knew I was back.

They gave us pen and paper to write down anything we'd lost in the war. Where do you start? My .303 and bayonet?

That was government issue and didn't belong to me anyway. My uniform? Ditto. And anyway, I'd got another one now. My pipes. My chess set. I'd had them stolen or had thrown them away. Four years of my life. Several stone in weight. And too many friends to think about. In the end most of us wrote nothing. That night we were allowed to hit town. I remember going into that pub as if it was yesterday. Anybody in uniform was still welcome then and the old niggles of peacetime had yet to return. The place was thick with smoke and the beer tasted wonderful. It wasn't Ansells yet, but it would do. I remember sitting next to a pretty girl in the snug and I asked her if I could stroke her cheek, just to make sure she was real and I wasn't still lying on my bamboo with the attap leaking rain above me.

'Course you can, chuck,' she laughed. And I did.

As chat-up lines go, it probably wasn't the most impressive she'd heard.

On Monday everybody went home. There were no more chances to phone Dad because the army had decreed that that should happen on Saturday. They gave us rail passes and we chugged south-east across country, through the towns we'd passed through nearly five years earlier. For a moment I was back on that other railway, the one we'd built with our blood, with the monkey chorus for company and that terrible river gliding alongside.

It was almost dark as the engine hissed and snorted to a halt at Leicester London Road station. There were knots of people standing there in their austerity clothes. Mums and wives in tears, little kids looking confused, wondering who this stranger called Daddy was. Like it had been for me, all those Christmases ago in 1919 when my dad was the genie from the

East. There were hugs and handshakes but no one there for me. Outside in the forecourt a fleet of black taxis waited and the fare was on His Majesty's Government. I'd never ridden in a taxi before and it was bizarre to think that of all the peculiar forms of transport I'd travelled in over the last five years, this was one of the most novel and it took me right to my doorstep.

I stood in my greatcoat and field cap outside 41 Burnside Road, Saffron Lane, with my kitbag by my side. About a minute after I'd knocked, I heard the bolts slide and Dad stood there. He hadn't changed and I wondered how far I had. I threw my arms round him, but he put out his hand and shook mine, like men did in those days, and he went upstairs to wake the girls. Sheila was eleven and Denise eight, real little girls in their own right. I didn't know where to start with them, but they made it easy and it was hugs and kisses and questions I couldn't answer. Then Peggy arrived with her husband, Tommy Kissane, and was shocked to see how yellow my skin was.

We went round to Cyril's house the next day. It was good to see him and to see that the family were still there, just a little older than I remembered them. But they weren't all still there. Evelyn had gone, leaving the girls behind with Dad, and I never did get to the bottom of that one. There are some things you don't ask about.

Some things like my football trophies. They'd gone too. Number 41 hadn't been my home, of course, before I'd left for all points east, but the furniture was the same, old and battered and a reminder that families like ours, thousands of families like ours, had had to scrimp and tighten their belts for a long time. There was the glass-fronted sideboard, but there wasn't a single trophy left. I didn't mention it for a while. With all that had happened along the Kwai, the disappearance of a few knick-knacks was neither here nor there.

But that was just it – they weren't here. Along with my pipes, my Red Cross parcel and my jungle carvings, another tangible part of my life had gone. And no one had an explanation, ever. I knew my dad would never have hocked them, no matter how bad times must have been, and anyway, what would they have been worth? In the scheme of things, I was lucky. So many of the poor buggers I'd known in the last four years had lost far more than that.

And so the rest of my life began. It started with Dad asking me casually when I was going back to work! So the 'hail the conquering hero' bit didn't last long and the anti-climax of reality kicked in soon enough. Astonishingly, they'd kept my old job open at Snaith's and it was quite touching that they thought I'd be back. I worked there until I retired, becoming something of a guru when it came to wallpapers and paints, in charge of the warehouse. 'What about this, Reg?' a junior member of staff would ask and I'd give him my oracle-like dispensation; I wasn't often wrong.

I'd only been home a day when there was a knock on the door. Dad answered it and I heard a voice I knew well, a gravel voice that took me back to my childhood, a voice from White Grit, Salop.

'Hello, Reg. Fancy a pint?'

Private Bob Hillier was standing there, still in his Desert Rat uniform and a broad grin surrounding the ubiquitous fag. And we sat like the old cronies we were at the City Arms, sipping our Ansells Best Bitter at last and talking about the best of times and the worst of times. Bob had had his share of 'moments' in North Africa. An Arab surgeon had made a complete hash of taking his appendix out and he'd nearly died. He'd nearly died from totally different causes when he'd told Field Marshal Bernard Montgomery that he was a cook and didn't really want to chase Jerry out of Africa. It was a brave, perhaps even reckless answer; but perhaps Monty should never have asked the question.

My generation, those who returned, had to try to fit back into a society which was also rebuilding itself. It was the 'age of austerity', with rationing and holes in the ground where homes had been. With no money at all, Clement Attlee's government set up the Welfare State and I voted Labour from then on. I cycled to work (and back again for lunch) every day, twelve miles. After the Railway, that was nothing. And what did I do on Sundays, the day of *yasumé*? You can be sure I never went to church – the vicar might want to talk to me about those missing apples! I taught Sheila and Denise to cycle and became, I suppose, a sort of father figure for them. Dad was always there, but he was a different generation, more of a grandfather to the girls, really. So it was me they'd natter to as we pedalled out to Great Glen with the rooks wheeling in the elms. When I got married, my new family and my sisters became my cycling partners. With our baby boy, Clive, Kathleen and I had picnics by the old canal, often with Bob Hillier and his wife. We'd sit and smoke on the banks of that altogether friendlier water than the one I remembered flowing through the jungle. And, like the overgrown schoolboys we were, we combed the hedgerows, looking for birds' eggs.

In the year of Waterloo, there was a sign in the London parks that read, 'No dogs and no soldiers in uniform'. It had always been like that and I've never seen the love–hate relationship of the British civilian and the British soldier better expressed than in Rudyard Kipling's 'Tommy Atkins':

For it's Tommy this, an' Tommy that, an' 'Chuck him out,
  the brute!'
But it's 'Saviour of 'is country' when the guns begin to
  shoot.

It was a bit like that for me on my first Christmas back home.
I was still wearing my uniform and if you've stayed with me
this long, you'll know what I'd been through. There was no
counselling for my generation – 'This is the Leicestershire
Regiment. Where do you think you are, man?' – but a little
understanding would have been nice. I was cycling in Wistow
that day with Cyril, somewhere between St Wistan's church
and the canal, when a lady pulled up in her car. Could I cut
some holly for her, growing wild in the hedge? She was
elderly and frail. It was Christmas. So I took her pair of clip-
pers and clipped away – a nice wreath for the old girl's door.

And for that, we were arrested, Cyril and me. I still have
the summons. 'Cyril Sidney Twigg (warehouseman) and Pte.
4863477 Reginald Twigg (Leicester Regiment) . . . Information has been laid this day . . . that you on the 16th day of
December 1945 at Wistow . . . did unlawfully steal a part of a
certain Holly Tree of the value of 1/- at least . . . the property
of Lord Cottesloe . . . contrary to Section 33 of the Larceny
Act 1861.'

And we duly appeared before the magistrate six days later
at the Court of Summary Jurisdiction at Leicester Castle. The
16th was my thirty-first birthday, and as for the third Baron
Cottesloe, I don't suppose he even knew he owned a holly
tree in that hedge, still less what it was worth. They fined us
fifteen shillings. We could have bought a couple of nice new
shirts each with that money and got some change in 1945.

Welcome home, Reg!

*

My discharge papers, on 5 May 1946, recorded that I had
served in the army for 5 years, 316 days. At that time, according to the official documentation, I 'ceased to fulfil army
physical requirements'. None of us were quite the same after
the Railway. And the testimonial the army gave me – what I
suppose you'd call a reference today – is, by definition, thin:

Circumstances beyond the control of the soldier and the service prevent
his testimonial being fully assessed. From such records as do exist, he is a
reliable, intelligent, hard-working man of sober habits.

Bob Hillier and I had a good laugh at that one in the City
Arms.

Epilogue: Reunion

Some survivors of the Railway could never talk about their memories. They were too painful, seared into their brains, burned there by the flames at Tonchan. They locked themselves away, couldn't face family, old friends, the routine of a day's work. Some were terrified by sounds – the clanging of a building site, the whistle of a train – *anything* that reminded them of the Railway. Some couldn't stand to be near a river or work in the claustrophobic humidity of a greenhouse. One I heard of in London would cross a road in his last years rather than walk past a Japanese tourist – and that tourist couldn't have been even a twinkle in his grandad's eye in the days of the Railway. 'Old men forget,' Shakespeare said in *Henry V*; no, they don't. They can't.

Me? Well, I just got on with my life, grateful every day for the chance to do just that. And time, they say, heals. I refused to buy Japanese goods for years – those hi-tech gadgets they copied, often in miniaturized form from somebody else. But eventually I cracked and bought a second-hand Nissan. That took a while – I didn't pass my driving test until I was sixty-eight. That's what being a confirmed cyclist does for you!

But no; old men don't forget. And we don't forgive. I have no animosity at all towards the Japanese people – to see how they coped with the nuclear disaster after the tsunami in 2011 has to impress you. It was born of the same stoicism that we saw in the Hiroshima generation. But the guards on the Railway? Yes, I hate them with a passion now as I did then. In that respect, nothing has changed. *Those* Japs and their Korean

counterparts came from a culture where cruelty was com-
monplace and their code of bushido meant that we had no
more rights than the ants that crawled the jungle floor at our
feet.

And, yes, we were forgotten. It's a cliché today – the
forgotten army. Nobody actually forgot us – Cyril wrote
to me but I never got his letter. How could I? What was he
supposed to write on the envelope? Pte. R. Twigg, he's-one-
of-the-thousands-of-poor-buggers-dying-somewhere-along-
the-Kwai; you can't miss him. Churchill and the army high
command knew to within a few miles where we were. What
they couldn't do was get us out; not until the summer of 1945,
anyway.

I'm not an armchair strategist, looking at the Burma campaign through balanced eyes with all the wisdom and hindsight
of the years. I was one of the lions led by donkeys who had to
go back for an officer's machine gun across a no-man's land
raked by Jap rifle fire. I was the one told to hold on to British
property even as General Percival was giving it away. I'm not
a hero; I did as I was told and I survived the Railway because
once there was nobody to tell me what to do, my tough childhood memories kicked in and I coped on my own.

And so the years rolled on. I joined a POW group after the
war and we held Christmas dinners until our numbers got too
few in the 1970s. The Blair government gave us compensation
of £10,000, which was very nice to have, but it was a token
gesture; no more. Tony Blair was a great one for apologizing
for the past; most Western politicians are. It's pointless, of
course, but it's well meant. The Japanese government have
never apologized for the Burma–Thailand Railway, though,
and short of a revolution the scale of which is unimaginable,
they never will.

It was my son, Clive, who sent for my medals. Personally I wouldn't have bothered. My football trophies meant more to me than they did, but I think my family were proud of me and they surround me still with their love. The Burma Star has six points and carries the cipher of the King Emperor. I occasionally wore it, as many men did with pride. I pinned it to my blazer with a ribbon of red, yellow and blue at regimental dinners. A small token of a war long ago and far away.

After Kathleen died in 1999, Bob Hillier's daughter, Sue, used to take me out for the odd drink at a pub at Queniborough. It was here that I met Richard Lane, the historian of the Leicester Regiment, and I probably bored him to death talking about the 'good' old days. It was Richard who invited me to a battalion officers' dinner in 2004, and who should I find sitting there but Lieutenant Savage, the officer I'd been batman to all those years ago. I'd last seen him at Chungkai and we'd saluted each other in our Jap-happies, looking forward to some vague, eventual end to the hell camps along the river. Suddenly, it wasn't 'Twigg' and 'sir' any more – it was Reg and Ray and there was a kind of comfort in that. Two old soldiers, sitting with our pints – actually, I think his was a Bloody Mary – both of us glad we'd made it. We drank to our comrades who made it and to those who didn't. We also drank to men like Wiggy, whose fate we didn't know.

And what about the blokes who didn't make it? Sergeant Seichi Okada actually did, but he didn't deserve to. Some men in other memoirs called him Dr Death, but to me he was the Konyo Kid's sidekick during 1943. He got ten years in a Japanese prison – not a bad tariff for killing hundreds of men like the bloke I knew only as George. The Kid himself didn't get off so lightly. They hanged Lieutenant Usuki at Changi prison in 1946. I don't believe in a heaven; I don't believe in a hell. But I hope I'm wrong and that somewhere beyond the edge of a universe, the Konyo Kid is rotting there, building the devil's railway. The Silver Bullet died too, executed for war crimes. Executed for the murder of my mate Harry Barnett. I'd have pulled the lever myself.

I went to see Harry's family after the war, and Albert Wingell's. There wasn't a lot to say. There were thousands of families then trying to come to terms with the loss of their loved ones and it wasn't easy. I told them how great their particular loved ones were, what good mates they'd been and of the laughs we'd had. I didn't tell the Barnetts I'd last seen Harry dying of dysentery in Tarso and shuffling off into the jungle to be bayoneted to death, his eyes hollow, his will broken. And I didn't tell the Wingells that the last time I'd seen their boy was in some God-awful jungle track south of Jitra. I'd told him to keep his head down and his chin up. But there had been something in his eyes that morning and I knew he wouldn't be able to do either. For the record – and as the years go by, it's all we have of the man – Thomas Albert Wingell's name appears on Column 66 of the Kranji War Cemetery in Singapore. He died on 12 February 1942 aged twenty-six. And he has no known grave.

Neither does Jackie Weston. He'd come down from Hellfire Pass when I'd seen him last and I'd scrounged some tobacco for him at Tarso. I'd sat on the bamboo until he'd fallen asleep and by the next morning he'd gone. I didn't have a chance to say goodbye. He may have died on the prison ship *Kachidoki Maru,* which was carrying 900 British POWs on the night of 12 September 1944 when it was sunk by torpedoes from the American submarine *Pampanito*. Column 65 at Kranji records Jackie's death for this date. He was aged thirty and his bones have long ago gone to the fish in the South China Sea.

Clive grew up with stories of the Railway and it's because of him you're reading these words today. He collated all of it – the big, the small, the trivial, the vital – and put it together as the testimony of one of the forgotten army from a generation that one day will also be forgotten. But Matthew played his part too. He's my eldest grandson and, fired up by my stories of the Railway, went out there in 2005 to find the places I'd talked about.

If you like, this was a personal pilgrimage for me so I didn't want to go with other ex-POWs. I wanted to go with my family. In the end, I went with Clive and Chris (my daughter-in-law) in the February of 2006 and we met Matthew out there. My wife had died seven years earlier or she'd have been at my side as I walked with those ghosts along the Kwai.

We flew to Bangkok in luxury. No more rattling Dakotas with more holes than a sieve, no more coffin trains jolting and swaying along a Railway we'd all built with our blood. It was a different world. They say you can't go back, that then was then and returning is a mistake. I couldn't believe the city now. The old pagodas were still there, but they were lost in the colossal new buildings of steel and glass. Air conditioning was everywhere and that faceless internationalism that is the hallmark of every city in the world today. I sat in the river bus with tourists who weren't born when I'd seen this place last. I was different. I was out of place and out of time.

Matthew took me to Soi Cowboy, Bangkok's best-known red-light district and not an area I remembered at all. I noticed Clive and Chris didn't go with us to the pole-dancing club and the pretty girls crowding round me wearing little more than their smiles had probably never had such an ancient customer before. Tilley would have had a field day but I hadn't come to enjoy myself. Matthew says that this was the part of the trip I talked about most afterwards – I must have words with that boy!

From the heavenly cocktails of the Oriental Hotel, we took a taxi to Kanchanaburi, the 'base camp' where my imprisonment along the Kwai had started all those years ago. I didn't recognize any of it. The jungle had grown and been felled and felled again in the seventy years since my last visit and anyway we were all too busy worrying about the professionalism of the taxi driver. Every time we passed a temple or a statue to Buddha, he took both hands off the wheel to make a prayer sign. I'm glad his god was with him.

We stopped at the Jolly Frog at Kanchanaburi, a watering hole well known to the young backpackers who were everywhere. They were of both sexes, in shorts, hiking boots and jungle hats of the type we'd never had in the jungle. And most of them were carrying cameras made in Japan. Five minutes away, at the bridge at Tamarkan, I had my first glimpse of it in nearly three-quarters of a century – the silent, deadly River Kwai, gliding peacefully past in a new and, I hope, better world. We sat on a pontoon and I dabbled my feet in the water. It was warm and comforting and yet I felt a chill. For a moment I was up to my waist in that water again and a torrent of emotions swept over me. I could see the Monkeys thudding down out into the river, hear the chanted screech of the guards – '*Ichi, ni, san, s̄ i, go.*' I could see the dots in the sky far away that became bombers and blew the bridge to bits as I watched, shaking and trembling.

I shook myself free of it. The Kwai and the Railway of Death are tourist resorts today. Look them up online and you'll see what I mean. You can ride the train that runs twice a day up the track from Kanchanaburi to Nam Tok – which is what they call Tarso nowadays – and it will cost you 100 baht, or about £3. The carriages are third class, like they still were when I was a boy in Leicester, with hard seats and open sides. Vendors wander the train selling beer and pre-packed fruit; the slices of pomelo in that stifling heat are like nectar.

We didn't take the railway north. It was late, it was hot and I wanted to find memorials to my mates. From Nam Tok, had we ridden the rails, we would have had to have walked beyond that because the rails have gone and only the sleepers remain. The sleepers that they say mark the graves of good men – 13,000 British, Australian and Dutch soldiers and 80,000 coolies – Malays, Tamils and Chinese. They had names, they had faces, they had families and hopes and dreams. And the Railway killed them all. The Railway and the heat and the Japs and Koreans. And I remember shaking my head as I looked out onto the Kwai at Tamarkan. So many good men. So much waste.

The wooden bridge I'd helped to build has gone now. The steel one, smashed by the Allied bombers in 1945, still stands and the tourist train rattles over it at a regulation ten miles an hour, past knots of tourists who stand in the recesses alongside the track to let it pass. Many of these, the kids with their backpacks, the armchair soldiers of another generation, have come here because this is the Bridge on the River Kwai, made famous by the film in 1957. Except, of course, they've come to the wrong place. The film was actually made on location in Ceylon, the country they call Sri Lanka today, and the novel was written by Pierre Boulle, who had never been to Thailand and didn't know there was no bridge on the Kwai; it was over the Mae Khong instead. Undeterred, the

Thai government just changed the name of the river in 1960 and now everybody's satisfied.

Am I glad I went back? Yes, because I could wander the cemeteries at Kanchanaburi and read the names of the men I knew. The memories came tumbling back in the sound of a voice, the tilt of a head, a smile. Mates. *My* mates, lying here under a savage sun. We chatted a while, those mates and me, though I have to confess the conversation was a little one-sided. I left them under their neat stones in rows with the grass clipped and the roses in bloom. They were at peace now. And they'd surely deserved that.

Little things. Things that might have been and never were. A beautiful Jewish girl on a magical beach under Table Mountain. I've tried to trace Sylvia Cohen. What for? Just to thank her. To thank a pretty girl for walking out with a soldier on his way to a war he'd live with for the rest of his life. I had no luck. Like my pipes and my old barber's knife and my chess pieces, they're all lost to time.

In 2005, I gave an interview to a young reporter from my local paper, the *Leicester Mercury*, and he quoted me as saying 'Some blokes say they wake up from nightmares about it all but I never dream about it.' No, I never dream about it. About the wild, dark jungle and the screaming rant of the guards, the lonely songs around the campfire and the crosses beside the track. I never dream about it. But my family say that sometimes I toss and turn in my sleep, shouting in an alien tongue that sounds a little like Japanese.

And, of course, Harry sits on my bed sometimes, talking . . .

Acknowledgements

Our thanks go to Chris Medway, Clive's wife, for her patient support and unstinted assistance when this book was in development. To Rebecca, Christopher and Chris Maj for their support, advice and encouragement and to Matthew, whose adventures brought about Reg's return to the River Kwai and found the memorials to long-lost friends. Also, to the wider family for searching out long forgotten pictures and memories.

We are grateful to Andrew Lownie for taking a chance that Reg's story was different and worth telling. To the boundless enthusiasm and support from the staff at Penguin, especially Eleo Gordon, and to Mei Trow who took an interesting family story with potential and gave it that professional touch which resulted in a finished book that so many are enthusiastic about.

Reg Twigg's
Japanese Index Card

'I was moved from Group IV to Group II, probably when I had beriberi, otherwise I would have been lost at sea with Jackie.'

Reg Twigg's
Air Drop Leaflet

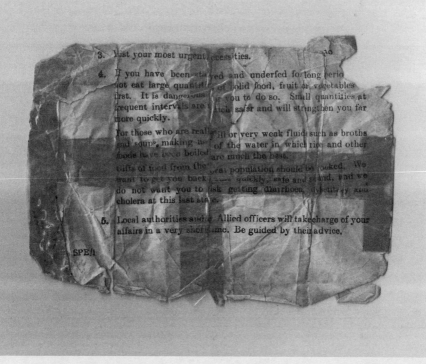

The leaflet from the sky that told me I was free and gave sensible advice – which we immediately ignored.

Reg Twigg's
Liberation Questionnaire

BLOCK
Nº 15
A.

NIL

‹FIDENTIAL

M.I. 9/JAP/ Nº 11472 A

WRITE IN BLOCK CAPITAL LETTERS IN PENCIL

No. _4863477_ Rank _PRIVATE_ Surname _TWIGG_

Christian Names _REGINALD_ Decorations _____

Ship (R.N., U.S.N. or Merchant Navy) _____ Unit & Div. (Army) _1ST BN LEICESTERS 11TH INDIAN DIVISION_

Squadron and Command (R.A.F., A.A.F.) _____

Date of Birth _16TH DECEMBER 1913_ Date of Enlistment _24TH JUNE 1940_

Private Address and ~~Telephone No.~~ _41 BURNSIDE RD. LEICESTER_

Place and Date of Original Capture (Aircrew R.A.F. to give place and date of a/c crash). _15TH FEBRUARY 1942 AT SINGAPORE_

1. What camps, detachments or hospitals were you in ? Give dates and names of the British Camp Leaders, Detachment (or Block) Leaders or, in the case of hospitals, the Senior British Medical Officers.

Camp or Hospital.	Dates.	Camp Leader.	Detachment or Block Leader (if any).
·CANU	1942 TO 1943	I THINK LT. CL. MOORE RA	
TARSOA	1943 TO 1944	LT. CL. KNIGHT (NORFOLKS)	
CONQUETTA	1944	LT. CL. KNIGHT "	
RIN TIN	1944	MJR. HUMPHEYS NORFOLK	
HARROW HILL	1945	SGT. MJR. PICKERING (SIGNS)	

2. ESCAPES OR ATTEMPTED ESCAPES. (Additional paper will be supplied on request if required).

(a) Give full description and approx. date of each attempt you made to escape, showing how you left the camp, and from which camp each attempt was made. State whether there was an air-raid in progress at the time or not. If an escape was made from a train or vehicle the approx. speed and how it was guarded should be included.

No

(b) Were you physically fit when you made these attempts ?

(c) Give Regimental particulars of anyone who accompanied you on each attempt.

What happened to them ?

(d) Give briefly your experiences during periods of freedom.

(e) How were you recaptured and on what date ?

Further Reading

Allen, Louis, *Burma: The Longest War*, London, Weidenfeld & Nicolson, 1998

Barnard, John T., *The Endless Years*, London, Chantry Publications, 1950

Braddon, Russell, *The Naked Island*, London, Werner Lawrie, 1952

Burton, Reginald, *Railway of Hell*, London, Macdonald, 1963

Chye, Kooi Loong, *The British Battalion in the Malayan Campaign 1941–1942* (revised edition), Kuala Lumpur, Dept of Museums and Antiquities, Malaysia, Ministry of Culture, Arts, and Tourism Malaysia, 2002

Dunlop, E. E., *The War Diaries of Weary Dunlop*, Victoria, Aus., Penguin, 1986

Kandler, Richard, *The Prisoner List*, London, Marsworth, 2010

Lomax, Eric, *The Railway Man*, London, Jonathan Cape, 1996

MacArthur, Brian, *Surviving the Sword*, London, Abacus, 2006

Pavillard, Stanley S., *Bamboo Doctor*, London, Macmillan, 1960

Peck, Ian, *One Fourteenth of an Elephant*, London, Bantam, 2005

Reed, Bill and Peeke, Mitch, *Lost Souls of the River Kwai*, Barnsley, Pen & Sword Military, 2004

Smith, Colin, *Singapore Burning*, Harmondsworth, Penguin, 2006

Summers, Julie, *The Colonel of Tamarkan*, London, Simon & Schuster, 2005

Urquhart, Alistair, *The Forgotten Highlander*, London, Little, Brown, 2010

Wyatt, John, *No Mercy from the Japanese*, Barnsley, Pen & Sword Military, 2008

Brief video-recorded wartime recollections of Fred Shenstone (see pages 121–2 for his story), Reg Twigg and a number of other veterans form part of the permanent exhibition in the Museum of the Royal Leicestershire Regiment gallery of the Newarke Houses Museum, Leicester.

Index

'Abe', Japanese guard 266

Alexandra Hospital, Singapore 2, 102,
103, 121, 284

Ansells Best Bitter 43, 68, 138, 143, 172,
289, 291

Arsenic and Old Lace (film) 285

Ausland organization 31

Bally (comrade in Singapore) 72, 73, 74

Bam Pong 132

Bangkok 247, 260, 261, 263, 264, 277, 278,
279, 281, 299

Barber, Arthur 29, 30

Barnett, Harry 1–5, 103, 191, 252, 254,
275, 288, 298, 302

barracks
  Aldershot 15–20, 134, 207
  Athlone 12
  Glen Parva 9, 35, 42, 108, 134, 152,
    160, 199, 207, 241, 249, 256, 273
  Selarang 119
  Bidadari Camp, Singapore 66

Basil (fellow prisoner) 220, 221

Bay of Biscay 52, 61, 287

beriberi 153, 171, 172, 174, 207, 224, 247

Bombay 61, 62, 63, 65, 69, 71, 119, 143,
278

Boultham Park Road, Lincoln 32

Bowley, Maj., Leicestershire Regt 106,
109, 111

Bridge on the River Kwai 301

Burrell, Sgt, Leicestershire Regt 268, 271,
273, 275

bushido 144, 165, 189, 190, 204, 275, 296

Butterworth, Penang 76, 77, 89, 98

Cagney, Jimmy 42

camps
  Arrow Hill 236, 238, 239, 242, 243,
    344, 345, 248, 257, 258, 264
  Bandoeng 221
  Chungkai 247, 248, 249, 297
  Kinsaiyok 227, 229
  Konkuita 263, 264, 265, 266
  Konyo 140, 142, 143, 149, 150, 155,
    156, 160, 161, 164, 172, 174, 177,
    180, 184, 185, 188, 199, 201, 260,
    268, 270, 285
  Konyo 2 159, 160, 161, 164, 167, 171,
    174, 177, 180, 270
  Rin Tin 225, 227, 229, 231, 238
  Takanun 267
  Tamarkan 253, 254, 258, 300, 301
  Tarso 1, 103, 140, 141, 155, 156, 171,
    174, 176, 177, 178, 180, 181,
    182–221, 235, 239, 249, 251, 252,
    253, 263–74, 298, 300, 301
  Tonchan 221, 222, 223, 224, 264, 280,
    295

Canal St, South Wigston 10, 12

Cape Town 58, 59, 61, 65, 143, 278, 287

Cart, Arthur 22, 24, 25

Chamberlain, Neville 32

Changi, Singapore 117, 119, 120, 121, 122,
123, 130, 161, 174, 249, 297

Chaplin, Charlie 217, 218

Chirk 29
cholera 222, 223, 224, 247, 280
Churchill, Winston 34, 116, 117, 147, 279, 284, 296
Clarence Hotel, South Wigston 42, 48–9
Clayton, Jack 1, 5, 230, 279
Cohen, Sylvia 59, 60, 61, 65, 140, 143, 244, 287, 302
Co-op, Long Street, Wigston Magna 42, 43
Crane, Sam 'Porky' 37, 46, 52, 100, 107, 249, 256, 272
Curtis, Cpl Roger 219

D-Day 288
Daniels, 'Paddy' 77, 78, 80, 182, 250, 251
Dawes racing bicycles 30
Dobson (fellow prisoner) 191, 192, 193, 195
Dublin 11–15
Dunkirk 33, 34, 48, 115
Dunlop, E. E. 'Weary' 247, 248
Dunmore's biscuit factory 10, 11, 42
dysentery 1, 2, 3, 130, 153, 172, 173, 174, 191, 252, 267, 298

Edwina, Lady Mountbatten 280

Flanagan and Allen 263
Flynn, Errol 105, 173
Foley, Harry 123, 249, 250
Foxton 47
Freeman Hardy and Willis factory 44
Freetown, Sierra Leone 55

Geneva Convention 144
George (fellow prisoner) 166, 167, 297
Georgetown 77, 79, 83
Gibson, Hoot 25

Grace Road cinema, Leicester 25, 55, 175, 217
Grant, Cary 285
Great Glen, Leicestershire 47, 129, 151, 284, 292
Grieves factory, Leicester 44

Hallam, Ginger 162, 163, 285
Happy World, Singapore 74, 75
Harc, Japanese guard 125
Harlech 30
Havelock Road, Singapore 123, 124, 249
Healey Street, South Wigston 9, 10, 12, 20, 42, 146
Hellfire Pass 185, 298
Hillier, Bob 24, 25, 46, 47, 48, 123, 151, 291, 294
Hillier, Sue 297
Hiroshima 270
Holmes, Sgt, Leicestershire Regt 79, 80
Hong Kong 88
Hwong Sisiwan 276

Irish Republican Army 13, 14

Japanese military police *see* Kempei
Jitra, Battle of 86, 93, 98, 101, 103, 105, 121, 132, 136, 138, 150, 152, 226, 248, 250, 270, 278, 284, 298
Joe (Australian prisoner) 231
Johnson, 'Jigger' 78, 79
Johore 149

Kampong Manggis 86
Kanchanaburi 135, 141, 255, 256, 268, 300, 301, 302
Keaton, Buster 25
Kempei 186, 187, 215, 228, 239, 248, 263
Keppel Harbour, Singapore 124, 128, 134, 145, 187, 232, 243, 280

Kilby Bridge 47
King Street, Leicester 27
Kirby Frith Hall, Glenfield 21, 24
Kirk White's Youth Club 28, 29
Kissane, Tommy 290
Konyo Kid (Lt Usuki) 144, 145, 148, 159,
    164, 165, 168, 169, 180, 187, 199, 225,
    248, 249, 274, 278, 279, 297, 298
Kota Bharu 88
Kranji War Cemetery, Singapore 298
Krung Thep *see* Bangkok

Lancaster, Burt 110
Lane, Richard 297
Langdon, Harry 25
Lansdowne Road School 25
Lavender Street, Singapore 69, 86, 261,
    283
Leggie Queue 154, 155
Leicester 8, 9, 11, 12, 20, 21, 23, 24, 27, 28,
    30, 33, 40, 41, 43, 50, 52, 55, 64, 71,
    72, 75, 80, 82, 95, 100, 103, 107, 123,
    129, 199, 239, 244, 261, 264, 284, 286,
    289, 293, 301, 302
Leicester Mercury 27, 302
Ley, Captain, Leicestershire Regt 91, 92,
    93, 94
Leyte, Battle of 250
Lincoln 28, 30, 103, 265
Liverpool 49, 50, 66, 218, 287, 288
Lloyd George, David 20, 25
Lockton, Albert 80, 81, 92, 93, 94, 152,
    254, 279
Long Street cinema, Wigston Magna 42,
    43
Lopburi 275, 277
Luther Street, Leicester 21

Maine, Ron 90, 94
malaria 3, 153, 230, 247, 249, 255, 261
McCrea, Joel 42
Medway, Chris 299

Medway, Clive 292, 297, 299
Midway, Battle of 250
Ministry of Information 34
Mix, Tom 25
Montgomery, Field Marshal Bernard 292
Moore, Sgt, Leicestershire Regt 38, 39,
    40, 52, 133, 249, 279
Morris, Matthew 299, 300

Nam Tok *see* Tarso
Nappi 82, 83, 180, 251

Oates, CSM Harry 67, 68

Parkin, Ray 221
Pathé News 42, 62
Pattani 88
Pearl Harbor 88, 250
Pelham Street, Leicester 20
Penang 67, 76, 77, 78, 79, 80, 95, 98, 183,
    250
Percival, General Arthur 116, 118, 296
Pickering, 'Pick' 255
pipe tobacco
    homemade 161, 162, 285
    St Bruno 49, 51, 57, 66, 91, 139, 162,
        266, 285
    Walter Raleigh 121, 128, 161
Port Said 287
Power, Tyrone 43
prickly heat 80, 82
public houses
    City Arms, Leicester 89, 143, 191, 291,
        294
    Jolly Frog, Kanchanaburi 300
    Victory, Leicester 32, 33
Pwllheli 30

RAF Butterworth *see* Butterworth
Raffles Hotel, Singapore 68, 69, 109, 116

Rangoon 284, 285

Reast, Howard 212, 213, 214, 215, 225,
    227, 229, 230, 232, 238, 240, 241, 242,
    243, 245, 248, 250, 263, 264, 266,
    268, 270, 275, 280, 281

Red Cross (Australian) 128, 129, 177, 278,
    291

regimental marches *see* songs

regiments (British)
    5th Infantry Division 103
    11th Indian Division 90, 117
    Leicestershire 7, 8, 11, 15, 36, 45, 47,
        48, 50, 57, 59, 66, 81, 83, 86, 87, 88,
        90, 93, 101, 105, 115, 116, 117, 120,
        121, 153, 177, 182, 230, 232, 249,
        268, 284, 287, 293, 297; Sixteen
        Platoon 38, 117, 248
    Lincolnshire 19, 20, 26
    Manchester 255, 265
    Norfolk 254
    Notts and Derby (Sherwood
        Foresters) 162, 189, 190, 194
    York and Lancaster 8

regiments (Japanese)
    5th Division, Japanese Imperial Army
        105
    18th Division, Japanese Imperial Army
        105
    Imperial Guard, Japanese Imperial
        Army 105

Reinforcement Camp, Singapore 103, 104

Rhyl 29

rivers
    Chao Phraya 261
    Krian 100
    Kwai Noi 100, 136, 137, 138, 152, 158,
        162, 197, 214, 218, 219, 222, 230,
        235, 236, 238, 242, 243, 244, 245,
        250, 251, 253, 254, 256, 258, 267,
        268, 269, 273, 278, 279, 283, 287,
        290, 296, 299, 300, 301
    Kwai Yai 136
    Mae Khong 136, 301
    Nan 269

Sence 47

Roosevelt, President F. D. 88

Saffron Lane, Leicester 9, 25, 28, 40, 48,
    117, 290

Saffron Lane Estate Working Men's Club
    28

Savage, Lt Raymond, Leicestershire Regt
    120, 249, 297

Seichi Okada, Sgt 297

Seishiro Hagaki, General 280

Sembawang naval base 102

Shenstone, Fred 121–2, 307

ships
    HMS *Hood* 52, 53, 89
    HMS *Prince of Wales* 89
    HMS *Repulse* 52, 53, 89
    Kachidoki Maru 298
    SS *Boissevain* 286
    SS *Duchess of York* 50, 51, 52, 54, 56,
        61, 65, 129, 160, 286
    USS *Pampanito* 298

Silent Forest 151, 230, 279

Silver Bullet 4, 5, 187, 188, 189, 190, 191,
    225, 248, 251, 266, 267, 298

Singapore 2, 53, 66, 67, 68, 74, 75, 76, 77,
    83, 99, 101, 120, 125, 126, 128, 129,
    133, 149, 153, 161, 164, 177, 180, 195,
    226, 242, 244, 251, 256, 261, 270,
    276, 279, 280, 284, 298
    battle for 102–18, 149
    Golf Club 105, 111, 114, 115, 116

Singora 88

Skegness 30, 49, 125

Slim, General William 250, 279

Smiling Joe, Korean guard 185, 186, 187,
    239, 248

Snaith's decorators' merchants 22, 33, 46,
    107, 184, 288, 291

Soi Cowboy, Singapore 299

songs
    'Colonel Bogey' 123, 129, 134, 262, 275
    'Dad Smoked a Pipe' 286

'General Monckton' 232
'Land of Hope and Glory' 240, 275
'Moon Over Malaya' 280
'Romaika/A Hunting Call' 48, 232, 287
'Run, Rabbit, Run' 263
'We'll Meet Again' 213
'When They Sound the Last
    "All-Clear"' 103
'Yours' 285
South East Asia Command Games 79, 80
South Wigston 9, 35, 41, 42, 48, 49, 76
Starkey, Lance-Cpl, Leicestershire Regt
    95, 96, 97, 98
Suez Canal 53, 286
Sungai Petani 80, 83, 180

Thompson (fellow prisoner) 1, 5, 248,
    249
Three Pagodas Pass 263
Tilley (fellow prisoner) 218, 219, 221, 300
Trinity Lane, Leicester 21
tropical ulcer 136, 155, 157, 225
Twigg, Constance 8, 10, 15, 20, 36, 43
Twigg, Cyril 7, 11, 15, 20, 46, 277, 282,
    290, 293, 296
Twigg, Denise (Bunty) 21, 46, 290, 292,
Twigg, Ethel 7, 8, 10, 11, 12, 19, 20, 21,
    26, 36
Twigg, Evelyn (née Thacker) 21, 277,
    290
Twigg, Kathleen 292, 297
Twigg, Ken 7, 11, 15, 20, 30, 46, 277, 286
Twigg, Margaret (Peggy) 21, 290
Twigg, Reg
    childhood 7–27
    enlistment and training 35–50
    homecoming 289
    in camps 117–270
    journey to Singapore 50–65
    liberation 271
    return to the Kwai 299–302

taken prisoner 117
work 27–35
Twigg, Sheila 21, 46, 290, 292
Twigg, Sidney 7, 8, 11, 13, 15, 17, 20, 21,
    22, 25, 26, 28, 32, 34, 37, 46, 64, 78,
    80, 84, 89, 90, 108, 109, 143, 157,
    160, 184, 201, 277, 286, 288, 289,
    290, 291, 292

Union Jack Club, Singapore 68, 70
Usuki, Lt *see* Konyo Kid
Uttaradit 269, 270, 271, 273, 274

VE Day 267
Victoria Hospital, Singapore 114, 116

Watkins, Sgt Benny, Leicestershire Regt
    85, 86, 89, 107, 133, 250
Wavell, Field Marshal Archibald 117
Wayne, John 105, 173
Webster, Pte, Leicestershire Regt 93, 94
Weston, Jackie 1, 5, 132, 133, 135, 136,
    154, 156, 157, 162, 168, 172, 184, 185,
    213, 279, 288, 298
White, 'Chalky' 222, 223, 224
White Grit, Shropshire 24, 291
Wigginton, 'Wiggy' 45, 99, 100, 249, 297
Wilton, Robb 212
Wingell, Albert 1, 5, 54, 57, 58, 59, 60, 61,
    65, 69, 84, 85, 89, 93, 94, 279, 288,
    298
Wistow 293
Worrell, Frederick 265

Xavier, Father 122

Yamashita Tomoyuki, General 88, 118

He just wanted a decent book to read ...

Not too much to ask, is it? It was in 1935 when Allen Lane, Managing Director of Bodley Head Publishers, stood on a platform at Exeter railway station looking for something good to read on his journey back to London. His choice was limited to popular magazines and poor-quality paperbacks – the same choice faced every day by the vast majority of readers, few of whom could afford hardbacks. Lane's disappointment and subsequent anger at the range of books generally available led him to found a company – and change the world.

'We believed in the existence in this country of a vast reading public for intelligent books at a low price, and staked everything on it'
Sir Allen Lane, 1902–1970, founder of Penguin Books

The quality paperback had arrived – and not just in bookshops. Lane was adamant that his Penguins should appear in chain stores and tobacconists, and should cost no more than a packet of cigarettes.

Reading habits (and cigarette prices) have changed since 1935, but Penguin still believes in publishing the best books for everybody to enjoy. We still believe that good design costs no more than bad design, and we still believe that quality books published passionately and responsibly make the world a better place.

So wherever you see the little bird – whether it's on a piece of prize-winning literary fiction or a celebrity autobiography, political tour de force or historical masterpiece, a serial-killer thriller, reference book, world classic or a piece of pure escapism – you can bet that it represents the very best that the genre has to offer.

Whatever you like to read – trust Penguin.